HEBREW WORD STUDY

EXPLORING THE MIND OF GOD

CHAIM BENTORAH

with LAURA BERTONE

WHITAKER HOUSE

Hebrew Word Study:
Exploring the Mind of God

Chaim Bentorah
www.chaimbentorah.com
chaimbentorah@gmail.com

ISBN 978-1-64123-223-4
eBook ISBN: 978-1-64123-224-1
Printed in the United States of America
© 2019 by Chaim Bentorah

Whitaker House
1030 Hunt Valley Circle
New Kensington, PA 15068
www.whitakerhouse.com

Library of Congress Cataloging-in-Publication Data (Pending)

1 2 3 4 5 6 7 8 9 10 11 ⨆⨆ 26 25 24 23 22 21 20 19

Dedication

To my precious nephews:
John, Michael, Nikko, and Dominic
—Auntie Laura (Lolo)

Contents

Author's Note

Please refer to the alphabetical Glossary at the end of this book for definitions and explanations of historical, cultural, and linguistic terms followed by an asterisk (*) where they initially occur in the text. Some of these terms may first appear in plural form. For clarity, in the case of a term consisting of two words, two asterisks (**) will follow the second word of the term, and in the case of a term consisting of three words, three asterisks (***) will follow the third word of the term.

As with other Semitic languages, the original Hebrew alphabet** is consonantal, with no separate letters for vowels. Nevertheless, vowel sounds were used in the Hebrew language, because it is impossible to pronounce a word without using the sounds represented by *a, e, i, o,* and *u*. In rabbinic Hebrew, the letters aleph, hei, yod, and vav can be used to denote a vowel. Additionally, around the seventh century AD, the Masoretic text introduced the *niqqud*, which are a series of dots and dashes placed near a consonantal letter to indicate a vowel. The normal pattern is: consonant, vowel, consonant, vowel. I use the *abajab*, or the consonantal alphabet, and follow a rabbinical tradition of defaulting to using the *a* whenever any vowel is needed, except in cases where I am explaining a certain word usage or grammatical expression. Additionally, while many academic texts use left-handed apostrophes for the aleph and right-handed apostrophes for the ayin, this text has been streamlined, using left-handed apostrophes for both.

Finally, in the Scripture quotations, brackets indicate words added or substituted for clarity and/or flow and boldface type indicates my emphasis.

Preface

In Romans 11:34, the apostle Paul asks this rhetorical question: *"Who hath known the mind of the Lord? or who hath been his counsellor?"* The Greek word translated *"known"* here is *egno*, which comes from the word *ginosko*. This is the same word Mary used when she asked the angel Gabriel, who told her that she would become the mother of the Messiah, *"How shall this be, seeing I know not a man?"* (Luke 1:34). In other words, she is asking how she could be pregnant given the fact she had never had a sexual relationship with a man. *Ginosko*, although rendered as "know," is a word that is often used to describe intimacy. It is similar to the word used in the Aramaic, which is the language Mary spoke. That word is *chekam* (אכמ), which also refers to knowing in an intimate sense.

The question Paul is asking, therefore, is this: "Who has an intimate knowledge of the mind of God enough to be His counselor or advisor?" This verse is not saying we cannot know the mind of God at all—we just cannot know it enough to offer Him any advice.

Even though we cannot know the depths of God's mind enough to be His counselor, God does reveal much about what is on His mind—especially about His relationship with us—through His Word. We may think we know the mind of God merely from studying the Scriptures. Yet we cannot really be sure that what we are reading is fully accurate in our modern English language versions. The Bible was written in ancient (Classical) Hebrew,* Aramaic,* and Greek*—all of which are now dead languages.

The Bible translators do their best with the knowledge and skills they have to give us an accurate translation, yet with over 115 modern English translations, there is still much dispute over the proper rendering of certain words. The fact is, many translations reflect an understanding of God that may be subjective—and very different from the one the reader has. Hence, our true teacher is the Holy Spirit, and no matter how skilled and knowledgeable the translator may be, we still must pray for the guidance of the Holy Spirit when reading God's Word in an English translation.

In fact, I do not want anyone to read this book without first asking for the guidance of the Holy Spirit and following the teaching found in Colossians 3:15: *"And let the peace of God rule in your hearts, to the which also ye are called in one body; and be ye thankful."* The Greek word translated *"peace"* here is *brabeueto,* which means "to arbitrate" or "to umpire." You don't need an umpire to call whether a baseball player is safe or out when the baseman catches the ball and touches the base before the runner ever reaches it. A call is needed when a runner touches the base at seemingly the same time the baseman touches the base with the ball. In the stands, fans of one team are screaming, "Safe!" while fans of the other team are shouting, "Out!" It is the umpire who makes the final decision.

In your study of God's Word, the "umpire" is not your pastor, teacher, study leader, or even Chaim Bentorah. It is the Holy Spirit and whether or not you feel His peace in your heart. If you feel no peace about something I write because it goes against what your preachers or teachers have taught you, or what your own Bible study has indicated, I would encourage you to pray about it and ask for the Holy Spirit's guidance. If, after asking for the Spirit to guide you, you still feel a lack of peace in your heart, then don't feel you need to accept it. All I ask is that you seek the Spirit's leading to bring you into the knowledge He wants you to have and not allow Chaim Bentorah or any other teacher or preacher to stand in your way.

Having said that, I would like to point out that it comes as a surprise to many Christians to learn that there are literally hundreds of words in the Hebrew over which scholars strongly disagree regarding their proper, twenty-first-century English renderings. In fact, many linguists will tell you that we cannot possibly know the real depth of certain words in the Hebrew and express them in our modern English language. For instance, the Hebrew word *racham* (רחם) could be translated as "love," "tender mercies," or "lovingkindness." It could also denote the following: a very personal and individualized blessing, strength, protection, assurances, guidance, consolation, support, spiritual gifts, the gift of faith, repentance and forgiveness, persistence, fortitude, and cheerfulness. The list can go on and on, and yet we still cannot find an adequate word for *racham* (רחם). Perhaps God never intended for us to have a sufficient English word for it. Perhaps He wanted that word to have a fluid meaning so it could speak to us individually, so the Holy Spirit could whisper a personal message to us.

I recently heard a rabbi say that Hebrew is a spiritual language, the language of God, and thus many words have an eternal meaning that we will never have a complete understanding of until we are joined with Him in eternity. I like that idea because it suggests we will spend eternity learning and coming to understand the mind of God.

This concept can be illustrated by the marriage relationship. A husband may spend a lifetime learning the mind and heart of his wife. The more time he spends with her, the more he learns what is going on in her mind, but he will never have a complete understanding of it, at least not in this life. As much as his wife might share her heart and mind with her husband, it would still take more than a lifetime for him to comprehend them completely.

Then again, is that not one of the joys of becoming one with your mate—learning what the person you love the most is thinking and then knowing their thoughts so well that you know exactly the right anniversary or birthday present to purchase for them? Is it not a couple's desire and quest to learn each other's minds that draws the two closer together to form a bond that no one else on this planet can share with them, not even their own parents?

But what is greater still is when husband and wife seek to understand the mind and heart of God together. The closer they draw to God's mind and heart, the closer their bond will be to each other and to Him, with the three sharing each other's hearts and minds.

Jewish tradition teaches that one is to never study Torah* alone. Some students of Torah will actually pay someone to study the Word of God with them so they will not have to do it by themselves. For over ten years, one of my former students, the coauthor of this book, has been my study partner. The word studies I have chosen to include in *Hebrew Word Study: Exploring the Mind of God* are ones my study partner and I have worked on together, and many of the insights about God's love came from her experience in caring for her nephews—all the loving things her heart expressed to them and the loving bond she created with them. Although she does not share my academic background in biblical languages, she has a lifetime of experiences that I do not have. Through her relationships with her nephews, and her intimate walk with Jesus, she revealed to me a deeper understanding of the heart and mind of God as a Parent and Guardian. And I discovered a deeper understanding of many of the words that we studied.

Again, there are numerous words in the original biblical languages that have secondary meanings and translations. In the following word studies, I have chosen many renderings that you may not find in any English version. For example, the Hebrew root word for "anger" is *'aneph* (אנף). The term originates from the sound a camel makes—a snorting. The word even sounds like a camel's snort! Why does a camel snort? For several reasons: anger, frustration, or because it is being forced to do something it does not want to do. A camel also snorts when it is in heat and desires intimacy. Thus, *'aneph* (אנף) is an expression of great emotion that could reflect anger, frustration, desire, passion, grief, and many other possibilities. Only the context and tradition will tell us which English word to use.

For instance, we may read in our English translation that God's anger was kindled, and the original Hebrew word rendered "anger" is *'aneph* (אנף). In such an instance, why could we not say that His grief, His disappointment, or His sorrow was kindled? Perhaps the sin that aroused this emotion in God has separated His people from Him. Why could we not say that His passion for them was aroused, His longing and desire for intimacy with them was kindled, but He cannot fulfill His longing for intimacy because it has been blocked by their sin? Once more, translators use the context, tradition, and cultural influences to determine their word choices. These elements are very important, but I ask again that we add to this the personal guidance of the Holy Spirit.

As I wrote in a previous book, *Hebrew Word Study: Revealing the Heart of God*, in no way does this book seek to undermine any of our modern translations. It is my belief that all of our contemporary English versions of the Bible were translated by men and women skilled in biblical languages and linguistics. Every word in the dozens of modern English translations was prayerfully considered, and it is my position that even though various translations may contain different meanings, expressions, and nuances, they all reflect the inspired Word of God. They also demonstrate the ambiguity of the Classical Hebrew language and the infinite greatness of God.

Yet, over the years, as I tried to be true to the traditional translations of many words, I was persuaded to consider many alternative renderings that are more in line with a love relationship with God than a business relationship, which seems to be what many Christians have with Him. Sadly, I believe the fear of punishment and going to hell drives many Christians' relationship with God. Perhaps a relationship with the Lord of "I scratch Your back, You scratch my back" is not what it is all about. Maybe our church attendance, tithing, and good deeds are not about winning rewards from God or gaining eternal life in heaven, but rather about having a deep connection with a God who wants to share His unconditional love with us. Did God send His Son to die for our sins merely so that we would accept Jesus as our Savior and have our ticket to heaven? Once that is accomplished, why serve God any longer? If He will forgive all our sins, why not go out and live it up in a sinful lifestyle? Perhaps God made the basis of our salvation faith and not works so that our reason for living a life that is pleasing to Him would be motivated by love and not by a desire to gain favors from Him.

Someone reading this preface might conclude from my emphasis on God's love that I do not believe in a hell, punishment for sins, or even a devil. The fact is, I believe in these things more than I have ever believed in them. Even so, as I draw closer to God in my love relationship with Him, as I increasingly learn not to be afraid of Him, to realize that no matter how many mistakes or sins I commit, they will all be placed under the blood of Jesus, I find that my motivation not to sin doesn't come from a fear of going to hell but a fear that I will break the heart of the God whom I love.

Speaking for my coauthor and myself, it is our prayer that after you read this book, you will no longer be afraid that God will punish you for your sins and send you to hell. We pray that your love for Him will grow to the extent that your greatest fear will be that you might disappoint the God whom you cherish, that you might wound or even break His heart. God doesn't send people to hell. What sends people to hell is their refusal to accept His free gift of salvation, their choice to leave God out of their life, their choice not to accept His love. Our ultimate prayer is that someone who does not know God will pick up this book, fall in love with Him, and choose to follow Him in an ever-deepening relationship of mutual devotion.

—*Chaim Bentorah*

Study 1

God Declares His Thoughts

"For who hath known the mind of the Lord?
or who hath been his counsellor?"
—Romans 11:34

As I wrote in the preface to this book, Paul is asking a rhetorical question in the above verse. The answer is obvious. Who has ever known the full mind of the Lord? No one has, just as people cannot fully know each other's minds. Sometimes we do not even know our own minds! In Romans 11:34, the Greek word translated *"mind"* is *nous*, which refers to the intellect or the reasoning capacity. In Aramaic, the word is *ra'ina*, which, in Judaic literature, is not only used for one's mind or reasoning capacity but also for one's desires.

Isaiah 55:8 gives us additional insight into God's thoughts: *"For my thoughts are not your thoughts, neither are your ways my ways, saith the LORD."* Here, the Hebrew word rendered *"thoughts"* is *machashabah* (מחשבה), from the root word *chashab* (חשב), which means "plans, purpose, thoughts, and imagination." It is used for someone who invents something new. It is also an ancient word for a machine.

God Expresses His Thoughts Through His Creation

It is true that we cannot really know the plans and thoughts of God that He does not voluntarily reveal to us. For one thing, if He did reveal something deep, most likely, we would not understand it. Thus, the thoughts He communicates are on a need-to-know basis.

Yet, let's look closely at another verse, Amos 4:13: *"For, lo, he that formeth the mountains, and createth the wind, and declareth unto man what is his thought, that maketh the morning darkness, and treadeth upon the high places of the earth, the LORD, the God of hosts, is his name."* God forms the mountains, creates the wind, declares His thoughts to man, makes the morning darkness…. Whoa, wait a minute. Back up. "Declares His thoughts to man"? Apparently, God reveals some of His thoughts to us in avenues others than words. He declares them in the mountains and in the winds. Throughout all of His creation, He reveals thoughts that He intends for us to understand and embrace.

When was the last time God declared His thoughts to you in this way? Was it when your pet dog jumped up on your lap and for no reason at all gave you a sloppy kiss or stood waiting at your door when you came home, all excited about your arrival? Did something inside of you say, "God has just shown me through one of His creatures something of the nature of His love"? Through even small aspects of His creation, God gives us examples of His unconditional love—loving us no matter who or what we are. A dog doesn't care if you are handsome, beautiful, plain, or disfigured. It doesn't care about the color of your skin, your nationality, your political inclinations, or your religious beliefs. It just loves you. And God has proven through His Word that He loves us just as we are. (See, for example, Romans 5:8.)

I read a news story about a little girl who became lost in a forest. A search party spent hours looking for her, bringing her pet dog with them, and when they drew close to where she was, the dog began to bark, leading the rescuers to her. The article said that afterward, the little dog never left the girl's side. Have you ever felt like a little lamb who was lost in the woods? Is God any less faithful to us than that little girl's pet dog was to her? You are never alone. God is always by your side. I believe the little girl's dog, a piece of God's creation, was given to show us the faithfulness of our heavenly Father.

God Looks into Our Eyes with Love

There are some people who have the mistaken idea that I am a pretty smart guy and can figure out things about God. However, like you, I have learned that there are some things about God I am able to figure out, but there are many other things about Him that I cannot figure out, many things I will never figure out while still on this planet. I mean, I would sure like to know just what God was thinking when He pulled off a few of His "stunts" in my life! But then, the prophet Isaiah told us that God declares His thoughts to us, and Isaiah made this declaration under the inspiration of God's Spirit. Well, I am ready, God: tell me what You are thinking, because I sure can't figure it out!

I think it would help if we began by exploring the different Hebrew words translated as "thought" in Isaiah 55:8 and Amos 4:13. As I pointed out earlier, the root word for *"thoughts"* in the verse from Isaiah is *chashab* (חשב), which means "plans, purpose, thoughts, and imagination." These are what God declares to us through His creation. However, in Amos 4:13, which says that God *"declareth unto man what is his thought,"* the Hebrew word for *"thought"* is *secho* (שׂחו). Before I tell you the origins of *secho* (שׂחו) and what it means, I need to interpret the Hebrew word for "declareth," or "tells." That word is *magid* (מגד), which comes from a Semitic root* word as well as the Persian word *magi*, from which we get our modern word *magic*. The Hebrew root is *nagad* (נגד), which was borrowed from the Persian and means "what is most precious."

To be fair, in his well-regarded lexicon,* Benjamin Davidson claims this word is in a hiphal* (causative) form. Hence, the root word is *nagad* (נגד), which is an Akkadian* term meaning "to make a declaration that is clear and straightforward." Therefore, we might say this means looking into someone's eyes when saying something. I believe the prophet was making a play on words*** and that the meanings of the Persian and Akkadian root words were intended to factor into this expression. In other words, when God *nagads* (נגד), He is in some supernatural way looking directly into our eyes and declaring His *secho* (שׂחו), His thoughts, to us. To use a simple illustration, God makes His thoughts to us as plain as my neighbor's dog, Sparky, carrying his food bowl over to his master and looking into his eyes with expectancy.

Secho (שׂחו) also comes from a Semitic root from which the Hebrew word *shachah* (שׂחה), meaning "to worship," is derived. I found this root word used in a Ugaritic* text that tells the story of the goddess Anat who fell in love with a mortal man and entered into intimacy with him. The word conveys that intimacy, that expression of total love.

The Masoretes,* a group of Jewish scribe scholars who worked between the sixth century and the tenth century AD, made the first letter of *shachah* (שׁחה) a sine (שׂ), which has an "s" sound, rather than a shin (שׁ), which has an "sh" sound. This change would make the root word *shayach* (שׂיה), meaning "to meditate" or "to make a complaint." With the sine (שׂ), the word would be *sacha*, meaning "to be intimate." The change comes from placing a dot on the right side of the shin rather than on the left side. Just one altered dot in the Masoretic text (written seven hundred years after the birth of Christ) changed "intimacy" to "complaining." That dot was not in the original inspired text; it was placed there by man. Although many Christians hold up the Masoretic text as being almost inspired, the Jews do not, and they are not afraid to disagree with the Masoretes. I disagree with them, too. I don't believe God looks into man's eyes and shares His complaints—or that He even meditates on His complaints about man. I believe God looks into man's eyes and declares His deep, intimate love for those whom He has created.

As you continue to read this book, whose purpose is to reveal the mind of God to you, know that the foremost thought that expresses the mind of God toward humanity is His love for us in Christ Jesus. That is the central theme in everything this book expresses about God's mind. Thus, when I deal with words like *anger, wrath,* or *jealousy,* I will be looking at them through the lenses of God's perfect, unconditional love. If a particular Hebrew word is traditionally incompatible with the word for "love," like the Hebrew word for "anger," I will be looking at the various alternative renderings for this word. You will find that every Hebrew word used in our relationship with God that has a negative English expression has a positive, loving expression as well. I will insert a positive English word in the particular study verse that is being considered and allow you to decide if it fits or not. I only offer a suggestion, a viewpoint, a possible alternative. It is up to you to decide if I hit the target or missed it.

Most Precious

In my work, I drive a disability bus, and once, as I was waiting for one of my wheelchair clients to finish shopping, a flock of seagulls landed in the parking lot. The seagulls migrate at that time of year, and they pass over Lake Michigan, often coming inland to find food. As I offered part of my Egg McMuffin to one of the seagulls, he walked up to me, opened his mouth, and said, "Yik." I watched this seagull as he began to dance around and fluff up his feathers. His feathers were pure white, almost like fur, with little areas of pure black. The contrast was beautiful; he was beautiful.

The seagull and his friends just danced around my bus, showing themselves off. When anyone else walked by, these birds would just politely move away, unflustered, and then return for more Egg McMuffin. I could not help but think that only a God of pure love could have created such beauty. But why create this beautiful creature? Maybe because these birds made me begin to feel God's loving presence, His *secho* (שׂחו), His mind.

Even as the seagulls took off to continue their migration, I remained basking in the warm, glowing intimacy of God. With that little piece of His creation, God had looked me in the eye and, in a supernatural way, declared to me that I was most precious to Him. That is the meaning of *magid* (מגד), or "declare." And in this *magid* (מגד), I found *secho* (שׂחו), His mind, bringing me into His loving intimacy. In that moment, when He revealed His mind to me, I realized that He was most precious to me, as I was to Him. Suddenly, all my problems no longer mattered.

Emily Dickinson once said, "A wounded deer leaps highest." All my troubles, all my wounds, only cause me to leap higher into the arms of Jesus. They only serve to make me to open my heart further to God so that I am able to enter His *secho* (שׂחו) and hear the words He is speaking to me.

Study 2

A House of Prayer

"For mine house shall be called an house of prayer for all people."
—Isaiah 56:7

"[Anna] did not depart from the temple, but served God with fastings and prayers night and day."
—Luke 2:37 (NKJV)

To really get to know someone and understand their mind, or thinking, you need to communicate with them. In the same way, communication with God is essential to understanding and knowing His mind. In Isaiah 56:7, we find that God encourages us to pray to Him. He wants us to communicate with Him. And in Luke 2:37, we learn that prayer is really a means of serving God. Thus, prayer is a very important element in establishing our relationship with the Lord.

Simple Faith Pleases God

What makes prayer difficult is that we are speaking to an unseen God. How do we really know there is a God out there? That is what faith is all about. Hebrew 11:1 says that *"faith is the substance of things hoped for, the evidence of things not seen."* Faith is simply believing in an unseen, yet real and eternal, God. The writer of Hebrews goes on to tell us that *"without faith it is impossible to **please** [God]"* (Hebrews 11:6). Faith is at the very root of pleasing our heavenly Father.

In Luke 7:9, Jesus *"marveled"* (NKJV) at the great faith of the centurion who asked Him to heal his servant. Today, the word *marvel* has the connotation of "awe" or "amazement." Indeed, this word in the Greek, *ethaumasin*, does carry that idea, but when we drill down a little further, we find that *ethaumasin* represents "a joyful or wonderful feeling." The Aramaic term for "marvel" is *dama'* (דמא). It is similar to the Hebrew word *zamar* (זמר), which is a term for "praise" but, in its Semitic root, has the idea of "pruning." I am sure that, as a Roman centurion, the man had done a lot of things in his life that he would not be proud of, but Jesus only saw his faith, and it pleased Him.

When people marvel at a natural wonder like the Grand Canyon, they have a feeling of joy at seeing something beautiful and magnificent, while perhaps overlooking the fact that it can also be a very dangerous and treacherous place to travel. The marvelous feelings we have when we see God's beauty in nature may be similar to the marvelous feeling God has when He sees simple, childlike faith in us. He *zamars* (זמר), He prunes or cuts away, all those things that we would be ashamed of and just focuses on our faith, finding delight and joy in it. Jesus looked beyond all the faults of the centurion and saw something that was different or special, and He rejoiced in that. So, it wasn't that Jesus was shocked or taken by surprise by the faith of the centurion; it was that His heart was warmed and made joyful at his faith.

Serving God in Pursuit of His Will

We know we can please God with our faith, but what about *serving* Him, as Anna did in the temple? How can we best serve Him? By going to church and giving our tithes and offerings, or doing full-time Christian work, such as being a missionary? I suppose so, but I think the Bible gives us a better understanding of what it means to serve God. In Luke 2:37, we learn that Anna served God with *"fastings and prayers."*

To fast is to go without food, right? Well, not exactly. Going without food is just an expression of fasting. The Aramaic word used for *"fastings"* is *tsom* (צוֹם), which is identical to the Hebrew word *tsom* (צוֹם). The Greek word used in this verse is *nesteials*, and the Septuagint* (the Old Testament translated into Greek) uses the word *nesteials* for the Hebrew word *tsom* (צוֹם). I could not drill down very far with the Greek word *nesteials* to find any meaning other than *fasting*. But the Aramaic word *tsom* (צוֹם), with its Hebrew equivalent, does offer some insight. In its Semitic form, the Aramaic and Hebrew word *tsom* (צוֹם) has the idea of submitting the very necessities of one's life in order to receive some knowledge. In ancient times, the term was used for a soldier who gave up his life to be recognized by one of his gods and receive the knowledge of the gods. In the biblical context, it means to submit to God's will in order to bring about a transformation through the revelation of His hidden knowledge. That is the very essence of fasting. It is why going without food, the very basic necessity of life, is one of the most common expressions of fasting. But there are other ways to fast.

Some people believe in and teach what is known as a "fasted lifestyle." I am led to understand that it involves denying yourself the things of this world (see, for example, 1 John 2:16), fleshly desires (see, for example, Ephesians 2:3), and anything that feeds the flesh, in order to submit to the divine will. This would be an excellent definition of the Aramaic and Hebrew word *tsom* (צוֹם). Anna lived a fasted lifestyle. She continually stayed in the temple, denying herself fleshly desires to pursue God's will. This was called a *service* to God.

Anna also prayed. The Greek word translated *"prayers"* in Luke 2:37 is *de'esesin*, which really means "petition." The word used in my Aramaic Bible is *tselutha* (צְלוֹתא). In Isaiah 56:7, the Septuagint uses *de'esesin* to translate the Hebrew word *thapol* (תפל), which is rendered as *"prayer."* However, the meaning of *prayer* in the Greek, Aramaic, and Hebrew is not only prayers of petition, but also intercessory prayers—prayers of petition for others rather than oneself. Anna continually remained in the temple living a life of fleshly denial and interceding for others day and night. That also is called a *service* to God. It was not being a prophetess that was called her service; it was her *"fastings and prayers."*

Prayer Is Verbalizing the Heart of God

In order to express spiritual truths, some Orthodox Jews** sought to find relationships between Hebrew words that have the same numerical value.** This practice is called "Gematria"* The root word for "prayer" in Hebrew, as it is in Aramaic, is *palal* (פלל), which has a numerical value of 140. The mind or heart of God also has a numerical value of 140. The Gematria indicates that *prayer is speaking out, or verbalizing, what is in the heart of God.* Is that not what we are doing when we pray a prayer of intercession?

It is interesting that when you trace the root word for "prayer," *palal* (פלל), to its Semitic root, you discover its origins lie in the notch in a tent peg. The peg is firmly planted into the ground and the tent is attached to the peg. It is the notch, however, that firmly secures the tent to the peg and thus to the ground so that if a storm or strong wind comes, the tent will not blow away. That is what our connection with God through prayer is all about: it is the "notch" that firmly attaches to God so that when the storms of life come, we will not be blown away.

Creating a House of Prayer

What, then, is this *"house of prayer"* that we read about in Isaiah 56:7? The word translated *"house"* is *byith* (בית), which can mean not only a physical place of dwelling but also a spiritual one. The physical dwelling place could be a tent, a palace, a tabernacle, or a house. The spiritual connotation could be the spirit, the heart, or the mind, where our desires dwell. We could then say that the *"house of prayer"* is a place where the heart and mind of God reside. It is a place that one enters to verbally express His heart and mind. That is one way to translate the words *byith tepilah* (בית תפלה), *"house of prayer."*

But wait—if faith pleases God, and it takes faith to enter the heart and mind of God, it would follow that when we enter His heart and mind, our faith has made His heart joyful, so we enter into His joy. Since God's joy is derived from our faith, it is our faith that is ultimately responsible for the joy of the Lord that we enter into and feel.

Thus, going back to Jesus's interaction with the centurion, when this man expressed his faith, it created joy in the heart of Jesus such that healing power came forth from Him. Jesus made it clear that it was the centurion's faith that activated this power: "'*I say to you, I have not found such great faith, not even in Israel!' And those who were sent, returning to the house, found the servant well who had been sick*" (Luke 7:9–10 NKJV). The combination of *faith*—pleasing God—and *prayer*—proclaiming the heart and mind of God—created a "house of prayer" that brought about the healing of the centurion's servant.

God's Pleasure

"But his delight is in the law of the LORD; and in his law doth he meditate day and night."
—Psalm 1:2

My father used to tell a story about a time from his boyhood when he lived on a farm located way back in the hills of Missouri. A stranger came through carrying a Y-shaped tree branch with a silver dollar attached to the end that could supposedly detect the presence of silver. This was called "dowsing." (Other people use dowsing rods, or "diving" rods, to look for water or minerals under the surface of the ground.) When something was apparently detected, the branch would dip, incline, or twitch. The stranger let my father try it, and he remembered actually feeling the pull of the rod; it almost jerked out of his hand at one point. The branch eventually led them to a tree with the image of a canoe paddle carved into it, and there it started to bob up and down. The stranger said there was silver buried by the tree. When the man left, my dad, uncle, and grandfather started to dig. Before long, my grandfather gave up, saying there was nothing buried there. My dad and uncle kept digging until they hit a rock, and then they, too, gave up.

My father always said, "If only we had removed that rock." He was convinced the treasure lay underneath it. Since then, it has been a tradition for some of our family members to make a pilgrimage to the old homestead to search for the treasure. Sometimes, they have even gone with a metal detector, but they never have found that tree with the canoe paddle carved into it.

Buried Treasure in the Scriptures

Many times, when my study time is approaching, I tell myself, "I won't study this evening. I am tired, and surely I deserve a break." Yet I feel the Holy Spirit drawing me, like a divining rod, to a particular verse, encouraging me to continue in my quest to discover the heart and mind of God. It rarely fails that when I look at a verse, I see something like that old canoe paddle carved into the tree, a hint that there is something buried in there. I dig and dig—and then I hit a rock. I am tempted to give up, but then I think, "Will I ever find the old canoe paddle again when I return to this passage?" So, I call my study partner, and together we continue to dig until we remove that rock and find the buried treasure. Deuteronomy 4:29 says, *"But if from thence thou shalt seek the LORD thy God, thou shalt find him, if thou seek him with all thy heart and with all thy soul."* God will reveal His heart and mind to us if we seek Him with all our heart and mind.

You can learn all the biblical languages you want and purchase all of my Hebrew Word Study books, but you will never find those hidden treasures yourself until you search for them with all your heart and mind. If you want a study partner, you will have to find someone with whom you can share your own heart and mind. Thus, your best study partner is your spouse, for you would naturally share your heart and mind with your husband or wife. I would warn against having a study partner who is married to someone else, because in doing these deep word studies, you are sharing something very intimate and personal that is not appropriate to share with someone else's mate. Yet, you need that kind of intimacy in order to discover such treasures.

Delighting in the Law

"But his delight is in the law of the LORD; and in his law doth he meditate day and night." In Psalm 1:2, the word that stands out to me like the carving

of the canoe paddle, suggesting a buried treasure, is "*delight.*" This word intrigues me. I mean, who takes *delight* in the law? As I mentioned previously, I drive a disability bus. As any bus driver knows, when you reach a set of train tracks, usually at an established railroad crossing, you must stop the bus, put on your flashers, open the doors to the bus (even in subzero weather), listen for a train, look both ways, and then slowly proceed over the tracks. At a railroad crossing, when the red lights flash, the crossing gate goes down, blocking the way. However, often, the red lights will flash for a few seconds even before the gate goes down. If those red lights flash, you stop even if the gate is up and you know it will take a little while for the train to arrive. When you are in a hurry because you are late getting a passenger to their appointment, that particular law can seem excessive, and I do not always appreciate it, even though I know it is for the protection of my passengers and myself. Yet David is saying he *delights* in the law.

The Hebrew word translated "*law*" here is *torah* (תורה), which, in this context, is a reference to the first five books of the Bible. That was all the Scripture David had during his time, so he needed God's prophets to fill in the gaps. David's delight was to study and meditate upon those first five books day and night. Can you imagine delighting in the book of Numbers? Or getting your thrills reading through the genealogies? What would motivate David to study the law day and night if it were not the anticipation of discovering some new treasure, some new knowledge, about the God whom he loved?

The Hebrew word rendered "*delight*" is *chaphats* (חפץ), which represents one's will, but also signifies that which brings pleasure. If I am mining a verse with my study partner and I do not feel the pleasure of God while studying it, I will abandon any attempt to write up a word study because I want to share only what brings the pleasure of God. Often, if we go off on some "bunny trail," I sense the pleasure of God disappearing.

I think David took great delight in studying the law not only because of it treasures, but also because he felt God's pleasure when he did. That is why the first thing I do when I get home from work is to begin studying the Word of God. I look forward to meeting with my study partner and *chaphats* (חפץ), delighting, in the chance to share the pleasure of God with someone else who gets excited about sharing the pleasure of God.

Feeling God's Pleasure

I have to admit that when I run across various pamphlets entitled "Read Through the Bible in One Year," it is actually heartrending to me. A friend showed me a study Bible someone had sent her with a similar title. It is considered an achievement to *read* through the Bible in one year. Yet many Christians who struggle to discipline themselves to read through the Bible in a year, feeling very spiritual and proud if they manage to accomplish this goal, will sit down with the latest bestselling novel and read it in a few days. The titles of such pamphlets and Bibles say it all: *read* through the Bible. They don't say to study or meditate on it—just read it. David did more than just read—he meditated on God's Word because he felt the *chaphats* (חפץ), the pleasure, of God when he did.

I am not suggesting that if you find it hard to read through the Bible in one year there is something wrong with you. Growing up, I lived near a forest preserve. We would drive by it, and it looked beautiful. But on Sunday mornings, I would rise early with my father, and we would get in the car with our dog and drive out to the forest preserve to walk through it. We wouldn't talk much because my father was praying. At those times, I could feel God walking with us. I would hear the birds singing what seemed to be a special song, and I would see little animals stop in their tracks as if to savor the presence of God. My father would sometimes pause and say to me, "Look, a rabbit." In God's presence, anything He created is a big deal.

So, I am telling you a secret. (Be careful about spreading it around lest you get trampled!) There's treasure in the Book. Don't just drive by the forest preserve of the Bible, but take a walk through the inner beauty of the Word of God and feel God's *chaphats* (חפץ), His *pleasure*.

Meditate Day and Night

"But his delight is in the law of the Lord; and in his law doth he meditate day and night."
—Psalm 1:2

Let's continue to explore the treasure in Psalm 1:2. I recall a particular discussion with my study partner, who practices what she calls "meditative prayer." She told me that she sheds a lot of tears while she is meditating and praying. Later, I met with a group of men from church for a morning prayer time. We spent most of our time sharing our experiences of God. Again, there was much weeping.

The Hebrew word for "I weep" is *baki* (בכי). This word is spelled beth (ב), whose numerical value is 2, kap (כ), whose value is 20, and yod (י), whose value is 10. Added together, the numerical value of the word is 32. The Hebrew word for "heart" is *lev* (לב), which is spelled lamed (ל), with a value of 30, and beth (ב), with a value of 2. Thus, the numerical value of *lev* (לב) also equals 32. As I mentioned previously, the ancient sages taught that when two words in Hebrew have the same numerical value, you are to look for a relationship between them. I believe the relationship is that *weeping is an expression of the heart.* Many times, when your meditation brings you into the heart and mind of God, you begin to weep. Other times, you might weep for pure joy. There is something so cleansing when you have a time of *weeping* before the Lord. Sometimes, you might weep out of heartbreak as God shares with you that part of His heart and mind that weeps for a lost world, for the suffering of the world.

When I meditate on God's Word, I, too, often end up weeping, sometimes out of pure joy and other times out of shared grief with Him. I have gone on several weeklong, silent retreats, and at times I have stayed at a particular monastery.[1] During my first time of silence at the monastery, I made a deal with God. I told Him that if He would weep with me when my heart was broken, I would weep with Him when He shared His broken heart with me. Many times, as I travel through the inner city of Chicago, for no reason at all, I sense a deep sadness, hurt, or brokenheartedness welling up inside of me. Before long, I am weeping deep, uncontrollable sobs. I know and recognize that God is calling me to keep my end of the bargain. Somewhere nearby is someone who has broken God's heart. One time, I stopped to look around to discover what had broken God's heart, and I found I was next to an abortion clinic.

I have been in many worship services where there was great joyfulness in worship and praise, with many people shedding tears out of pure joy. Rarely, however, have I been in a worship service where there were tears of grief over God's broken heart for a lost world. Perhaps if we would occasionally dedicate a worship service to the broken heart of God and become silent before Him, searching for His heart and mind, we might end up spending that worship service weeping with Him over the pain of a lost world.

Focusing Intently on the Word

The Hebrew word for *"meditate"* in Psalm 1:2 is *hagah* (הגה), which has many usages. It is sometimes rendered as "to moan," "to growl," "to utter," "to muse," "to devise," "to plot," "to roar," or "to imagine." I can see "imagining" and "musing" as meditation, but what is this "moaning" and "roaring" business?

I attended a prayer meeting where a woman was so intense in her praying that it sounded as if she were moaning or even growling. Although this

---

1. See *Journey into Silence* (New Kensington, PA: Whitaker House, 2018).

might seem strange, a friend of mine offered the following illustration. If you go to the exercise room at a gym to work out, you hear a lot of grunting and groaning because the room is filled with people who are putting their whole hearts, minds, and bodies into their workouts. They are focusing all their concentration on lifting weights or doing other forms of exercise. Whenever anyone gets that intense, they usually let out a groan or moan. Perhaps you, too, have been so intense in your meditation that you have actually started to groan.

I heard an art history professor tell how he met an elderly curator at a Paris museum. The curator shared how, as a small child, he had once met Monet, the great Impressionist painter. The weather was subzero and the Rhine River was frozen over. His father took him for a walk along the river and said, "I bet we will meet Monet today." Sure enough, they came upon an elderly man sitting on a stool before an easel in the middle of the frozen river, intensely focused on his work. I am not sure if it was the color or shapes he was concentrating on in the scene. But whatever it was that Monet was studying, he was very intense in his study. As they went up to the painter, he stood and removed his hat. This curator said that even as a young child, he had been impressed by the fact that, when Monet took off his hat, steam rose from his head. He had been so intense in his concentration that even in subzero weather, he was working up a sweat.

Thus, meditation is more than just musing over something. It is intense concentration, focusing all of your attention on the Word of God. If you are to know God's heart and mind, you must focus your own heart and mind on Him. You must concentrate as if you were preparing for a final exam.

I used to teach a college class on speed-reading. When you speed-read through a book, you have to center all your attention on that material; you must have no distractions. If you allow one distraction, you will overlook an important word that ties everything together. I found the biggest reason a student could not pick up speed-reading was an inability to focus in that way. Such concentration is not natural for most people. It is something you must train your mind to do.

Receiving Spiritual Nourishment

My study partner mentioned that when she meditates, it is like eating or ingesting the Word of God. Rabbi Samson Hirsch relates the Hebrew word for "meditate," *hagah* (הגה), to the word *'aqah* (קה), meaning "encircle" or "surround." Encircling or surrounding is actually the same idea as eating. You encircle the Word of God and ingest it. Once it is ingested, like food, it begins to nourish you and give you energy.

This is what David did with the Word of God. He encircled it, ingested it, and let it become a part of him, giving him spiritual nourishment and energy. When God's Word becomes that much a part of you, you just cannot wait to dive into the Scriptures again. It is like looking forward to a three-course dinner of your favorite foods.

Such hunger for the Word of God does not happen naturally, at least for most people. Unless the Holy Spirit gives you this desire, it is something that takes discipline and time, but you soon acquire a taste for the Word. Then, before long, as can happen with physical hunger, you develop a craving for the Scriptures. And, as with physical starvation, you cannot concentrate on anything else until you feed well on God's Word.

Study 5

God Loves to Be in Love

"The LORD thy God in the midst of thee is mighty; he will save,
he will rejoice over thee with joy; he will rest in his love,
he will joy over thee with singing."
—Zephaniah 3:17

W hen I read the above verse in the Hebrew, the first thing that struck me was the word *qarav* (קרב), which is rendered *"in the midst of thee."* This word does not contain a definite article, even though most translators include one. I can understand why. It would be very awkward to say, "The Lord your God in midst of you." But perhaps there is another reason for the lack of a definite article.

The word *qarav* (קרו) can have two very distinct meanings. The difference between the two is indicated by using a pathah (vowel, short *a*) under the resh (ר) rather than a qammits (vowel, long *a*). This takes us back to the Masoretes, who used their own discretion in making such decisions. If we follow their thinking, we have a pathah, and hence the meaning "the Lord in your midst," or "nearby is mighty." However, since there is no definite article, I suspect a qammits would be more appropriate, and hence the phrase would mean, "The Lord in your inward parts" or "your heart is mighty."

God Will Save You

The Hebrew word for "*mighty*" is qavar (קור). This term means "strong" or "powerful," but it is a strength or power to help or rescue another person. Hence, the phrase could be rendered, "The Lord your God in your heart is a strength or power that will rescue or save you." The words qarav (קרו) and qavar (קור) play off of each other, expressing the idea that for God to be mighty means that He is in our midst and for God to be in our midst means that He is mighty. Not only is the power present to save you, but, as the verse says, "*He **will** save* [you]."

I once read a story in the newspaper about two teenagers who drowned. The lifeguards were aware of the life-threatening situation, and they had the equipment and training to rescue the teenagers, but they were also under strict instructions and regulations that prevented them from acting and could only call for the fire department to help. By the time the fire department arrived, it was too late. The point is that it takes more than just having the power of God in the midst of you to be rescued. There must also be a willingness and "authorization" on God's part to do the rescuing. Hence, this verse especially says, "*He will save*." Don't get too spiritual about the word "saved." I have no doubt it refers to our soul salvation, but it also means a physical salvation, or being rescued from our troubles.

God Will Rejoice over You

"*He will rejoice over thee with joy*." After reading this statement, we might ask, "Well, what else would you rejoice with?" However, there is no redundancy here. The word translated "*rejoice*" is sus (סוס), which is a pure form of joy that is not at the expense of others. You can rejoice in your favorite team winning a game, but that is because there is a loser involved. That is not sus (סוס).

The word translated "*joy*" is besimchah (בסמחה), which simply means being joyful. When I was a child, I would watch the comedian Bob Hope on television with my family. Half of the things he would say were not really funny and made little sense to me. But my family would laugh anyway. Just watching him perform made us relax and feel good. We were happy being together and finding pleasure in each other's happiness, and hence we laughed out of sheer joy. Years later, I watched someone laugh with what was called "holy laughter." There was nothing humorous happening; they were just laughing out of pure joy in the Lord. That is *sus* (סוס). God will rejoice over us out of pure joy. He feels joyful around us and takes pleasure in our happiness when we desire to make Him feel good.

God Will Rest in His Love

"He will rest in his love." The syntax* in this sentence is difficult, and it is a very troubling one for translators. How does God "rest" in His love? The Hebrew word translated "rest" is *charash* (חרש), which is in a hiphal (causative) form. *Charash* (חרש) can have a number of usages, including the concepts of fabricating, enchanting (more on this usage later), ploughing, or engraving. The basic idea is to produce something. Thus, "he will rest in His love" contains the idea that His love will cause something to be produced. In this context, His love will produce joy, such joy that "he will joy over thee with singing."

God Will Have Great Jubilation over You

In the final portion of the verse, a different Hebrew word for "joy" is used. It is *gadal* (גדל), which means "great and mighty." The word for "singing" is *ranan* (רנן), which is a celebration or jubilation. God will have great jubilation over us. From this verse, it appears that He can find much pleasure in us if that is our desire. But it is really more than that, so let's put all of this together.

The "Granddaddy" of Romance

God is saying that He will rejoice over us with joy, He will rest in His love, and He will joy over us with singing. This description caused me to think back to when I was a middle-school English teacher and I had a ninth-grade student in my class who was experiencing her first love. I mean, she was "gone," totally smitten by this young man. She was normally an attentive student, but now I had difficulty keeping her on target. She would drift off onto cloud nine and actually sigh.

One of the class assignments was to write a poem. You can guess what she wrote about. I had wanted my students to express something from their heart, which she did. Her poem went something like this:

> When he looked at me
> I was happy, so happy
> I was happy in my happiness
>
> I sang to him in my heart
> I sang to him a song of love
> A love song from my heart.
>
> And then he touched me
> His touched enchanted me
> And I fell into nothingness.

I gave her an A, although I was a little concerned about this "nothingness" business. I also told her that she needed to be careful to express only what she had personally experienced. But looking at her poem, it bears a striking resemblance to Zephaniah 3:17. It is almost as if God is a giddy schoolgirl experiencing her first love. Note my little student's words: "His touch enchanted me." We can get away with the word *enchant* in a love poem. We understand that the word means her love for this young man had totally captivated her, as if he had put a spell on her—but we know that no such thing actually happened.

So, what does it signify that God *"will rest in his love"*? As I mentioned earlier, the Hebrew word rendered "*rest,*" *charash* (חרש), has various meanings. There is one meaning of this word in its root that would make perfect sense if we used it here, applying it in a proper context. However, if the Bible translators used this word, a reader might not be as quick to assume the innocence of the word, similar to the context it was used by my student. You see, the word *charash* (חרש) also means to be "enchanted" or "bewitched." Those are not words we like to associate with God because of the implication of putting a spell on someone. We obviously do not put a spell on God. However, if we trace *charash* (חרש) to its Semitic root, it does not really imply an actual spell, but rather the idea of being so taken with an object or person that you become obsessed with them. In other words, *cha-rash* (חרש) really signifies an obsession, which would fit my little student's situation perfectly. But would we dare to put that word into this verse, say-ing, "'*He will rejoice over thee with joy.*' He will be obsessed/enchanted with His love for you. '*He will joy over thee with singing*'"?

To me, this idea of "enchanted" merely indicates that God loves to be in love—just like my student, and just like you, me, and almost every other human being. We love to be in love—no matter what our age. I heard on the radio about a retirement community in Florida called The Village. All the residents are in their "golden years." The community has a practice that if you are available for a little romance, then on a certain day, you wear a certain color. If you wear that color, you will likely have an elderly gentle-man or lady ask you out.

Let us never forget that we are created in the image of God—and He is the "Granddaddy of romance" who loves to be in love. When we return His love, He is *charash* (חרש)—*enchanted.*

Study 6

A Lover's Quarrel?

"And if ye will not for all this hearken unto me, but walk contrary
unto me; then I will walk contrary unto you also in fury; and I, even
I, will chastise you seven times for your sins."
—Leviticus 26:27–28

In Leviticus 26:27–28, God is revealing His mind-set in a very unusual way. However, many translations do not put it into the emotional context that I find many Jewish commentators do. I was reading a Jewish commentary on this passage that gave an enlightening insight, and I had to pause and wonder why I had never seen that insight before. So, I opened my King James Version and found out why.

The KJV, as do most other modern Christian translations, renders the Hebrew word *qari* (קרי), from the root word *qarah* (קרה), as *"contrary."* That is, if you walk *contrary* to God, He will walk *contrary* to you. Some Bible versions even render the word as "hostile" or "resistant." If you are hostile or resistant toward God, He will be hostile or resistant toward you with fury. Not one modern English translation that I have looked at renders this as the Jewish masters render it, and that is to use the English word *casual*. This is really the most common rendering of *qarah* (קרה). The English words *contrary, hostile,* and *resistant* are not the normal translations for this word. The only reason they are translated in this obscure way is because the text says God will answer the Israelites' disobedience in fury and chastise them seven times for their sins.

Really? Is this the God I love? Is this the God who said, "Love your enemies, and pray for those who persecute you?" Does God not apply this principle to Himself? Are there two sets of laws, two standards? God's Son teaching us to turn the other cheek and His Father still saying, "An eye for an eye?" (See Matthew 5:38–45; Leviticus 24:19–20.) Sorry, Christian scholars and teachers, I'm not buying it. The God I love will not return hostility with greater hostility that includes fury and punishment for sins seven times over.

Directly Connected with God

I am taking the side of the Jewish Hebrew masters and saying that *qarah* (קרה) is not to be rendered as *hostile* or *contrary* in Leviticus 26. Again, *casual* is the best translation. The word *qarah* (קרה) signifies "to meet without prior intent," "an accommodating arrangement," or "a marriage of convenience." Its origins lie in the concept of a structure whose roof is connected to its walls by beams. By appearances, a roof looks as if it is merely placed on top of four walls. Yet the roof is not directly connected to those walls but to the beams that are connected to them. Thus, the roof has only a "casual" connection to the walls.

What this means is that God wants to be directly connected to us, not to the support beams of our good works, pastor, church, or anything else. If we do not directly connect to Him, He will not connect to us—He can't. He can't connect to us any more than the roof can connect directly to the walls or the walls to the roof; they are separated by the support beams. As a result, God can only have a casual connection with us.

Often, the beams that separate us from Him are our sins. God is not saying, "Well, if you live contrary to My laws, then I am just going to be contrary toward you. How do you like them apples?" What He is saying is, "I don't want a *qarah* (קרה), a 'marriage of convenience.'"

A marriage of convenience means two people are together not out of love and passion, but rather because each derives some practical benefit from the relationship, whether it is financial security, protection, status, or any other reason. God is not interested in a one-sided marriage or a relationship in which only benefits are emphasized. He loves us deeply and wants to pour out His love and passion on us.

Unrequited Love

As we discussed in an earlier study, God doesn't want merely a relationship with us in which we scratch His back with good works and He scratches ours with gifts. If that is what you want, fine. He will give it to you—but with "*fury*." The Hebrew word translated "*fury*" in Leviticus 26:28 is *chemah* (חמה), from the root *yacham* (יחם), which is a term used for sexual excitement. In other words, you may desire God merely as a sugar daddy who will take care of you, but He is filled with such passionate love for you that when you discover what you have been missing, you will be "chastised" seven times.

The Hebrew word for "*chastise*" is *yasar* (יסר), which means "to influence toward a goal," "instruction," or "correction." God will be filled with such passion for you that He will keep demonstrating His love until you find that the love you have been looking for has been right in your own backyard the whole time, and you will love Him in return.

Too many people go to church every Sunday and pay their tithe thinking that God will consequently bless and "repay" them. With this approach, there is no real exchange of love. It is merely a marriage of convenience. Maybe God will bless them, but He will do so with *chemah* (חמה), with "*fury*," or better yet, with loving passion; and He will *yasar* (יסר), or "*chastise*," them seven times. Perhaps we could say He will instruct, guide, or influence them seven times.

Seven is the number of perfection. When God gives a blessing to someone, He is trying to influence them to see His genuine love. He does this "for their sins," as Leviticus 26:28 states. The Hebrew word translated "sins" is *chatah* (חטה), which is an archer's term for "missing the target." When God blesses people, they often just take that blessing and run with it, thus moving the target the blessing was meant to hit. That target was their heart. They just keep diverting the mark, never realizing that true love is right there waiting for them.

This is really a story of unrequited love, a theme Charles Dickens liked to write about. In *A Tale of Two Cities*, Sydney Carton is secretly in love with Lucie Manette. He sacrifices his life in the place of Charles Darnay, who is also in love with Lucie and whom Lucie loves in return. In *David Copperfield*, Agnes is in love with David, who only sees her as a friend throughout most of his life. In *Great Expectations*, Pip goes through great lengths to be worthy of Estella, his lifelong love. Even in *A Christmas Carol*, Scrooge's nephew dearly loves him, but Scrooge only scorns his affection.

In all these stories, I cannot help but think of God's love for us and how we feel unworthy of receiving that love, like Sydney Carton felt toward Lucie; or how we are oblivious to His love, like David Copperfield was to Agnes's devotion; or how we think we have to prove ourselves worthy of that love, like Pip felt he had to do for Estella; or how we are just too busy to even recognize that love, like Scrooge was about his nephew's affection. In each case, the common denominator is that there was unreciprocated love. God is making every effort to expose His deep love for us even as we pursue other "gods," never realizing that True Love has been with us all along.

Study 7

A Broken Heart

"The LORD is nigh unto them that are of a broken heart;
and saveth such as be of a contrite spirit."
—Psalm 34:18

An orthodox rabbi once told me, "You Christians do not understand the heart of David; you are so one dimensional." Indeed, we often are. For instance, we automatically assume that the expression *"a broken heart"* means only one thing. We never seek to examine the dynamics of what a broken heart refers to when it comes from the lips of David. Practically every modern translation will render *lenisheveri* (לנשברי) as *"broken."* This gives the impression that God's love is somehow special to those who have suffered a wounded heart. Although such a thought can be of great comfort during a time of brokenness, I believe David was trying to express something much deeper.

Most modern Bible translations use the King James Version as a model. In doing so, they often move in lockstep with old and established renderings beloved by Christians throughout the centuries. Although the rendering of *"broken heart"* from *lenisheveri lev* (לב לנשברי) is fully appropriate, it does not allow for the ambiguity of the text. My younger brother, who is a linguist and executive with Wycliffe Bible Translators, gave me some notes published by Wycliffe to assist me with my doctoral dissertation. In those notes, I read a statement from a former professor at Dallas Seminary who is now at Yale University. He said that many of our modern renderings often reflect the doctrine of the particular denomination or church that the translator represents. In translating, it is important to retain the ambiguity of many Hebrew words so that the readers will have the freedom to allow the Spirit of God to speak to them in ways that the teachings of their particular churches might limit.

The phrase *lenisheveri lev* (לב לנשברי) is a perfect example of this. By rendering it as *"broken heart"* in keeping with tradition, we limit what the Holy Spirit can reveal to us personally. Again, let me say that *"broken heart"* is not a mistranslation or an incorrect translation; it is just a limiting one, for these words express so much more of what was going on in David's heart. *Lenisheveri* (לנשברי), *"broken,"* comes from the root word *shavar* (שבר). The lamed (ל) that comes at the beginning is a preposition (to), and the nun (נ) that follows it indicates that it is in a niphal* (reflexive) form. Rather than limiting our range of renderings, this only broadens it and gives the Holy Spirit a lot of leverage with which to speak to people's hearts.

An Opportunity for a Breakthrough

One possible rendering for *shavar* (שבר) is "a breakthrough." The Lord is near to those who are experiencing a breakthrough in their hearts. A broken heart is often an opportunity for a *breakthrough* in one's heart. You frequently hear about someone being on the "rebound" after a broken relationship. For their own sake, people are usually advised to wait a period of time before starting a new relationship after a breakup because their heart is very tender and they may seek to fill their emptiness with another relationship too quickly and end up making a serious mistake of judgment.

David knew that when his heart was broken by a false "god" in his life (such as lust, wealth, power, advisers, or even friends), there was another Suitor waiting at the door. When those other gods failed him, the Lord was there, ready for His chance to recapture David's heart. Thus, David saw his broken heart as an opportunity. Just as a wound that is in the process of healing is very tender to the touch, his wounded heart would be very tender to the touch of God and would feel His touch in a way he never would have felt prior to his loss.

You see, David had a heart after God's heart. (See 1 Samuel 13:14; Acts 13:22.) This did not only mean he understood God's heart but that his heart was constantly seeking to be joined with God's heart. Hence, every wound he felt was an occasion to experience the touch of God in a way he could not experience when all was well, when every rose in his life was in bloom and healthy.

The Suitor at the Door

When that *rose* in your life fades or dies and you are left with a broken heart, what do you do? You may express your sorrow in different ways, such as weeping and mourning. These are normal responses, and grieving must be allowed, but don't let your wound blind you to the Suitor who is waiting at the door. He is ready to touch your wounded heart, and like David, you can welcome your *lenisheveri lev* (לב לנשברי), or *"broken heart,"* as an opportunity, a *breakthrough*, to feel the touch of God in a way you could never feel it when your rose was in full bloom.

When you suffer a broken heart, you might just want to be alone, but your Suitor wants to be alone with you in your hurt. Consider the mind of God and comprehend what He is quietly saying to you: "I understand what a broken heart is like, for My people have broken My heart many, many times. I will stay with you, comfort you, and heal your heart."

The Secrets of the Lord

"The secret of the LORD is with them that fear him."
—Psalm 25:14

"Never to make a line that I have not heard in my own heart."
—Edmond Rostand, *Cyrano de Bergerac*[2]

A poem, as with any art form, is a means of expressing one's heart. The play *Cyrano de Bergerac*, written by Edmond Rostand, is the story about a man who is very gifted both with words and skills of daring. He cuts a romantic figure, except for one glaring physical defect—a very large nose. He is desperately in love with a beautiful woman named Roxane, but he believes she cannot love him because of his nose. Roxane is also a romantic and longs for a man to speak of his love for her in skillful poetic verse. Enter a man named Christian who is also in love with Roxane. He is very handsome but cannot put enough words together to write a grocery list. So Cyrano fulfills his need to tell Roxane how much he loves her by writing her beautiful, poetic verse and then signing Christian's name to it, knowing she will not reject these words of love from such a handsome

---

2. Edmond Rostand, *Cyrano de Bergerac*, ed. Brian Hooker (New York: Henry Holt and Company, 1951), Act II, Scene 8.

man. Roxane falls in love with Christian, believing he is the one who is writing these deeply romantic words to her.

Expressing the Depths of Our Love

I think it is fitting that the character Rostand created who is such a dumb ox is named *Christian*. We Christians love God, but like "Christian," we find it difficult to express our love for Him in beautiful words. There is a scene in *Cyrano de Bergerac* where Christian is alone with Roxane and now has the opportunity to express his deep love and yearning in person, but all he can say is, "I love you." Roxanne grows frustrated and asks that he tell her *how* he loves her. But rather than say something like Cyrano would have said, such as, "My soul, be satisfied with flowers, with fruit, with weeds even; but gather them in the one garden you may call your own"—all he can say, once again, is simply, "I love you." Cyrano has to jump in and express the words that not only he feels for Roxane, but Christian feels too. Then Christian can state, in effect, "Yeah, like he said."

Toward the end of his life as one of the world's greatest evangelists, D. L. Moody reportedly said this to songwriter Will L. Thompson, author of the hymn "Softly and Tenderly": "Will, I would rather have written 'Softly and Tenderly Jesus is Calling' than anything I have been able to do in my whole life." Apparently, that hymn expressed the very depths of D. L. Moody's love and understanding of God. He just wished he could have penned it. But God gifted him with the words to preach, not the words to write poetry. God gave the gift of poetry to someone else who used it to write a hymn that expressed D. L. Moody's heart toward God, just as it has expressed the hearts of millions of other Christians toward the Lord.

This is why music is so important in worship and praise. We can say "I love You" just so many times. Lifting our hands in the air and repeating over and over, "I praise You, I love You," tends to become mere ritual. There is a yearning in our souls to say more, to express the very depths of the love for God that lies within our hearts.

The Words of the Master Poet

As a child, I used to sing an old hymn by Charles Wesley that begins, "O for a thousand tongues to sing my great Redeemer's praise."[3] God has provided us with poets and songwriters who love Him with all their hearts and can put that love into words that most of us could never dream of writing. The words in the old hymns, gospel songs, and modern worship and praise music are tools for us to express verbally what our hearts are crying out to communicate to the God whom we love. In this sense, we have access to literally thousands of "tongues" to sing our great Redeemer's praise! And sing it we must, or our love might just shrivel up and die. Love needs to be expressed. A lover needs to hear the words of his or her beloved, or that love may die.

Yet, what if the very depths of the love we have for God have also been put into words for us by the Master Poet Himself, the One who expresses His heart's longing for us? Not only has God published these words in a Book, but also, we can use those same words by which He expresses His deep love for us to speak of the love we have for Him. That Book, of course, is the Bible, which is filled with beautiful words of love and endearment.

Has your heart ever sung, "The LORD is my shepherd; I shall not want" (Psalm 23:1)? If so, at such times, have you felt tremendous love for God flowing from you? In a way, that is an expression of your own heart, even if the words were written under the inspiration of the Holy Spirit by someone who lived three thousand years ago. It will still sing from your heart to the God who inspired it. Yet, too often, these biblical words of endearment are muddied by translators who, while in the process of seeking an accurate translation, take the heart and soul out of the words. That is okay, for it challenges us to study the Word of God, to dig for a deeper understanding of it.

For example, we must stop and ponder just what it means for God to be our Shepherd and to love us like a Shepherd. We might read books on how a shepherd cares for, nurtures, and loves his flock and still feel there is more to understand about this verse. In the original language, the word rendered "shepherd" is ra'ah, (רעה) which is usually translated as "evil." How

---

3. "O for a Thousand Tongues to Sing," 1739.

do you get the term *shepherd* from the word *evil?* The more common rendering refers to an evil consuming passion. To have a consuming passion for drugs, alcohol, money, or other worldly devices is an evil. But a husband having a consuming passion for his wife or a mother having a consuming passion for her child is not evil as long as it draws them to God. By this understanding, we can discover a new depth to our love for God and cry out, "The Lord is my consuming passion. I have need of nothing else!"

Falling in Love with the Author

In my book *Hebrew Word Study: Revealing the Heart of God*, I told a story that is fitting in this context as well. A woman met a man at a social function, and when she inquired about his vocation, he said he was a writer. As far as her idea of a romantic partner, she saw no future with a writer—especially a writer of science fiction, a genre that she hated. He gave her a copy of his book, and she put it on her bookshelf and moved on, seeking a soul mate elsewhere. However, this writer was persistent in courting her, and before long, they began dating and fell in love.

One night, he asked her to marry him and she agreed. When she went home, she began to wonder about this deeply intellectual man with whom she had fallen in love. Oh, how she wished to understand his mind so she could know what to do to bring him pleasure, joy, and happiness. Suddenly, she remembered that he had given her his book. The woman ran to her bookshelf, dusted off the cover, and began to read. In fact, she read through the whole book that night.

Why would someone who hates science fiction give up a night's sleep to read through a science-fiction book? The answer, of course, is that she fell in love with its author. She read his book to understand his mind, because in understanding his mind, she grew to love him even more deeply and learned how to say "I love you" in a way that would reach his heart.

Thus, there is no "magic" in reading the Bible. God is not going to give you a special blessing just because you read a couple of verses every morning. You will not draw closer to God by a cursory reading of His Word. Intimacy with God comes when you learn about His mind through reading His Book and, in learning His mind, you fall more deeply in love with

Him and understand how to better express that love. Then, you will know how to say "I love you" in a way that reaches His heart.

Honoring and Respecting the Lord

All this leads us to our main study verse: *"The secret of the LORD is with them that fear him."* The Hebrew word translated *"fear"* is *yare'* (ירא). During the time the King James Version was written, the word *fear* had a much different meaning than it does today. To render *yare'* (ירא) as *"fear"* in the early seventeenth century would have been very correct. In that period, the word had the context of chivalry. Chivalry comprises the ideal qualities of a knight, including courtesy, generosity, gallantry, and valor. A chivalrous man showed respect where respect was due. If someone disrespected a woman, he would defend the woman's honor in a duel. The "fear" aspect was found in the concern that one might offend someone else's honor or disrespect them in some way. Thus, it was used to express the idea of reverence and respect.

It was none other than Charles Darwin in the nineteenth century who took the word *fear* and added the concept of concern for one's own gizzard. Therefore, today, when we hear the word *fear* as in "fear the Lord," we think of being afraid of God, of keeping our distance lest He hurt us in some way. (That is just another disservice given to Christianity by that Darwin guy.)

Learning Words from the Heart of God

"The secret of the LORD." The Hebrew word rendered *"secret"* is *sod* (סוד), which means the mysteries of God, the mind and heart of God. God will share His mind with those who fear that they may offend Him.

A woman will not share her *sod* (סוד), or the depths of her mind or heart, with a man if she doesn't trust him, because then he will have the knowledge to deeply wound her, to break her heart. However, if she is confident that the man respects and honors her and wants to know her heart so he can protect it and bring her pleasure and joy—she will feel free to reveal her heart to him. Similarly, God will not reveal His mind and heart to anyone who would use that knowledge to offend Him or break His heart.

If you truly want to know what brings God joy, happiness, and pleasure, then He will freely share His heart and mind with you.

Once again, there is no magic or special blessing in just reading some words from the Bible. The real blessing comes in learning the mind and heart of God as He has revealed them in His Word, in order to know and love Him more intimately. It comes in knowing words from the heart of God that express His love for you and realizing you can offer those same words back to Him. It comes in discovering words used by others who loved God thousands of years ago, like David, and finding them still fresh and relevant to express your own love toward Him.

Study 9

My Precious One

*"As the apple tree among the trees of the wood, so is my beloved
among the sons. I sat down under his shadow with great delight, and
his fruit was sweet to my taste."*
—Song of Solomon 2:3

To illustrate a theme from our previous study, Song of Solomon gives us many words that express God's love for us in a poetic form that we can use to express our own love for Him. Consider this: Does Song of Solomon 2:3 depict God telling us that we are *the apple tree among the trees of the wood*? Or could it be that we are the ones telling God that He is the tree among the trees of the wood? That is the beauty of poetry. You can use it whichever way your heart leads you to express it.

Still, poetry can be difficult to understand at times, and you need to study a poem to get the full benefit and beauty of it. This is especially true if the poem was written thousands of years ago in another language. (And frankly, many of our English Bible translators could use a little training in understanding the nature of poetry.)

Forbidden Fruit?

When reading Song of Solomon 2:3 in my Hebrew Bible, I was struck by the word *chimadeti* (חמדתי). The word seemed strangely out of place in this sweet, romantic verse. I was intrigued to find out how our English translators had handled it. I first went to your friend and mine, the King James Version, which rendered it as *"great delight."* This seemed to be the good, cowardly way out. The Authorized King James Version (AKJV), the *New American Standard Bible* (NASB), the American Standard Version (ASV), the *Bible in Basic English* (BBE), the *English Standard Version* (ESV), and the World English Bible (WEB) all said the same. The *New International Version* (NIV) and Young's Literal Translation (YLT) simply rendered it as *"delight"* and *"delighted."* The Douay-Rheims 1899 American Edition (DRA) was a little braver, using the phrase *"whom I desired."* But the version with the most guts, the Darby Bible Translation (DARBY), renders the phrase as *"have I rapture."*

What caught my attention in the use of the word *chimadeti* (חמדתי) is that it is found only once in Song of Solomon, and it is rooted in the Hebrew word for "covet," *chamed* (חמד), which is found in Exodus 20:17: *"Thou shalt not covet."* If you ever go to a synagogue, look at the Ten Commandments above the ark (which contains the Torah scrolls) and scan down to the tenth commandment. There, you will see in Hebrew script the words *Lo tachmod* (לו תחמד), which literally mean "No you will covet." Yet, in the same synagogue, I saw a Jewish woman pick up her granddaughter, kiss her, and say, "Come, *chamudi* [חמדי]." I took a look at the tenth commandment and asked my host, "What did she just call the child?" He explained that this was modern Hebrew for "my precious one." I followed up by asking, "Is that not rooted in the same word in the tenth commandment?" He merely shrugged, as if to say, "Go figure."

How the Hebrew language managed to meander around the guilt-inducing *"Thou shalt not covet"* to the Modern Hebrew term "my precious one" proved to be an irresistible topic of study for me. First, I realized that the commandment was not a blanket prohibition, "You will not covet," but rather, "You will not covet anything that belongs to your neighbor." We often interpret the word *chamed* (חמד), or *"covet,"* as "having a desire for something that does not belong to us." That idea has always been troubling to me because I can barely walk out the door in the morning before I start desiring things that I do not have. The command is specific: you do not desire what is intimate to, or being consumed by, your neighbor. In other words, a simple desire for something does not hurt. *Chamed* (חמד) has to carry a little more punch than that.

I had an e-mail from someone asking about the term "garden of Eden," and the inquiry drew me to Genesis 2:9: *"And out of the ground made the LORD God to grow every tree that is pleasant to the sight."* In that verse, I found the word *chamed* (חמד) again, only it is translated by most Bible versions as *"pleasant," "pleasing," "beautiful,"* or, as the *God's Word* (GW) translation puts it, *"nice to look at."* Of all the versions I surveyed, only Young's Literal Translation (YLT) uses the word *"desirable."* Of course, we learn in Genesis 3 just how seductive something desirable can be.

Early rabbinic literature showed a sexual connotation to *chamed* (חמד) in the word *chamdam* (חמדם), using it as a reference to a lustful person. *Chimmud* (חמד) is even more blunt as a reference to a sexual appetite. As a verb, *chamed* (חמד) means "to be excited" or "to be hot." The medieval Hebrew grammarian David Kimhi, also known by the acronym Radak, stated that it is no coincidence that the word *cham* (חם), or "hot," makes up two thirds of the root. He pointed out that *lechem chamudot* (לחם חמדת) is taken by some to mean "fresh, hot, tasty bread."

So, what conclusion am I drawing from all this? Is Solomon's beloved saying she is sitting under the apple tree with "one hot number"? The writer is making a very distinct play on the word *chamed* (חמד) by bringing it into association with the *"apple tree among the trees of the wood."* Although we do not know what the forbidden fruit in the garden of Eden was, if it was indeed a literal fruit at all, this is still a direct reference to the forbidden fruit of the garden. The lover sits under her beloved's shadow with *chamed* (חמד), or covertness, eating this forbidden fruit. The love King Solomon felt for the Shulamite woman was a forbidden love, as was her love for the king. She was already betrothed or pledged to a shepherd. Even so, in that particular culture, if a woman had two men seeking her attention, she was given the right to choose which one she wanted.

The word *chamed* (חמד) ultimately has the idea of intimacy or totally possessing or consuming something. This fruit is not forbidden as long as the Shulamite woman consumes it within the bounds of intimacy born out of love with her beloved. Just as a sexual relationship is forbidden outside of marriage born of love, so was the fruit in the garden forbidden outside of a relationship of love and intimacy with God.

The Intimate Presence of God

Adam and Eve were permitted to possess everything in the garden of Eden except the fruit of one tree. Jewish oral tradition teaches that this forbidden fruit wasn't totally off limits to Adam or Eve; it was only off limits without the intimate presence of God and a love relationship with Him. With this view, the fruit was designed by God to be something that was intimate between the three of them, to be shared only between man and woman *with* God—God and His beloved. Just as a husband and wife will share the fruits of their intimacy in a bedroom totally alone with no one around watching or listening, so too God created this "tree" with its fruit to be shared with Himself and Adam alone or Eve alone or Adam and Eve together. Sin did not occur until Eve took the fruit on her own and shared it with Adam, who ate it too; she was sharing with her husband the one thing she was not allowed to share with him outside of God's presence.

One penalty for Eve and her female descendants was that her *teshuqah* (תשקה), or "*desire*," would be for her husband, but he would, *mashal* (משל), or "*rule over*," her. (See Genesis 3:16.) The Hebrew word *teshuqah* (תשקה) is from the root word *shuwq* (שוק), which signifies a longing and reaching out. It implies that a woman will try to reach out to her husband to fill a longing that only God can fill. If her husband tries to fulfill her longing without the presence of God—in other words, if he *mashals* (משל), or rules over, what God is meant to give—she will become frustrated and perhaps angry with him because He will be unable to give her what she deeply desires, something only God can give. In turn, her husband will become frustrated because he cannot provide this special intimacy for her. Again, only God can fill this gap in their relationship.

God is a personal God. Although He allows us to share almost everything about our relationship with Him with other believers in the deepest *koinonia* (communion by intimate participation), there is still a special intimacy that He has reserved for us, and us alone, where our love for Him and His love for us is consummated. No one else in our lives can share in the fruit of this union, for it belongs to God and no one else—except when a husband and wife who are one can experience it together with Him. God longs for a special, intimate time with each one of us that is shared with no one else, just as a husband and wife share an intimacy with each other that no one else in the world should share.

We enter into intimacy with God through the blood of Jesus Christ, and it is through His blood that we can eat of the "forbidden fruit." Only by the complete cleansing of the blood of Jesus are we worthy to partake of this most intimate fruit that we are to share with God alone.

Study 10

Drawing Near to God

"Then Judah came near unto him, and said, Oh my lord, let thy
servant, I pray thee, speak a word in my lord's ears."
—Genesis 44:18

I read something interesting about the above verse in the Jewish Talmud,* an ancient collection derived from oral tradition and commentaries. The Hebrew word translated *"come near"* is *nagash* (נגשׁ), which contains the idea of drawing near or approaching with an offering, a present, or a request. The sages believe this verse is teaching the way in which we can approach God in prayer with a request.

When I first started to study the Talmud, it was with the intention of honing my skills in Aramaic, not to gain any spiritual insights. After all, I was a Christian. What did Judaism, another religion, have to offer me? However, I came to realize that even though, in general, the Jews had rejected Jesus as their Messiah, this did not mean they had lost their anointing to be the guardians of the Holy Scriptures. Additionally, I found that by substituting "Jesus Christ" for "Abraham, Isaac, and Jacob," many teachings of the sages had deep application for my own faith.

Three Suggestions for Approaching God

The sages believe that Genesis 44:18 is giving three suggestions, and that when we follow any of them, we will be able to have the strength to approach God in prayer.

Come on the Merits of Jesus Christ

The first suggestion is to consider that we are sinful and have no right to approach a holy God. All our deeds are filled with foolishness and emptiness. Yet, we can still approach God, not on our own merit, but on that of the holy ancestors, Abraham, Isaac, and Jacob.

In thinking about this suggestion, I know that the patriarchs are not my physical ancestors. And even if they were, I recognize that they were sinners just like me, so I can't approach God on that basis. But suppose I say it in this way: "We can approach God, not on our own merit, but on the merit of Jesus Christ, the sinless Son of God, the perfectly holy and obedient One, who died for our sins"? Now, that makes a lot of sense to me.

Take the Initiative to Move Toward God

The second suggestion for consideration is that God has placed within us a soul (comprised of mind, will, and emotions) that has been designed to attach itself to God as its source. However, I know there's a problem with this suggestion: we have been given a free will and can rebel against God if we choose to do so. Let's think about this idea with the following illustration: A magnet will attract a metal object. Yet that metal object must be close enough to the magnet for the magnet's force to draw the piece to it. In the same way, we must go near enough to God to be drawn into His life. *"Judah came near unto him."*

Continuing with the analogy, suppose there is another magnet on the other side of the metal object that is likewise exercising its force upon it. Spiritually speaking, the first force is God, and the second force is that of "the world, the flesh, or the devil" (see Ephesians 2:1–3); that second force is contrary to God and is exerting its force to draw our soul toward it. What should we do in this situation? The Bible says, *"Draw near to God and He will draw near to you"* (James 4:8 NKJV). The verse clearly indicates that the initial step is ours. We need to make the first move toward God, and when we get close enough, He will draw us to Himself like a magnet, pulling us away from the opposing force.

It is an interesting idea that prayer is the instrument God uses to draw our minds to Him. But again, my Jewish teachers seem to overlook the problem of sin separating us from God, which we cannot overcome through any merit of our own or of our forebears. This perplexing problem was solved by Jesus Christ two thousand years ago, so that, in Him, I am made pure and holy before God, and I may use prayer to draw my mind and heart to the God of the universe. (See 1 Thessalonians 5:23.)

Take Time to Prepare Your Heart and Mind

The third suggestion is that God spoke through the mouth of Moses. As our mind attaches to God, He will put His words in our mouth as we pray. By His mercy (and, I would add, the finished work of Jesus Christ), He will place His words, often the answer to our prayers, on our tongues so that we will pray *with* Him. I have heard some Christians criticize Jews and others for reciting prayers over and over, perhaps in light of Jesus's warnings against *"vain repetitions"* (Matthew 6:7). These believers say, in effect, "They think God hears prayers that are recited. How foolish. I speak my own words to God; I don't need a prayer book."

Yet consider what the sages are teaching. The recited prayers that the Jews speak are only used to *prepare* themselves for prayer. The recitation of prayers is meant to focus our soul and body on God and help us draw near to Him so that, when we get close enough, we are suddenly no longer praying *to* God but *with* Him. We are drawn into Him, and His words and our prayers become one.

Many Christians will drive to church arguing with a family member over some matter or yelling at another driver who cuts them off, and then, when they arrive at church, they will dive right into prayer. Biblically, I believe there is a need for a cleansing time before we approach the throne of God; there is a need to get our body and mind "in line with the program." I am not suggesting just reciting prayers, but really doing something of a spiritual nature—spending time in the Word, singing songs of worship, or just meditating on the Lord. We need to get our minds on God before we pray.

That is why I usually decline when someone asks me to open in prayer at a meeting or say the blessing over a meal. I am not going to jump before the throne until I have prepared my body and mind; after that, I will walk boldly before the throne of grace. (See Hebrews 4:14–16.) Consider this illustration: A husband and wife get into a little argument before bedtime and say some hurtful things to each other. They will not share intimacy until they spend some time in preparation: seeking forgiveness, expressing their honest feelings to each other, and entering into a little love talk. After this, they can get to the "good stuff," because then the two shall become one. In a similar way, we become one with God when we approach the throne, but not until after we have aired out our sins and shared some love talk with Him. Then, we can converse with God in unity.

Do you ever find yourself praying for guidance from God and saying things like, "Lord, I need Your help right now. Come on, I have tried to do my best, and I really need You to come through for me now"? That approach is like Aladdin rubbing the lamp and calling for his genie. God is your Father, your Lover, and your Friend, and you need to treat Him accordingly. Spend a little time in preparation, getting your mind and body in line with His.

I watched an episode of a TV program where a single mother took her two young children to meet her fiancé's parents for the first time. She had bathed the children and dressed them in clean, appropriate clothing. Just before entering the parents' home, the mother made a few adjustments to one child's hair and straightened the collar of the other child. After that, they were all ready to meet the soon-to-be in-laws. In the same way, if you love someone, you want to put your best foot forward. You are not going to greet your beloved unbathed and dressed in sloppy clothes with your hair disheveled. Yet that is exactly what many of us do when we come before our Spiritual Lover.

"Let This Mind Be in You"

Paul said, *"Let this mind be in you, which was also in Christ Jesus"* (Philippians 2:5). If we prepare our mind and body properly, then, when we draw near to God, He will draw us to Himself. Often, the words we speak in prayer will suddenly become the words of God, leading to the answer to our prayers.

We may pray, "Lord, I don't know what to tell Charlie. I really need Your.... Uh, yeah, I know I should be honest with him.... Yeah, I need to love him as You love him." It's curious how the answers just seem to flow when you enter the heart and mind of God and your thoughts and His become one.

"Thou Shalt Love..."

*"Hear, O Israel: the LORD our God is one LORD: and thou shalt love
the LORD thy God with all thine heart, and with all thy soul,
and with all thy might."*
—Deuteronomy 6:4–5

*"Love is a canvass furnished by Nature and
embroidered by imagination."*
—Voltaire

Each day, all Orthodox Jews in nations around the world recite Deuteronomy 6:4–5 in Hebrew. This passage is part of the Shema, a declaration of faith and devotion to God. Why do they recite this passage in Hebrew and not in their native languages? To be sure, there are ceremonial reasons, but one fundamental reason is that you cannot recite the Shema in another language, particularly in English, with exactly the same meaning that it has in Hebrew. With something as fundamental as this primary statement of faith and devotion to God, you want to be sure you are reciting it with its exact intent.

In Deuteronomy 6:5, the Hebrew word translated *"love"* is *ahav* (אהב). The Septuagint uses the Greek word *agapos*. *Agape*, as you are probably aware, is a word used for unconditional love. What is really interesting is that, in the Hebrew, the word *ahav* (אהב) is preceded by the letter vav (ו) and forms a vav construct state. Grammatically, this converts the imperfect value to the perfect value, denoting a completed action in the past, present, or future.

Therefore, when Jews recite this verse every day, what they are really saying is, "I have loved, I do love, and I will continue to love the Lord my God with all my heart, soul, and mind." Not a bad promise to make. I think most Christians have expressed to God that they will love Him unconditionally—that they have loved Him in the past, that they love Him in the present, and that they will love Him in the future. Such a commitment to loving God should be foundational to our relationship with Him.

A Command to Love?

However, when we hear the phrase *"Thou shalt love the* LORD *thy God…"* it sounds like a command. Rabbi Dov Baer Ben Abraham, an eighteenth-century Hebrew scholar and linguist who is called the Maggid of Mezeritch, asked this question: "How can there be a command to love? Love is a feeling of the heart; one who has the feeling, loves." In other words, love for God is embedded in the heart of man.

The Maggid of Mezeritch continued by pointing out that the meaning of the commandment to love the Lord lies in the previous verse: *"Hear, O Israel…."* The word *shema* [שמע], meaning "to hear," can also signify "to comprehend." Thus, Torah is commanding a person to study, reflect on, and comprehend the nature of God, because one of the functions of the mind is to rule the heart. Such contemplation will inevitably lead from the mind to the heart and reveal the love of God that is embedded there. A person's study of God and His Word will refine and purify them of the things that stifle their capacity to sense God and relate to Him. Once your meditation on God shifts from the mind to the heart, the love you have for Him will not be blocked, and the more you worship God with your heart, the more your love for Him will be revealed.

For the past ten years, I have been searching for the heart and mind of God. I have spent a minimum of three to four hours a day studying God's

Word in Greek, Hebrew, and Aramaic, and countless hours just meditating on the nature of God. As a result, I have come to realize the truth of a statement I read in a story in Jewish literature. A student went to his rabbi to complain about another student. His objection was that the other student was always bragging about his knowledge of Torah and how one day he would become a well-known and respected teacher. The first student went on to say that the only reason his fellow scholar studied Torah was so that he could gain fame and respectability. The rabbi simply replied, "It is okay, for the Torah will purify his motives."

I realize now that I began my journey to discover the heart and mind of God so that I could gain deep insights into His Word, impress people with my knowledge, and write books. I have accomplished all these things, but in the accomplishment, I discover I have found no joy or sense of fulfillment in any compliments I have received about my knowledge of the Word of God. What brings me great joy and a sense of fulfillment is when someone writes to me and says, "I have grown to love God more and more through your books and teachings."

Those years of studying God's Word have moved me from my mind to my heart, and in doing so, I have found a deeper and richer love for Him. That love has been in my heart since the day when, at twelve years of age, I accepted Jesus as my Savior. The moment I accepted Jesus, all my sins were removed, and my love for God was revealed. To this day, I reflect on the joy and love I felt for God at that time. But as the years went by, wrong motives and personal agendas began to cover that love. Through my daily studies of the Word of God in the original languages and my quest for God's heart and mind, I have reclaimed the joy and love I felt for the Lord when I accepted Jesus as my Savior.

Love Works Two Ways

Now that I have completed a full decade of searching for the heart and mind of God, I am embarking on the next decade, if God so chooses to keep breath in me, to encourage others to uncover the love for God that is buried in their hearts—to encourage them to study and worship Him with their hearts and not just their minds.

You see, love works two ways. If you learn to love God with all your mind and heart, God will return that love to you with all His mind and heart. You will begin to know and understand Him in new ways. You have loved Him in the past, you are learning to love Him more deeply in the present, and you will love Him more and more for all of eternity.

Study 12

"Let This Cup Pass from Me"

*"And he went a little farther, and fell on his face, and prayed, saying,
O my Father, if it be possible, let this cup pass from me: nevertheless
not as I will, but as thou wilt."*
—Matthew 26:39

For me, one of the great mysteries of the gospel story is that, when Jesus was praying in the garden of Gethsemane, He asked that the *"cup"* would pass from Him. I have always been troubled by this passage of Scripture. Just what is this cup? Even as a child, I was taught that Jesus's surrender to God in this situation was the greatest example of obedience. He was facing torture and death and was struggling against the will of His Father, not wanting to give up His life. Yet, in the end, He submitted and voluntarily yielded to the torture and death that awaited Him, saying, *"Nevertheless not as I will, but as thou wilt."* Or, as it reads in Luke, *"Nevertheless not my will, but thine, be done"* (Luke 22:42).

What was going through the mind of Jesus when He asked for the cup to pass from Him? Was it a fear of death or was it something else?

The other day, as I was driving the disability bus, I went past the Olive–Harvey College in Chicago, and I asked my passenger who Olive and Harvey were. I was told that this community college was formed from two colleges that merged, and it is named after two Vietnam soldiers who won the Medal of Honor. Both were killed in action. Infantryman Carmel Bernon Harvey Jr. died when he charged a machine-gun position to allow his comrades to carry two wounded soldiers into a helicopter, and PFC Milton Lee Olive died when he threw himself on a grenade to save his fellow soldiers. Both knew exactly what they were doing and did not hesitate to act, even though it would cost them their own lives.

If human beings are capable of such heroic acts, then how much more is the God who created them capable of? This begs the question, "If God is perfect in love and loves us with this perfect love, why did He hesitate to go to the cross, as this passage suggests? Did Jesus really have a time of indecision, worried about giving up His life, and then finally, after a long struggle, surrender and say, 'All right, already, Father, You win. I'll go if You order Me to'"? Okay, maybe you read this passage differently than I do. Maybe it doesn't trouble you as it does me. I have spent forty years of my life studying Greek, Hebrew, and Aramaic so I could come to a degree of peace over passages such as this one. So, you will have to forgive me if I happen to read my own bias into it.

Overwhelmed by Love

The dialect Jesus spoke was an Old Galilean form of Aramaic (not Greek), which scholars are just beginning to understand. When I read this passage from the Aramaic version of the Bible, called the Peshittta, I come up with a somewhat different rendering. First and foremost, the Aramaic word that is used for "cup" is *kasa*, meaning "ask." It is identical to the Hebrew word *kavas* (כבס), which is also the word found in other Semitic languages that is used for a stork and/or a pelican. In ancient times, these two were considered the same bird.

The stork was noted for its tender, loving care of its young. Legend teaches that, in times of famine, the mother stork would peck at her breast until it bled and them feed her chicks with her own blood. Legend also has it that if one of the stork's chicks died, she would resurrect her young with her own blood. This is the same word Jesus used at the Last Supper when He said, "*This cup* [not this wine] *is the new testament* [covenant] *in my blood*" (Luke 22:20). In other words, "This *nurturing love* is the new covenant in My blood." The Semitic mind-set of the disciples would have allowed them to see the little play on words in this context. It would be Jesus's blood that would restore us to a rightful position with God and enable our spirits to be resurrected.

In the garden, Jesus was praying that this *kasa* (cup, nurturing love) would *"pass"* from Him. The Greek word translated *"pass"* is *parelthato*, which means "to avert," "to avoid," or "to pass over." But if Jesus spoke this word in Aramaic, which was later translated into Greek, it is possible that He used the term *'avar* (אבר). The Aramaic *'avar* (אבר) has a comparable word in Hebrew with a wide range of meanings. The word itself is the picture of a river overflowing onto its banks. You could say that it is "passing over," but more correctly, it would be rendered as "overwhelming." Yes, the human part of Jesus was not looking forward to the imminent torture and pain, but I don't think He was praying to get out of that situation. Instead, He was praying that this cup, or this nurturing, sacrificial love would *overwhelm* Him so that His mind and emotions would not dread the coming pain.

Note that, in verse 37, it says that Jesus became *"sorrowful."* In Aramaic, the word for "sorrowful" is *kamar* (כמר), which means "to burn" or "to kindle." It is used to signify a burning love or compassion. As Jesus was about to make the sacrifice of His own life, His entire being was filled with a burning love and compassion for humankind, such that He says, "If it is possible, let this cup, or this nurturing love, *'avar* (אבר), or overwhelm, Me." In Aramaic, the word that is translated here as *"if possible"* is *shekev* (שכב), which literally means "if this happens." Once more, Jesus was saying that if this suffering was going to happen, then let a burning, nurturing love for humankind overwhelm Him so that all He would think about was that love. Olive and Harvey thought only of their love for their buddies when they faced their final moments, and that love helped them to endure the agony they experienced. Likewise, it was the sacrificial love Jesus had for each one of us that helped Him to endure the horrendous pain and torture He went through in His sufferings.

Taking on Our Suffering and Pain

Thus, in the garden of Gethsemane, I don't believe Jesus sweat drops of blood due to a fear of His impending torture and death, or even the pressure of taking on our sins. (See Luke 22:44.) At that moment, I believe He saw and knew the tremendous agony, pain, and suffering *of humankind*. He was so filled with love for each one of us that He could not endure the knowledge of what *our* pain and suffering was like.

God could not fully understand human suffering until He took on human flesh. And being sinless, Jesus did not fully understand the torment of sin until the cross. But when He carried the sins of the world, He understood what the torment of guilt and condemnation was really like. Often, the mother of a sick child will pray that her child's suffering and pain could somehow be placed upon her. At Gethsemane, Jesus understood our suffering and pain and knew He could take it on. It was His knowledge and understanding of what sin had done to us and His empathy for our suffering that caused Him to sweat drops of blood.

Study 13

A Man After God's Own Heart

"But now thy kingdom shall not continue; the Lord hath sought him
a man after his own heart."
—1 Samuel 13:14

"I have found David the son of Jesse, a man after mine own heart,
which shall fulfil all my will."
—Acts 13:22

As a teacher, one of the top ten questions I am asked is, "What does the Bible mean when it says that David was 'a man after God's own heart'"? When we take at good look at David's life, that is an excellent question. He had multiple wives. He was apparently a lousy father, as evidenced from the uncontrollable behavior of two of his sons: Amnon raped his half-sister, Tamar, and her brother Absalom subsequently killed him. Absalom later started a rebellion and tried to usurp the kingdom from his father. David was also an adulterer and a murderer. (See 2 Samuel 11–18.) Additionally, he was *"a man of war"* who had so much blood on his hands that God would not allow him to build His temple. (See 1 Chronicles 22:7–8; 28:2–3.)

However, we read in 1 Kings 15:5 that David *"did what was right in the eyes of the Lord…, except in the matter of Uriah the Hittite"* (NKJV). The phrase *"except in the matter"* does not mean that David never committed any other sinful acts. Instead, it references a continued apostasy against God. It is similar to the phrase "turning aside from God." All David's other sins were transient—they were sudden and followed by repentance. However, this matter with Bathsheba was a willful, "I know it is wrong, but I am going to do it anyway" act. This act came after God had allowed David to enter the special, fragile areas of His heart and mind. David's willful rebellion had bruised and broken God's heart.

Aligning Our Desires with God's

A man after God's heart is not a sinless man who locks himself in a room and prays and reads the Bible all day. In 1 Samuel 13:14, the preposition *kap* (כ), which is used before the Hebrew word translated "*heart*," *levav* (לבב), is traditionally rendered as "like" or "as" rather than "after." So, we could render this phrase as "a man with a heart like God's heart." In the quote from Acts 13:22, the Greek preposition *taka* is used, which is often rendered as "according to." Therefore, David was a man who had "a heart like God's heart," or "a heart according to God's heart." The Peshitta uses the Aramaic preposition *kia* (כיא), which is often rendered as "such as" or "as though." David had "a heart such as God's heart" or "as though it were God's heart."

The question as to what it means to be a man after God's heart can be answered only if you know what God's heart is and if your heart's desires are the same as His. It was in this way that David was a man after God's heart, and the Lord allowed him into the very secret rooms of His heart; He exposed himself to possible heartbreak in order to share a special intimacy with David.

As I mentioned previously, for many years, I have been on a quest to discover God's heart and mind. I have completed over two thousand daily Hebrew word studies and published four books about this journey. Yet, the quest continues, and each day, I discover something new about God's heart and mind. I am beginning to believe that David was a man *after* or *according to* God's heart because he spent his life seeking to know God's heart and mind, to do what would bring pleasure to God's heart, and to avoid that which would break His heart.

In my journey, I have caught a glimpse of God's heart, which I discovered has twenty-two "guards"—the twenty-two letters of the Hebrew alphabet. As my quest has progressed, and I have grown closer to the heart and mind of God, I have found the little, hidden codes in each letter, whose secrets have been taught by the ancient Jewish sages. These codes carry even greater access to the inner depths of God's heart and mind. However, I have learned that the letters do not easily share their codes and combinations. Additionally, even though we may read the various meanings that the ancient sages assigned to each letter, we cannot really apply a combination of these meanings to discover a personal message from God without seeking this understanding with all our heart, soul, and mind.

Again, I can only say that I have caught a *glimpse* of the inner depths of God's heart and mind, but there are higher levels, levels that are much more fragile but offer even greater intimacy with Him. The greater the intimacy we gain, the greater the responsibility we have to be as careful as possible not to break God's heart. As you approach these levels of His heart, you will find that it affects your emotions. You begin to weep over things that you would not normally feel any grief over, and to rejoice over things that would not normally bring you joy. But they are what cause God's heart to grieve or rejoice, and as you approach those depths of His heart and mind, having, like David, a heart according to His heart, you will feel His grief or His joy. You will weep with Him and you will rejoice with Him—and you will feel His pleasure.

Intimacy Means Responsibility

It seems as if Christians are constantly talking about "intimacy with God." I know that this intimacy starts with God's heart and mind, and that the very nature of intimacy means we must make ourselves vulnerable to Him. In human relationships, when two people are intimate, they give one another access to a special part, a very fragile part, of their hearts and minds. They also give each other the opportunity to break their respective hearts. Is it not the same in our relationship with God? If He allows us to enter a very fragile part of His heart, could not our negative, self-centered attitudes or actions break His heart? Therefore, if we wish to enter into intimacy with God, we must be aware of our responsibility. We will have the twenty-two guards of the Hebrew alphabet watching us very closely. They will not reveal their secrets if we are reckless with God's heart and mind.

The Holy Spirit is often pictured as a gentle dove who would be easily bruised if you were to be reckless with the heart of God. (See, for example, Ephesians 4:30.) Men are often frustrated by what they perceive as women's tendency to get overly emotional and offended. Yet God created women with a sensitive nature as a *helpmeet* for men so they can better understand His heart and mind. God's heart can become offended, and yes, there are times when we men can get pretty reckless with a woman's heart—and we do the same with God's heart.

David had been allowed into the fragile chambers of God's heart, but then he became reckless with the life of another human being—Uriah, who was completely loyal to him. David slept with Uriah's wife, and when she became pregnant, he arranged for Uriah to be killed. As a result, he broke God's heart. Later, David's brokenness over his sins with Bathsheba and Uriah was not over the consequences he suffered, but over the fact that he had broken God's heart after the Lord had entrusted special areas of His heart and mind to him.

If you want to be a person after God's heart, you must first resolve that if God grants you entrance into the fragile areas of His heart and mind, you will enter reverently, carefully, and prayerfully, with every intention of protecting His heart. During prayer meetings, I have heard people talk about "protecting the anointing." I suspect what they are really talking about is that one must be careful, upon entering those secret chambers of God's heart and mind, not to bruise His heart with personal agendas, pride, or showing off. In my view, they are not protecting an "anointing" but rather the very heart and mind of God.

"Intimacy with God" is not to be considered a new fad in Christianity, something you put on your Christian "You Gotta Experience It" list. We are talking about the very heart and mind of our God. Do you want a heart after God? Do you want intimacy with Him? Then consider the great responsibility He will put in your hands when you enter special areas of His heart and mind. Expect to weep as much as you rejoice and to find yourself avoiding those annoying little sins you used to commit as you learn to *fear God*—that is, fear you might wound the fragile area of His heart that He has opened up to you. Remember that David said, "*The secret of the LORD is with them that fear him*" (Psalm 25:14).

Study 14

"Bless the Lord, Ye His Angels"

*"Bless the LORD, ye his angels, that excel in strength, that do his
commandments, hearkening unto the voice of his word."*
—Psalm 103:20

Sometimes I ask myself, "Do other people wonder about things in the Bible like I do?" What I wonder about in the above study verse is the idea of David seemingly ordering the angels around! Is he actually reminding the angels to praise or bless the Lord? The Hebrew word translated *"bless"* here is simply *baraku* (ברכו), which means "to bless," "to make happy," or "to praise." However, it's interesting that this word is in a piel* (intensive), imperative* (command) form. It is not just a command but an *intense* command—do it or else!

I know this psalm is written in a poetic style and David is just excitedly saying, "Come on, angels, join in the fun! Let's dive into this praise pool together. 'Blest be the ties that bind' and all that." Well, perhaps that is what he is saying. Poetry is poetry after all, and when speaking poetically, I guess we can command the angels to do something they are already doing, have been doing, and will continue to do.

A Test of Devotion

I have another theory, however. It is outside of the box, so I am sure most Christian Hebrew scholars will throw salt in the air if they read this.

Yet, I think I might get an "amen" from some Jewish rabbis. The word translated "*angels*" is *melek'an* (מלכן), which is the term for "king," "royalty," "ruler," "kingly messenger," "teacher," "prophet," "angel," or really anyone who takes on a leadership role to deliver a message or proclamation. Why do we plug the English word *angel* into this verse? Well, tradition and the context seem to suggest it. But if we used the word *teacher, prophet,* or even *preacher,* each of whom is a messenger of God like the angels, then who is to say it cannot fit the context? In fact, I think it fits the context much better than a supernatural angel.

We have no record that David ever saw angels, so how much did he really know about them? Yet, he *had* seen prophets and teachers—various messengers from God. Unfortunately, some of them were not really God's messengers, but rather messengers of their own flesh who claimed their message was from Him.

For many years, I worked for pastor and evangelist Dr. Lester Sumrall, and I remember him telling me what he would do whenever members of a religious cult came to his door: "I won't call them a cult. I will simply say, 'Praise the Lord. You love Jesus, you like to study His Word, then let's just get down on our knees right now and have some fellowship in prayer.'" Dr. Sumrall told me they usually found some excuse to leave. He concluded, "If they don't want to get on their knees and pray and praise the Lord, I don't want to hear any message they have about God."

I think David had the same idea in this Scripture passage. I don't believe he was talking about angels. He said that the angels "*excel in strength.*" The Hebrew word translated "*strength*" is *koach* (כּוח), which signifies human strength and/or power. This is not necessarily physical strength. It could be intellectual strength. I believe David is calling all the great teachers to account by saying, "If you really are teachers and messengers of God, then start praising and blessing Him!"

True Messengers of God

In our Western culture, we place our teachers and preachers on a high pedestal. If they have a megachurch or a large television audience, or if they have a PhD or degrees from a well-known school or seminary, we listen to them with awe. We heap honors upon them. We have pastor appreciation days and weeks. David did not look at the educational degrees or the number of followers of the great teachers, prophets, or preachers of his day. He watched how they worshipped and praised God, and if their hearts were not in it, he did not have much use for their message.

I think it is time that we, like David, called our leaders to account. We should invite them to praise and worship God with us. If they are uncomfortable doing it, I am not sure I want to hear their message. I don't want to hear a teaching from someone with a lot of charisma who can merely preach a good sermon and build a large audience. I don't want to hear a message from someone just because they have advanced academic degrees. I want to hear a message from someone who loves God with all their heart, soul, and mind, and diligently seeks to know His heart and mind. I want to hear from those who are so in love with God that they are constantly praising Him, just like the *"angels…that excel in strength."* These are the messages I want to listen to.

So, bless the Lord, you His teachers, preachers, scholars, and prophets, you *melek'an* (מלבן), who excel in "strength" (of members, book sales, degrees, Nielsen ratings, and social media followers). Prove that you are real messengers of God!

Study 15

A Song of Love

"And they come unto thee as the people cometh, and they sit before thee as my people, and they hear thy words, but they will not do them: for with their mouth they show much love, but their heart goeth after their covetousness. And, lo, thou art unto them as a very lovely song of one that hath a pleasant voice, and can play well on an instrument: for they hear thy words, but they do them not."
—Ezekiel 33:31–32

If the nightingales could sing like you,
They'd sing much sweeter than they do,
For you brought a new kind of love to me.
—Irving Kahal[4]

I recall hearing the term *making love* for the first time many years ago. The phrase threw me. How can you *make* love? I quickly learned that it was a carnal expression for a man and woman who have a sexual relationship.

Whatever is important in a culture is reflected in its language. We have over a million words in the English language, but somehow we can come up with only one word, *love*, for a variety of meanings. That one word can

---

4. "You Brought a New Kind of Love to Me," 1930, words and music by Sammy Fain, Irving Kahal, and Pierre Connor.

expresses anything from fondness to pure lust. *Love* might refer to parental love, romantic love, affectionate love, sexual love, friendship love, physical love, emotional love, and so on. We need to add adjectives to the word to communicate the difference in meaning.

Greek has only three words for love: *agape*, *phileo*, and *eros* (some people include a fourth, *storge*). Yet, Classical Hebrew** (the language of the Old Testament), which has only 7,500 words, has a number of terms that can be rendered as *love*. So, I ask you: which culture found love more important? We call a sexual relationship "making love." The Hebrews called a sexual relationship *yada'* (ידע), meaning "to know." The emphasis is on knowing someone intimately.

"Feel Good" Love

The lyricist Irving Kahal, in a song made famous by entertainers Maurice Chevalier and Frank Sinatra, expresses the idea that you can learn "a new kind of love." You might say that Ezekiel 33:32 speaks about a new kind of love. The phrase *"thou art unto them as a very lovely song"* is more correctly translated as "You are a love song." The word *"love"* here is not *ahav* (אהב), the general word for "love," nor is it *racham* (רחם), a deeply affectionate and romantic love. The word is *'agav* (עגב), which fits our colloquial expression "making love." This is selfish love or lust, and it is often used for a sexual relationship with a prostitute. Someone enters into a sexual act purely for personal pleasure and desire; the other person involved is of little consequence.

Ezekiel was preaching about the love and protection of God to the Israelites in captivity in Babylon, and they were eating it up. Yet, it was as if the prophet were merely singing a popular love song rather than talking about a real relationship with the living God. To the people of Israel, it was not an *ahav* (אהב) song, or a *racham* (רחם) song, but an *'agav* (עגב) song—one catering to their own personal desires and pleasure. They loved to hear about all the good things God would do for them, but He Himself did not mean much to them. God essentially told Ezekiel, "They hear these words of love, but they do not act upon them." The people's attitude was, "Give me, give me, thank You, God." But they didn't take His words to heart; they didn't live according to them.

Before we throw rocks at the Israelites, we may need to pause and take a good look at ourselves. I have heard some people say, "I am not going to that church anymore because I just don't feel the presence of God." What they are usually saying is that the music is not to their liking or the style of worship is not what they are comfortable with. They tramp around to different churches, trying them out like they are shopping for a new mattress, until they get one that feels just right. When they do, they might not actually be sensing the presence of God there. They might be feeling their own emotions and passion. Their own passion demands a certain type of music, a certain type of sermon, a certain type of style. Yes, they love God, all right, but not really with *ahav* (אהב) or *racham* (רחם) love, but with *'agav* (עגב), a selfish, "feel good" type of love. Genuine love does not always feel good. Sometimes, it needs to feel pain as it shares the pain of the one who is loved.

So, ask yourself, "Do I attend church in the same way the people of Israel listened to Ezekiel?" They listened to a love song, but what they heard was not *ahav* (אהב) or *racham* (רחם). It was *'agav* (עגב). In other words, "If I am not getting satisfied and fulfilled, then I will just pick up my tithe and find a 'god' who will satisfy me. I deserve to be satisfied."

What do you suppose is running through God's mind when He encounters such an attitude? How would you feel if you found out that someone loved you only for your money or fame? It would be heartbreaking, just as it is with God. Read carefully what the Lord says in Hosea 6:6: *"For I desired mercy, and not sacrifice; and the knowledge of God more than burnt offerings."* What is God going to do with a sacrifice or burnt offering? The whole point of the sacrifices and burnt offerings was for people to receive forgiveness, draw close to God, and have a vehicle in which to express their love for Him.

Suppose a man comes home with some roses for his wife and says, "Okay, here are some flowers. Now you have to let me go fishing this weekend." I tell you, most wives in that situation would plant those flowers somewhere other than in a vase. But now, imagine the husband brings home some flowers and says, "Honey, I have been thinking about you day, and I decided that the money I was going to use to buy my lunch, I would use to buy these flowers for you." Of course, those flowers would find their way to his wife's favorite vase. The flowers are a symbol of his love and willingness to make a sacrifice to bring her a small joy.

Which Love Song Will You Hear?

The old saying "You can't buy love" is not only true among us earthly creatures. but it is also true in our relationship with God. However, some Christians still try to buy God's love by doing good deeds, giving 10 percent of their income to the church, and attending services every Sunday. They hear the love song of God, but to them, that love is *'agav* (עגב), or "What's in it for me?" They are essentially religious gold diggers, trying to charm their way into God's storehouse of riches. God has them pegged before they utter their first "Hallelujah."

Many churches fill their empty chairs by promising people great things from God—prosperity, healing, success, restored relationships, and all sorts of other goodies—and people flock to hear sermons with those messages. If the Israelites had listened to Ezekiel with a heart of *racham* (רחם) love and not *'agav* (עגב) love, they would have felt God's broken heart, God's longing for them, God's weeping for them. Instead, all they wanted to hear was, "Happy, happy, happy; no problems, just rich and fulfilled."

When you go to church this week, which love song will you hear—an *'agav* (עגב), selfish, "me, me, me" song, or a song from a Singer whose heart and mind is always set on you and who longs to have a relationship with you?

His Passionate Love

"The Lord will perfect that which concerneth me: thy mercy, O Lord, endureth for ever: forsake not the works of thine own hands."
—Psalm 138:8

"It was the best of times, it was the worst of times."
—Charles Dickens, *A Tale of Two Cities*

With the above quote, Charles Dickens begins his novel *A Tale of Two Cities* with one of the major motifs of the book. Throughout his novel, there are contrasting pairs: England at relative peace; France in revolution. Charles Darney the perfect gentleman; Sydney Carton the self-centered profligate. In the end, all the contrasts tie together for a perfect conclusion.

Coming Full Circle

In Psalm 138:8, we see a very clear picture of something that is on God's mind with regard to bringing a matter to its conclusion. In Hebrew, the phrase *"the Lord will perfect that which concerneth me"* literally means "The Lord will bring to an end, or to completion, that which is about me." This is a picture of something coming full circle. It has the idea of starting something and then finishing it.

The Hebrew word for "bring to an end" or "bring to completion"—or, as the King James translation renders it, *"perfect"*—is *gamar* (גמר). Rabbi Samson Hirsch, the nineteenth-century Hebrew scholar and linguist, suggested that *gamar* (גמר) could be a play on the word *kamar* (כמר), which means "to kindle a fire of passion or love." In other words, "The Lord will kindle a fire of passionate love in me as He puts me through this process of perfecting me."

There are different ways we can look at this verse, which was written by David. We can view it in the sense that, from the beginning to the end of our lives, God will fulfill the purposes for which He has created us. But we can also look at it from the perspective that, during our lives, God starts many different works, all of which are meant to kindle a passionate love in us for Him. The Lord finishes everything that He starts; He has no abandoned projects. All the works He begins in our lives will be brought to completion, ending with His passionate love.

Sometimes, God starts a work in the middle of someone's life or even in their later years. Two biblical examples are Abraham becoming the father of the promised child, Isaac, at the age of one hundred (see Genesis 17:15–21) and Moses being called to lead the Israelites out of slavery in Egypt at the age of eighty (see Exodus 7:7). God's work in our lives may begin with a tragedy, the loss of a job, or a health crisis. If you find yourself in this situation, always remember that the work is built on His passionate love. When you look back over that tragedy or crisis after having come full circle, you will see God's great love in the midst of it, and you will say, like Dickens, that "it was the best of times and the worst of times." Every disappointment and every crisis is contrasted with God's faithfulness and lovingkindness. You can be assured that, one day, you will come full circle and be able to praise God in every situation as He embraces you with His passionate love.

God Knows Our Life Story

Psalm 138:8 seems to make clear that God is the author of our life story. He is designing us to be profitable servants (contrast Luke 17:7–10), vessels through whom He can be glorified (see, for example, 2 Corinthians 4:7), and beloved sons and daughters who reflect His image (see, for example,

2 Corinthians 3:18). He will finish our story. Right now, we do not and cannot know the full mind of God, and we do not yet know how our story will end—but God knows. As gospel music songwriter Ira Stanphill wrote,

Many things about tomorrow
I don't seem to understand
But I know who holds tomorrow
And I know who holds my hand.[5]

If you have committed yourself to God, make sure to put Him at the helm of your life. Then, whatever happens is not the luck of the draw—it is part of an overall plan and purpose to show you His passionate love and take extreme pride in you. You can rest assured that your welfare is on God's mind. He has shared with us His thoughts about this, as we find in Jeremiah 29:11: *"For I know the thoughts that I think toward you, saith the* Lord, *thoughts of peace, and not of evil, to give you an expected end."* God's revelation of even that much of His mind is more than adequate for us.

A New Beginning

The Hebrew word *gamar* (גמר), meaning "to perfect" or "to complete," is spelled gimmel (ג), mem (מ), resh (ר). This word gives us a built-in commentary, telling us what to expect from the perfecting process.

The first letter, gimmel (ג), tells us that as we go through this process, whatever the nature of the crisis or tragedy, it will be surrounded by the passionate love of God. The sages picture the next letter, mem (מ), as water or the womb. This is the process of birthing something new. When it is complete, we will have been born into a new season of our lives. During a human birthing process, a mother feels immense love for her child. Likewise, you can be assured that God is showering you with His love during your spiritual birthing process. The final letter is resh (ר). I recently read that one rabbi called the resh (ר) a mini-Rosh Hashanah, or mini-New Year.

Thus, when the process is complete, it is not really an end but a beginning. Lately, many Christian leaders and authors on TV, on the Internet, and in books have been talking about the need for a "breakthrough"; they

---

5. "I Know Who Holds Tomorrow," 1950.

tell people their breakthrough is coming and that they will experience a new beginning in their lives. I believe David had a similar experience, which he expressed in Psalm 138:8. People use various terms for the period during which God does His work—such as "season," "refining process," "cleansing process," "wilderness experience," and so forth—but they all have one common denominator. It is the fact that this is a process initiated by God to ultimately show His passionate love for us. God promises that He will finish the process. He will not abandon us in the middle of it, and we will find His passionate love as we go through it. Then, when the process is complete, we will have a new beginning in our love relationship with Him.

Air Kiss

*"But the hour cometh, and now is, when the true worshippers shall
worship the Father in spirit and in truth:
for the Father seeketh such to worship him."*
—John 4:23

"A kiss is a lovely trick designed by nature to stop speech
when words become superfluous."
—Ingrid Bergman

As I have traveled around visiting various churches, I have found that many of the worship leaders were apparently hired or given the position to lead worship solely due to their musical ability. I find that few worship leaders really have a biblical perspective on the nature of worship. I remember one worship leader who felt sorry for a worship leader in another church who could not find a good drummer. It was hard to imagine that God would not bless this church with a good drummer because they sincerely wanted to worship Him, and of course, without a drummer, your worship will suffer. (I wanted to ask if he felt such empathy for King David, who did not have the benefit of electric guitars and keyboards.) My point is that it seems even our leaders spend little time trying to understand what true worship really is. Most tend to go with what seems to work or what others are doing.

What Is True Worship?

But who am I to criticize? I think of the woman at the well, who was from Samaria and was under the impression that worship could take place only in a certain geographical location. Her worship leaders said Samaritans could worship on a specific mountain, but the Jews said worship should take place in Jerusalem. Even in those days, people differed on the correct way to worship. But Jesus revealed to this woman what true worship is. (See John 4:5–26.) He told her that worship is not a geographical location, but rather a matter of the heart, and that true worshippers worship God *"in spirit and in truth."* The Greek word translated *"spirit"* here is *pneuma*, which is the term used for the Spirit of God, the human spirit, breath, or wind. But the woman with whom Jesus was talking did not speak Greek; she spoke Aramaic. In the Aramaic, the word He used was *rucha* (רוחא), which is identical to the Hebrew word *ruch* (רוח) and has the same meaning as the Greek word *pneuma*, whose meaning I described above.

Actually, it is the word translated *"worship"* that has me intrigued. In an earlier study, I mentioned that *shachah* (שחה) is a Hebrew word for "worship." There are other words rendered as "worship" that depict a certain aspect of worship. The Greek word for *"worship"* in John 4:23 is *proskyneo*. This is a compound word, combining *pros*, denoting "throw" or "toward," with *kyneo*, meaning "kiss." Thus, to worship is to essentially throw a kiss to God.

It is helpful to look at some cultural background regarding this Greek word. In the Aramaic, the word is *segad* (סגד), which comes from a term borrowed from Middle Egyptian. When the Egyptians worshipped their gods, they would breathe onto the idol through their nostrils, and that was considered an "air kiss." So, air passing through the nostrils became known as *segad* (סגד), or an air kiss. Later, in the Greek, it was known as a *proskyneo*, which, being interpreted, means "to worship."

Worshipping by the Holy Spirit

Remember that in Genesis 2:7, when God created the first human being, He breathed into Adam's nostrils the *nashem* (נשם), or breath, of life. Yet, here we are not worshiping God with our *nashem* (נשם) or natural breath, but with *rucha* (רוחא), which is the word used for the *Ruch Kodesh* (רוח קדש), or the Holy Spirit. In John 4:23, in the Aramaic, the word *rucha* (רוחא) is preceded by a beth (ב), meaning "by." Hence, we do not worship *in* the Holy Spirit but *by* the Holy Spirit. God breathed *nashem* (נשם), or physical life, into human beings through the nostrils, but we breathe His Spirit, our spiritual life, out of our nostrils to Him. We worship *by the Holy Spirit*.

Purified Motives

Thus, without the Holy Spirit, we cannot worship the Lord. But if we allow the Spirit to take control of our lives, He will draw out of us our love for God. In Mark 9:39, Jesus said something interesting about an individual who was not one of His disciples but was casting out demons in His name: *"Do not hinder him, for there is no one who will perform a miracle in My name, and be able soon afterward to speak evil of Me"* (NASB). As I mentioned in an earlier study, the Jewish sages believed that even if your motives for studying Torah were selfish, Torah would soon purify those motives. Similarly, Jesus indicated that if you are working and performing miracles in His name, such service will purify your motives.

I sort of censured worship leaders at the beginning of this study, so let me qualify my statements with the following: There may be some worship leaders who are frustrated rock star wannabes or who merely desire to show off their talents. There may also be worshippers who seek to impress others with their holiness by loud expressions of praise or performing physical contortions. If they are expressing the name of Jesus, then perhaps, rather than hinder them, we need to let the Holy Spirit purify their motives. For it is only by the Holy Spirit that any of us can worship God in truth.

In Aramaic, the word for "truth" is *sharara* (שררא), which means "to be tightly bound together." It is like strands of fabric tightly bound with each other to form a rope. *Sharar* (שרר) is the word used to express that tight bonding, a bonding that nothing can break. When we *segad* (סגד), or worship God, giving Him an *air kiss* and sharing the life of His Spirit with Him, we create a bond with the Lord that can never be broken.

Therefore, worship is *segad sharara* (סגד שררא), that is, allowing the Holy Spirit to bind us tightly with God. The more tightly we are bonded with God, the more we will know His mind; and the more we know the mind of God, the purer our motives will become.

A Hardened Heart

"And I, behold, I will harden the hearts of the Egyptians."
—Exodus 14:17

Exodus 14:17 would almost suggest that God's mind is filled with vengeance and revenge. Why harden the hearts of the Egyptians, including Pharaoh, their leader? Why not soften them? There seem to be many theories as to what was going through God's mind when He hardened Pharaoh's heart. (See, for example, Exodus 14:4, 8.) Let me share my own thoughts on this.

I recently read Tom Clancy's book *The Cardinal of the Kremlin*. In one chapter, sharpshooters for the FBI are ordered by the president to shoot the Russian spies holding an American scientist hostage, even though the spies are not threatening to kill the American. The sharpshooters were shocked that they had to shoot another human being in cold blood. They had been trained to shoot only if there was no other alternative to saving an American life, and it completely went against their nature and training to shoot down a man who posed no direct threat to them or to the hostage.

In war, a soldier will kill an enemy only because he knows, "It's him or me." This is the idea behind the phrase that describes God as *"a man of war"* (Exodus 15:3). God is a "sharpshooter" who will "waste" the enemy, but only if there is no alternative to saving His people. He will give them every possible chance, as He did with Pharaoh and the rest of the Egyptians, to turn to Him. Indeed, we learn that some Egyptians did believe in God and followed the Hebrews out of Egypt, although they caused a lot of problems later. (See Exodus 12:38; Numbers 11:4.)

Did God "Cause" or "Permit"?

So, we have a benevolent God who "shoots" only when there is no other recourse. Then, how do we explain the fact that just when the hearts of Pharaoh and the Egyptians begin to soften, God turns around and hardens their hearts so He can inflict more suffering on them? That does not seem fair. It also seems to make Scripture contradictory, because 1 Samuel 6:6 tells us, *"Wherefore then do ye harden your hearts, as the Egyptians and Pharaoh hardened their hearts?"* In one passage, it is God hardening their hearts, and in another, they are hardening their own hearts.

Until a few years ago, we really could not explain this apparent contradiction. Christians either took the Calvinist position, "God can do what He wants, and who are we to question it?" or they considered the attempts made by some to explain that this was just a Hebrew idiom.* The idea was that, when God said, "I will harden the heart of Pharaoh" (see, for example, Exodus 7:3; 14:4), this was an idiomatic expression for "I will permit his heart to be hardened." That sounds good, but few Hebrew scholars bought into this interpretation, and therefore you will not find any modern translation that renders this as "I will permit Pharaoh's heart to be hardened." At least, I have not found any that express it in that way.

However, in recent years, there have been many new discoveries about the Classical Hebrew language, not the least of which are being learned from the Dead Sea Scrolls.*** We now know a few things about the Classical Hebrew that the rabbis of the middle ages and John Calvin did not know, and we are still learning new things.

One piece of information we have learned is the nature of the active voice in Hebrew. The word translated *"harden"* in Exodus 14:17 is *chazaq* (חזק), which means "to be hardened," "to be stubborn," or similar connotations. It is in a hiphal (causative), imperfect form in the first person singular. You cannot get much more direct than that. God is saying, "I will cause

Pharaoh's heart to be hardened." However, this word is also in an active voice, and we have now learned from the Dead Sea Scrolls and the discovery of the Ugaritic language that when a verb is in a hiphal active form, *it becomes permissive.*

Only by Grace

This sheds new light on what God was thinking with regard to Pharaoh. We now have grammatical evidence that this phrase should be rendered, "I will permit Pharaoh's heart to be hardened." Calvin would have loved that. Only by the efficacious grace of God would his heart not be hardened. In other words, our hearts are hardened against God to begin with, and it is only through His special grace or what we call the conviction of the Holy Spirit that our hearts start to soften toward Him. Yet, we learn in Genesis 6:3 that God's Spirit will not always strive with humankind. If we keep resisting Him, there will come a time when, as with Pharaoh and the Egyptians, God will remove the convicting power of His Spirit and we will go back to our hardened hearts.

It is by grace that we are saved through faith, and this is a gift of God. (See Ephesians 2:8.) It would appear that Calvin was right after all; even when our hearts long for God, that a gift from Him. It is God who makes the overtures to us, and we respond. Unlike Calvin, however, I believe that this grace is offered to everyone and God will strive with people for a long time in order to draw them to Himself. However, one day, if they continue in their sins, God may just remove His convicting Spirit and allow their hearts to go back to their normal, hardened state. In thinking about this, I am reminded of the little sins that I continually commit, rationalizing, "Oh well, He is a loving God—He will forgive." That is true, but there might come a time when I would not care to seek His forgiveness, and He will *permit* me to go back to a hardened heart.

The point is that any desire you have for God comes from Him. It is a gift. You don't have to beg, plead, bargain, or do something in order to be forgiven and have a life of fellowship with God. He is the One who gave you the desire to begin with. Without that gift, you would be like old Pharaoh and have a hard heart. Pharaoh had his chance and blew it, but then God came in and softened his heart—yet still he refused to yield to

Him. So God again withdrew His convicting Spirit, and Pharaoh let his sinful nature rule. Let us not follow his example, but instead turn whole-heartedly to the Lord and receive the gifts of His forgiveness and grace.

"The Lord Is My Story"

"Unto thee will I cry, O Lord my rock; be not silent to me: lest, if thou be silent to me, I become like them that go down into the pit."
—Psalm 28:1

I don't know about you, but I find this verse to be very curious. David calls the Lord his *"rock,"* but then he asks the Lord not to be silent. Maybe I am reading too much into this, but if I am going to call someone a *rock*, I am not going to follow that statement by asking them to refrain from silence. Okay, maybe David is metaphorically asking God to be his Rock, his source of stability and dependability, but not to be silent like a real rock. It is not my intent here to discredit the thousands of sermons that have been given based on this verse, proclaiming the stability and dependability of God. Rather, I am asking that, just for a moment, we think outside the box and examine some alternative meanings.

There are at least eight other words in biblical Hebrew that have been rendered as "rock." The most common are *sala'* (סלע) and *tarash* (תרש). These words would fit the idea of solid rock or a boulder, and thus better depict the picture of dependability than the word used here, which is *tsur* (צור). *Tsur* (צור) signifies a rocky cliff, a rocky wall, or the wall of a mountain. I can buy the idea of God being the side of a mountain—I can hide behind that wall of rock and feel pretty secure. So, the old sermons are safe.

Carvings on Rock

Still, while researching the word *tsur* (צוּר) through its Semitic origins, I spent some time at the Oriental Institute at the University of Chicago to confirm my findings. I believe there is an identical word in the Akkadian language that was used to signify designing, forming, sculpturing, or carving in or on rocks. Therefore, I believe *tsur* (צוּר) was likely borrowed from the Akkadian language. If this was the case, then we have a whole new understanding of what David meant when he said the Lord was his *tsur* (צוּר).

I had been meditating on all this to see if there was a relationship between the meanings of the Akkadian and Hebrew words, but I had been coming up with nothing until a friend of mine suggested that, possibly, David was not referring to the Lord as a rock of stability but rather to his own story (referencing the carving in or on rocks) and that the Lord *is* his story. That set off all sorts of bells in me from my prior research into the Akkadian language.

Akkadian was written in cuneiform* (wedge-shaped letters) on a *tsur* (צוּר). There is an interesting account about King Sennacherib, who abandoned his siege on Jerusalem in 721 when his army came down with dysentery. When he told the story about this incident, he was the hero of the day. However, we read this in 2 Kings 19:35: *"And it came to pass that night, that the angel of the LORD went out, and smote in the camp of the Assyrians an hundred fourscore and five thousand: and when they arose early in the morning, behold, they were all dead corpses."* Nonetheless, it was not unusual for a king to record his exploits or story in stone so that all future generations would honor and revere him.

Whose Story Are We Communicating?

Thus, in Psalm 28:1, I don't believe David was making a reference to God as a solid Rock of stability. Of course, He is our Rock of stability. I can testify to that in my own life, and there are Scriptures that confirm this fact—but not this particular verse. Instead, this psalm is saying something very important to us today, especially to those of us who happen to be in a leadership role in the church or are published authors and have our names and pictures shown throughout the Christian world through electronic and broadcast media and in bookstores. The question is, "Whose story are we communicating?"

I have personally requested that my publisher leave my real name and photo off of my books, which they have graciously agreed to, even though my contract calls for a photo. The name Chaim Bentorah is just a pseudonym. It is nowhere close to my real name, and for me personally, it means "Life through the Son of the Law." To me, Jesus is the Son of the Law, and I find life through Him. So, for those of you hoping to get a glimpse of what this dusty old Hebrew teacher looks like, you will not find it by purchasing my books. The only picture I want you to see is of Jesus, and the only name I want you to read is Jesus's.

You see, this book is not my story—it is God's story. In my view, this is confirmed by Psalm 28:1, where David says that the Lord is his *tsur* (צור), or *"rock."* David did not desire that his own story be told. When future generations saw the account of David's life engraved in stone, they would not really be reading David's story, but rather a portion of God's story. As my friend said, "God *is* his story."

Study 20

Howling

"And they have not cried unto me with their heart,
when they howled upon their beds: they assemble themselves for corn
and wine, and they rebel against me."
—Hosea 7:14

Hosea is prophesying to the northern kingdom during the reign of Jeroboam II in the eighth century BC. This was the time just before the Israelites in the north were taken into captivity by the Assyrians. King Jeroboam encouraged the worship of Baal, the god of the Assyrians, in hopes of appeasing them. He also tried to gain a little more security by introducing the worship of the calf, the god of Egypt, with a strategy of winning an alliance with the Egyptians to fight off the Assyrians. But when famine hit the land, guess who the Israelites turned to?

This is where Hosea comes in. Under God's instructions, he married an unfaithful woman to symbolize the relationship between the Lord and Israel at that time. Hosea was in love with his wife, but she would continually run off with other men. When she became destitute, Hosea would take her back. However, no sooner would she find herself in a good position again than she would run off with another man. That was so like the northern kingdom's treatment of God.

In Hosea 7:14, what is being expressed is that after the Lord comes to their rescue, the Israelites rebel against Him. The Hebrew word translated "*rebel*" is *sur* (סור), which means "to withdraw." The verb is in an imperfect form and should be translated in the future tense. Hence, we would render this as, "'*They assemble themselves for corn and wine,*' but they will withdraw from Me." Once they get what they need, they will forget about God again.

Crying Out with Our Heart

The key problem with this whole matter is not that the Israelites were calling out to God in a time of trouble after having strayed from Him. In fact, David says in Psalm 119:71 that if it hadn't been for his affliction, he wouldn't have sought the Lord. Moreover, it is not that the Israelites' call to God was indifferent. The verse says that they "*howled*" from their beds. It seems that the worst moments of our struggles or problems often come in the middle of the night when we are trying to sleep. The Hebrew word rendered as "*howled*" is *yalal* (ילל), which means "to wail." It is spelled yod (י), lamed (ל), lamed (ל). The two lameds picture someone in bed with their arms raised up, tearfully crying out to God. The yod (י) indicates that their attention is directed to Him. So, they were crying out to God with their attention focused on Him, but still the Bible says that they did not call upon Him "*with their heart.*"

It is our heart that connects with God. But surely, someone sitting up in bed with their arms raised to heaven, tearfully crying out to God, giving Him their full attention, must be crying from the heart, right? According to Hosea 7:14, not necessarily. Too often, when we find ourselves in trouble, we just lash out at God, saying, "How could You do this to me?" or "Why don't You *do* something?" We are so focused on our situation that we don't stop to consider that He may be hurting as well (especially if we have turned away from Him) and that what He really wants to do is what Hosea wanted to do for his wife when she was hurting as a result of her wrong choices. God wants to take us in His arms, speak soothingly to us, and comfort us.

Connecting with God

If the Lord loves us as much as the Scriptures say He does, and He is perfect in His love, then it stands to reason that when we hurt, He also hurts. If we are truly crying out to Him with our heart, we will have a connection with Him, and when we do, we will feel His hurt as well. Instead, like a spoiled child, we push Him away and tell Him to do something *now* about our situation or we will run after some other "god"—just as Hosea's wife ran to other men, and as Israel ran to make foreign alliances and take on foreign gods. Such reactions are not in keeping with calling to the Lord with our heart. We are merely calling to Him out of our immediate desires and hurting soul.

When you are in a difficult situation, especially one of your own making, and you want God's help, consider how you are about to approach Him. How will you cry out to Him? Will you cry out of fear and anger? Or from a heart that loves and seeks Him? And when you are tempted to turn away from Him, seeking help from other "gods," will you remember His deep love and concern for you? Will you remember His hurt? Run back to Him and let Him take you in His arms and comfort you. *"Then they shall be My people, and I will be their God"* (Ezekiel 37:23 NKJV).

Study 21

As a Father

"As a father pitieth his children,
so the LORD pitieth them that fear him."
—Psalm 103:13

There are certain nuances in the original Hebrew of the above verse that many people might feel are unimportant. Yet, when you are seeking the heart of God, such nuances can carry life-changing implications. Does it really matter how we render the Hebrew word *'al* (עַל), which could mean either "upon" or "over"? Some translations render the first phrase, "As a father has compassion *upon* (or *on*) His children...." Still others translate it as "...*over* His children." Perhaps, as the King James Version does, we should just ignore the word and leave it out altogether.

"Over" or "Upon"?

There is a difference in nuance between the English words *over* and *upon*. That difference is not reflected in the Hebrew word *'al* (עַל), so it is up to you and what the Holy Spirit whispers in your ear as to which word you will use in this verse, if you choose to translate the preposition at all. What word a particular Bible version uses may be an indication of the translator's view of God. To say "over His children" gives the impression of God covering them with compassion. But to say "upon His children" suggests the idea of God not only covering them, but also touching them. Or again, we can take the route of the KJV (and other translations) and simply phrase it, "As a father pitieth his children...."

While working on this word study, I was sitting in a coffee shop, and I saw an excellent illustration of the difference between "over" and "upon." There was a young couple there who were either newly married or freshly in love—they were totally absorbed with each other. All of a sudden, there was a sound like a bang or a pop from outside. It sounded like it might have been a firecracker or even a gunshot. Instantly, our gallant young man got up and placed himself in front of his beloved, covering her with his body. At first, he just stood over her protectively, not even touching her. But after everything seemed well and the concern had passed, perhaps he realized he was about to pass up a good opportunity. Now, instead of just placing himself over his sweetheart, his protective covering became a little hug in which the couple exchanged a quick kiss and then resumed their socially acceptable position of sitting next to one another. However, during that hug, the young man was not just "over" his sweetheart but "upon" her with a touch of love.

When it comes to our relationship with God, such nuances between "over" and "upon" are important too. Yes, I would like God to show compassion *over* me, but I would much prefer that He show His compassion *upon* me. I don't know about you, but hugs are a very rare occurrence for me, and if God is going to show me some compassion, I really wouldn't mind if He topped it off with a little hug as well. Therefore, if you don't mind, I will choose the word *upon* rather than *over*. It makes it a little more personal and fits the nature of my God very nicely.

"Compassion" or "Pity"?

Continuing our study, what is this "compassion" or "pity" business, anyway? Looking at the original term in the Hebrew, it turns out to be my favorite word, *racham* (רחם). David seems to really love that word too. There are many faces to *racham* (רחם), a term that signifies romantic love, a love that is reciprocated—like that of the young couple who sat across from me in the coffee shop and took little sips each other's coffee and gazed into each other's eyes.

Most translations render *racham* (רחם) as "compassion." I think that's a good choice. One translation uses "tender and compassionate." While I was in the coffee shop, I also saw a young mother with her little daughter, who was about three years old, standing in line to order. The daughter was bouncing up and down, wanting a piece of cake she saw in the glass case. The mother knelt down to her level and pointed to something else in the case as the little girl squealed with delight. The mother's face beamed as she tenderly wiped the hair away from her daughter's eyes. Ah, *tender and compassionate*—I really like that rendering too. I like to have God beside me taking delight in the things I find joyful.

Again, the King James Version uses *"pitieth,"* and this can also be a meaning for *racham* (רחם). When I first walked into the coffee shop, I saw a homeless man in filthy clothes sitting in a corner. After a few minutes, I noticed another man, who had purchased an extra cup of coffee, simply set one of the cups down in front of the homeless man and walk away. Thus, the man in dirty clothes was now officially a customer, and he could stay in the coffee shop and keep warm.

That day was one of those dark, chilly, rain-swept autumn days, and it didn't seem as if the homeless man was ready to go outside and face that dank weather again right away. His beneficiary had walked to the other side of the shop and sat down with a woman, perhaps his wife. They looked like a prosperous and happy couple, and it is obvious that this man had *pitied* the homeless man. He had felt sorry for him. Regarding our relationship with God, I still prefer the *tender and compassionate* rendering over *pity*, although both are correct. It is up to you to make your choice.

Other Bible translations use the phrase "has mercy." *Mercy* is a correct translation of *racham* (רחם) as well. A little while ago, an older man sitting on the other side of the coffee shop accidently knocked his cup of coffee off the table when he tried to move his laptop. (As is often the case in the coffee shops I visit, I am not the only one sitting there using a computer. Considering that the shop is in the artistic district, you could probably walk up to anyone working on a laptop, ask, "How's your book coming?" and be correct in your assumption.)

This older man was obviously embarrassed at having spilled his coffee, but the young, female employee was there in an instant with a mop, reassuring her customer that it was okay and they would get him another cup of coffee. This young woman was showing the man *mercy*. The store was not obligated to give him another cup of coffee, but they did, and in that act, they showed him mercy, or undeserved favor.

I could use some mercy from God, and I would be happy rendering *racham* (רחם) as *mercy* in this verse. However, since I have a choice, I think I still like the idea of "tender and compassionate." So, it is the mother and daughter who get the prize for helping this dusty old professor choose his own word for *racham* (רחם) in this passage. Of course, you are free to make. your own decision. Let the Holy Spirit whisper the best choice for you to fit your present situation.

Daddy's Little Girl

*"I have likened the daughter of Zion to
a comely and delicate woman."*
—Jeremiah 6:2 (KJV)

"I will destroy Daughter Zion, so beautiful and delicate."
—Jeremiah 6:2 (NIV)

What a contrast! Which of the above translations is correct? The first speaks in gentle, loving terms, calling the daughter of Zion a *"comely and delicate"* woman, and the second, which is a modern translation, affirms that *"Daughter Zion* [is] *so beautiful and delicate"* but then talks of "destroying" her. How can two translations be so different? Which is expressing the true mind of God in this situation?

I looked at this verse in twenty-one different English translations, and nine of them essentially say that the daughter of Zion is beautiful and comely, while twelve essentially say, "Let's get her." There are about 150 English translations of the Bible, and I don't plan to go through all of them to tally up the score. Let's just say that, based on my preliminary research, this is a big problem. Many commentators admit that Jeremiah 6:2 is probably the most difficult verse in the book of Jeremiah to translate. Thus, what you will get from me in this word study is just another paraphrase, another opinion. I will leave it to you to decide if God is simply calling the daughter of Zion beautiful or if He is also getting ready to destroy her. You may have already guessed my choice.

Beloved Children

First, we need to establish the identity of this *"daughter of Zion."* The word *"daughter"* is obviously used metaphorically, as it references both the male and female members of Zion. The word *"Zion"* is derived from one of the following two root words: the first is spelled sade (צ), vav (ו) hei (ה), which means "to stand erect to be charged with a mission," and the second is spelled sade (צ), yod (י), hei (ה), which means "to be dry, dusty, and barren." Since *Zion* is always a reference to Israel, I'm inclined to go with the first option, because Israel had been charged with revealing to the world the reality and nature of God. That is why they are the chosen race. They had the mission to bring the Messiah into the world—the One who is God in human form and is the ultimate revelation of God the Father to humanity.

Zion is also a word used in Scripture when God is expressing His love for Israel. It is a term of endearment for Him, sort of like a father calling his daughter "Princess" or "My Little Cupcake." It is always used when God is pictured as a father. It is only natural that the word *daughter* would be used to modify the word *Zion*, for with *"daughter of Zion,"* we have the picture of a father doting on his beloved child; she is purely "daddy's little girl." Even if she is a naughty little girl, nobody lays a hand on her without paying the consequences. The father will not think twice about giving his life for his little princess. Now, a son is just as loved by a father, but a father is not apt to be as gentle with a son as he is with a daughter. The father's heart swells with pride when, for instance, he sees his son, after getting tackled by some giant on the football field, get up and knock that giant on his backside in the next play. But if any one of those football players were to so much as touch his cheerleader daughter—look out!

Beautiful Children

It is no wonder that the daughter of Zion is called *"comely"* or *"beautiful."* This word in the Hebrew is *na'veh* (נאוה), from the root word *na'ah* (נאה), which means "to dwell" or "to sit." It comes from an old Canaanite word used in the worship of Astarte. In those days, once in her life, a young woman had to adorn herself, looking her absolute best, and then sit at the feet of the statue of the goddess and wait for some man to come along who found her truly beautiful to—how can I put this delicately?—have his way with her. After that one-time seduction, the young woman would be free to live out her life without any other obligations to the goddess (although there was no rule against a woman performing her religious duty more than once, and indeed many did). There were some poor souls who would sit on the chair for years, waiting for some guy to have pity on her. But this is how the word *na'ah* (נאה), meaning "to sit," came into the Hebrew language with the meaning of "to be beautiful." It is a word applied to a young woman at the height of her beauty.

Pampered Children

The Lord also calls the daughter of Zion *"delicate."* The Hebrew word is *'anag* (ענג) and is used for a princess who is spoiled and pampered. She never had to work a day in her life because her father had servants to see to her every need and desire. Thus, her skin remained soft and delicate, free from the ravishes of the sun that most women experienced from laboring in the fields. Their skin soon became hard and leathery. But the *'anag* (ענג), the delicate one, was the joy of the king's court. Everyone fawned over her and went out of their way to be gentle with her, for she could easily be bruised—and heaven help the man who bruised this soft, gentle creature! Her daddy was the king, and he had a guy wearing a pointed black hood and carrying a big ax, just itching for the chance to test out the sharp blade of his weapon.

Jeremiah 6:2 is expressing one central idea: Israel, and each one of us as God's children, is like "daddy's little girl" whom He spoils and pampers. A father's emotions are easily moved by his daughter's silly little gestures, and his heart is warmed by her gentle embraces and kisses. Daddy may be a powerful man, perhaps a king or another ruler, but in the hands of his little girl, he is mere putty.

God's Own Children

Therefore, picture yourself before God as "Daddy's little girl." His heart is melted by your presence. His powerful position of ruling the universe is "placed on hold" when you, His beloved child, say, "Daddy, I cut my finger and it hurts. Kiss it and make it better." He stops everything else to kiss your cut finger. And if anyone would dare to lay a hand on you, that bruiser had better run and hide because Daddy will come after him.

Yet, what will happen if Daddy's little girl is disobedient and misbehaves? Well, according to twelve out of twenty-one translations, He is going to destroy her. But according to the nine remaining translations, He is going to weep as He sees His little girl get beaten by a bad man, because her sins have tied Daddy's hands. However, once she confesses and repents, His hands will be untied, and then, look out for Daddy's wrath!

A Quiet Place

"Until I went into the sanctuary of God; then understood I their end."
—Psalm 73:17

Asaph, the author of Psalm 73, was a close friend of King David and collaborated with him on much of his poetry and music. Asaph was also a "seer." The Bible shows a difference between a "seer," *ra'ah* (ראה), and a "prophet," *nebim* (נבם). Simply put, people would go to consult with a seer, but a prophet would go to proclaim to the people.

Serving God in Vain?

As a Levite who functioned in the role of a seer, Asaph would have had many people come to him for counsel, just as people would go to their pastor or priest today. Like many present-day pastors, Asaph saw the sufferings and anguish of God's people, and he could not help but contrast their situation with the prosperity and seemingly problem-free life of the wicked.

In the first part of Psalm 73, I think Aspah is most likely only repeating a question he has been asked by the many people who have come to him for counsel. This is a question that only a revelation from the mind of God can answer. That question goes something like this: "I have served

God, sacrificed for Him, and lived for Him, and yet I am suffering. God has made many promises, but it seems as if He has not kept them. Why?"

On top of this, there is the issue expressed in verse 13: "*I have cleansed my heart in vain.*" In other words, what good is there in serving God if you receive nothing in return? Of course, we Christians today never have such doubts!

I have heard a number of people comment that they tried Christianity but felt it just did not work. I think what they were saying is that they had bought into all the hype propagated about Christianity that God will be certain to solve all their problems, restore their marriage and other relationships, and grant them prosperity. Then, when they accepted Jesus as their Savior, things only seemed to get worse. These people were really expressing, like Asaph, "*I have cleansed my heart in vain.*"

Well, I understand their frustrations. I have prayed for healing, only to get worse. I have prayed for the restoration of relationships, but they were too far gone to be repaired. I could keep you up all night telling you about my unanswered prayers. But you know what? That is not the reason I signed on with God. I signed on for love of my Creator—"for better or for worse, for richer or for poorer, in sickness and in health." As Asaph wrote toward the end of the psalm, "*Whom have I in heaven but thee? and there is none upon earth that I desire beside thee*" (Psalm 73:25).

Go into the Sanctuary

This matter of why the righteous suffer while the wicked seem to get a pass on suffering is an age-old question, and it usually goes unanswered. It remains unanswered because few who ask the question go into the "*sanctuary,*" as Asaph did, where they could discover the answer. Sometimes, we just need to find a "sanctuary" in which to sit with God in the quietness, where He can reveal His mind to us.

The Hebrew word translated "*sanctuary*" in Psalm 73:17 is a rather mysterious one. It is *miqodeshi* (מקדשי), which literally means "my place of separation" or "my place of holiness." The Masoretes ended the word with a sere yod, which would give it a plural ending and thus be an allusion to the Holy of Holies. Some say it is in the plural because there are three divisions to the sanctuary: the court, the Holy Place, and the Holy of Holies. Nevertheless, I question this explanation because Asaph was not a high priest and could not have entered the Holy of Holies. As a seer, however, he would have had a separate or holy place where he would go to receive his revelations from God. Thus, I take issue with the Masorete interpretation. Instead, as many rabbis do, I would end the word with a chireq yod, which would create the pronoun *my*. This is important because it shows that when Asaph needed an answer from God, even as a seer, he had a special place, a quiet place, where he would go to pray and meet with the Lord. He could even have called it "my place."

It was in Asaph's *miqodeshi* (מקדש), his special, quiet place, that God revealed His secrets to him. And it was there that Asaph found the answer to that age-old question of why the righteous suffer while the wicked prosper.

Many translators render the last word in this verse, which comes from the root word *'achar* (אחר), as "end." However, its primary meaning is "after" or "behind," or, in its verb form, "to tarry." Stretch the meaning, and you can arrive at "end." Thus, if we say that "end" is the sense here, it suggests that in this quiet place, Asaph saw the end of the lives of the wicked, which is everlasting torment. In contrast, the righteous, after a life of suffering, will be received into heaven. In other words, the translators wanted to answer the question of why the righteous suffer and the wicked prosper with something like this: "It will all pan out in the end."

However, suppose we stay with the general meaning of *'achar* (אחר) in its verb form, which means "to tarry" and not try to stretch it to fit our agenda or personal bias. If we say the meaning is "tarry," then what Asaph would have been saying is that in this quiet place, he understood why the wicked *continued* or *tarried* in prosperity. What Asaph came to understand is this: it was the presence of God that he felt in his quiet place, the peace and joy he experienced with God, that answered the question for him. Let the "wicked" have their prosperity, for in the presence of God, wealth and possessions mean absolutely nothing. The people of the world may have their fortunes, but we have the great riches of God's presence, which are infinitely more valuable.

God Will Be There When We Need Him

Still, the idea that "it will all pan out in the end" is not always very comforting, even with the promise of heaven. So, this thought was not satisfying to me until I entered my own *miqodeshi* (מקדש), or quiet place. About the time I was working on this word study, I received an email newsletter from the organization Voice of the Martyrs, and I read yet another story about a Christian who was shot to death by ISIS, the militant Islamic fundamentalist group. The only crime this Christian committed was to love Jesus and try to share that love with others, and for that he was murdered. After reading about this, I went to my *miqodeshi* (מקדש), my quiet place, my sanctuary, where I sought an answer from God as to why He had not delivered this faithful servant from death.

As sometimes happens in my quiet place, I entered the heart and mind of God, and He allowed me feel what this Christian felt when a terrorist pointed a gun to his head. It was as if I were looking into the face of Jesus, and all I felt was peace, serenity, and joy. I felt a longing to reach out and hug Jesus, and I believed that at any moment, my arms would be around Him and His arms would be around me. Then I heard a bang, and suddenly I was outside the heart of God again.

I felt such a letdown that I almost wept. I actually began to feel depressed that I hadn't been able to physically hug Jesus. I had to return to my world, my life, my problems and frustrations, without being able to hug Jesus in His life. I actually envied that Christian martyr. That is when I comprehended the last words of Psalm 73:17: "*Then understood I their end* [or continuing]." I sensed God saying, "I will be there when you need Me." I knew and understood that those who seemingly prosper when we who are faithful get the short end of the stick are missing something vital that we have: the very living, loving life of Jesus when we need it. Nothing this world has to offer can come close to that. God will be there for us when we need Him. We can't depend upon our jobs, bank accounts, or anything else in this crazy physical world. But we can always depend on Him.

Study 24

Cruel with Wrath and Fierce Anger

"Behold, the day of the LORD cometh,
cruel both with wrath and fierce anger, to lay the land desolate:
and he shall destroy the sinners thereof out of it."
—Isaiah 13:9

This *"day of the LORD"* business sounds like serious stuff. We are talking about a desolate land and sinners being destroyed. I know this verse is speaking about the destruction of Babylon—and indeed, using the Medo-Persian Empire, God really did a number on the land of Babylon. But note that Babylon is not named, leaving this verse open-ended as a warning to other sinners who cross God.

I once heard a preacher say, in reference to God's love, "You have nothing to be afraid of with God." Then he caught himself and added, "But you had better be afraid of God." So, which is it?

Some Christians use phrases such as *"cruel both with wrath and fierce anger"* to scare people into receiving salvation, attending church, or paying their tithe. Actually, there's an English word for getting people to pay their tithe out of a fear that God will be wrathful and angry toward them if they don't: it's called *extortion*, and extortion is illegal, both in heaven and on earth.

Fiercely Protective

So, how should we understand the above verse? First, let's look at the Hebrew word for "*cruel*," '*akazari* (אכזרי), which comes from the root word *kazar* (כזר), meaning "to be valiant, daring, and courageous." Such a fearless person can be a terrible foe to face. They can be relentless and capable of doing things someone who is fearful for their life would not do. A person who has nothing to lose is capable of committing horrendously cruel acts. But just because someone is daring and courageous does not make them a cruel person.

Let's think about what might be going through God's mind on "*the day of the* Lord." That "*day*" will be a time of saving His people. He will be courageous in that He will deliver those whom He loves at any cost, just as a mother bear will protect her cubs at any cost. You can look at a momma bear in such a situation either as cruel or as determined to fight to the death to save her offspring. Thus, I don't like the word *cruel* applied to God, and I don't believe it is the best rendering for '*akazari* (אכזרי) in this context. Instead, I would go with "fiercely protective" wrath.

Overflowing Anger

Next, let's look at the word "*wrath.*" This is a scary word, particularly when applied to God. No one wants to face the wrath of the Lord. *Wrath* denotes something terrible—how can we associate it with a loving God? The Hebrew word rendered "*wrath*" is '*ebrah* (עברה), which comes from the root word *ebar* (עבר). In its Semitic root, it is a term used when a river overflows it banks. It has the idea of "overwhelming" or "all-encompassing." Thus, instead of "*wrath,*" I prefer to go with the original intent of the word and call it an "overflowing" anger.

Passionate Determination

In Isaiah 13:9, the Hebrew word for "*fierce*" is *charon* (חרון), from the root word *charah* (חרה), and it can mean "anger" or "wrath." It is often used to express displeasure. In its Semitic root, *charah* (חרה) has the idea of a raging fire. This is where the idea of anger comes in. However, *charah* (חרה) is merely a picture.

What is a picture of a raging fire when applied to an emotion? It might be anger, but it might also be other emotions, such as raging fear, sexual rage, raging passion, or consuming passion. There are any number of ways to render this word depending on the context. And much of this context depends on how you view God. If we are to view Him as perfect in love, with a love that casts out all fear (see 1 John 4:18), then I don't think the word *fierce* is our best choice.

Some time ago, a movie came out about a soldier who won the medal of honor. He rescued seventy-five wounded soldiers under enemy-controlled territory, carrying each one on his shoulder or dragging them to the ridge of a mountain and lowering them to safety. He was a Christian, and each time he rescued a comrade, he would pray to God, "Just one more. Help me save just one more." This soldier did not even carry a rifle because he was a medic. Many people said that what he accomplished was beyond human strength, yet he did it. He was filled with *charah* (חרה), a passion to rescue his fellow soldiers that consumed him to the point where he cared nothing for his own safety. He was *'akazari* (אכזרי), courageous, and filled with *charah* (חרה), passionate determination.

The Hebrew word translated *"anger"* is not clearly defined. As I wrote in the preface to this book, its root word is *'aneph* (אנף), which means "to snort," and it comes from the snorting of a camel. Why does a camel snort? There are many reasons. Yes, it might snort out of anger. But it might also snort when forced to do something it does not want to do, or out of frustration, or out of grief if its mate or calf dies. Additionally, it will snort when it is in heat and desires intimacy.

So, here is how I would translate the first part of this verse, even though many people in the church might find it unacceptable. I believe these words fit the Hebrew just as much as the ones in our current English translations do: "The day of the Lord is coming, and He will be courageous and filled with overwhelming determination and consuming passion to lay waste the land." This describes a very brave act and shows God's determination to rescue His people, because He is willing to lay waste the land that He created. He will sacrifice His creation for His people, and He will destroy the sinner.

A Day of Closure

We have two more words to look at in this verse: *"destroy"* and *"sinners."* The Hebrew word translated *"destroy"* is *shamad* (שמד), which means "to destroy" or "to exterminate." The use of these words reminds me of something I experienced one day while driving my disability bus. I pulled up to a house and beeped the horn to summon my passenger, who did not come. Therefore, I picked up my phone and called her. She did not speak much English, and when she answered my call, I heard the pages of a book turning, so I figured she was looking for the right English words with which to answer me. Finally, she said, "I am totally ignoring you," and then she hung up. A few minutes later, my dispatcher called to say the woman had canceled her ride. I thought about this, and to say, "I am totally ignoring you" *is* one way to express that you are canceling your ride. However, her choice of words was not the best; it was not appropriate for the context. Similarly, to use the word *destroy* or *exterminate* is correct with regard to the word alone, but in the context of a loving God, I doubt either is the best term to use.

In its Semitic origins, *shamad* (שמד) means "to bring to a conclusion," "closure," or "ending." The Hebrew word for *"sinners"* is *chatah* (חטה), which is an archer's term for "missing the target." In other words, this *"day of the* LORD*"* is a time of closure, bringing to an end the rule of those who cannot hit the target of God's laws.

All the renderings we have of this passage are correct—it is just how you want to spin it. Do you have an angry God who waves His hands and destroys everything and everyone that displeases Him? Or, do you have a loving God who is filled with such passion for His people that He will one day bring all the evil and suffering in the world to a conclusion—a God who will come as a valiant "knight in shining armor," rescuing His people from those who failed to follow His laws, which resulted in harm to His children? The choice is really yours. As I previously encouraged you, let the peace of God rule your heart (see Colossians 3:15) regarding whatever choice you make about what will be going through God's mind on *"the day of the* LORD*."*

Study 25

An Intimate Knowing

"The heart of the prudent getteth knowledge;
and the ear of the wise seeketh knowledge."
—Proverbs 18:15

I have always struggled with accepting the translation *"knowledge"* in the above verse because I felt there was something much deeper indicated there than just gaining an understanding of God. When I studied the Hebrew word, I discovered this was true—there was something much deeper and more wonderful being expressed.

Our English word *knowledge* is defined as "acquaintance with facts, truths, or principles, as from study or investigation; general erudition." Hence, when we read the above verse, probably the first thing that comes to mind is that the prudent person studies hard and acquires facts, truths, and principles. However, in the Hebrew, the word *knowledge* takes on characteristics not often assumed by one who speaks English.

Practical Knowledge for Survival

The root word of the Hebrew term translated *"knowledge"* is *yada'* (ידע). Indeed, it means "acquiring knowledge," but the word was birthed in a simple, uneducated, and illiterate culture. Today, with the prevalence of colleges and universities and the wide range of training and learning available to us, we automatically think of "knowledge" as book knowledge or information learned from teachers. In ancient times, only the elite went to schools, such as they were. The vast majority of people had little time for education; they spent most of their existence struggling to survive year to year. The main factual knowledge they acquired was about how to plant seeds, harvest crops, and tend animals—and the sheer need to survive made the acquisition of this knowledge essential. They needed little encouragement to obtain it.

Relational Knowledge

In those days, a person also needed knowledge about the people in their family and circle of friends. Their continued existence depended heavily upon their ability to trust, work effectively with, and get along with other people. There were no lone wolves. They survived by the relationships they developed.

In my writings, I have often emphasized that Hebrew is a relational language. This is true not only regarding the relationship between certain words, but also in how we are to look at each word and consider it in light of a relationship. I mentioned previously that my younger brother is a linguist and executive with Wycliffe Bible Translators. He has taught linguistics on the college level, and he is the one who first told me that whatever is important in a culture is reflected in its language. For instance, the Eskimos have dozens of words for snow because snow is integral to their culture. They might want to describe a wet snow that is good for packing and building igloos. Or, they might want to indicate a dry, powdery snow that is good for hunting and tracking. In our culture, snow is just not important enough to merit multiple words, despite attempts by the Weather Channel to add new words to our vocabulary such as *snain* (snow mixed with rain). Such words don't catch on in America and elsewhere because they're not perceived to be very important.

What our English language *does* have is more adjectives than any other language. Adjectives describe things (as well as people), and of course, "things" are of primary importance in our society. But, again, in ancient Semitic culture, relationships were most important. Whole families and clans often lived under the same roof and shared life communally. They had to know how to get along with each other, so understanding relationships was important.

An Intimate Knowledge of God

This brings us back to the word *"knowledge"* in Proverbs 18:15. To review, in our culture, we acquire knowledge so we can either get a good job or advance in a position in order to make more money and buy more things. In ancient Semitic culture, knowledge was acquired so people could learn how to get along with others whom they needed to depend upon, and know how to provide food for themselves so they could survive. Therefore, when you read the word *knowledge* in the Bible, think like an ancient Semite—think in terms of relationships.

Consider this: when you acquire knowledge about a subject, you become intimate with that knowledge. Likewise, the more knowledge you have about a person, the more intimate you are with that person. As indicated in an earlier study, the word *yada'* (ידע) is used for sexual intercourse between a husband and wife. To the ancient Hebrews, a sexual relationship in marriage was the ultimate in *knowing* another person; it was the ultimate in *being intimate* with someone. Both parties expose themselves physically and emotionally when they share such intimacy. In fact, they know each other better than anyone else in the world, and they would be pretty upset to learn that someone else knew their spouse better than they did.

Thus, because our twenty-first-century understanding of the English word *knowledge* detracts from the biblical, Hebraic understanding, I don't like to use the word *knowledge* in most passages that include the Hebrew term *yada'* (ידע). I am not saying the word *"knowledge"* is a mistranslation; I am only saying it is obsolete, made so by our cultural perspective. We need to use a different word, and in my view, that word should be *intimacy*. The next time you see the word *knowledge* in the Old Testament, as in Hosea 6:6, where God says that He desires *"the knowledge of God more than burnt offerings,"* just insert the word *intimacy*. God is saying that He desires intimacy with us more than offerings.

Do you see that, when studying the Bible, it can be helpful to take a closer look at the English words that are used? Even though they may be correct, and our lexicons and *Strong's Concordance* may be correct, we must ask ourselves, "What is my understanding of this English word, and does it really line up with the intent behind the Hebrew word?"

Let's read our entire study verse again: "*The heart of the prudent getteth knowledge; and the ear of the wise seeketh knowledge.*" If we paraphrase this Scripture in twenty-first-century English, it could read like this: "The heart of the prudent becomes intimate with God, and the ear of the wise seeks words of intimacy." Does that improve your comprehension of the verse? Again, it is not that using the word "*knowledge*" is wrong, but the word *intimacy* adds the frosting and special topping to our understanding of what that knowledge consists of.

Study 26

Betrothed to Jesus

"And I will betroth thee unto me for ever; yea,
I will betroth thee unto me in righteousness, and in judgment,
and in lovingkindness, and in mercies."
—Hosea 2:19

There is much talk among Christians about being the "bride of Christ" and "married to Christ." This is, of course, a very biblical picture of our spiritual union with Jesus. In fact, many Christians see Song of Solomon, which is the story of the love relationship between King Solomon and the Shulamite woman, as a picture of our relationship with Christ. This is not only a Christian concept but also a very Jewish idea. I read a story in Jewish literature about a rabbi who would literally dress up in a wedding outfit on the Sabbath in anticipation of the coming of the Messiah to receive him as His bride.

Marital love is such a strong and beautiful image of our relationship with God that the enemy seeks to strike at the very heart and core of the marriage relationship to distort it with the many sexual perversions that exist today. He seeks to corrupt the sanctity of marriage with selfishness, unfaithfulness, and abuse—turning marriage into something that becomes almost a mockery in order to warp the very picture God has given us to understand our relationship with Him.

Yet, even though the divorce rate is high and many people are living together outside of matrimony, marriage is still very popular. Stories about romantic love sell novels, movies, and tabloid magazines. As some famous movie star enters her fifth marriage, we all grab the latest edition of *People* magazine to find out if she has finally found her true romantic partner. We fill movie theaters to capacity to watch a story about a man and woman who find true love and begin "living happily ever after." Our hearts are warmed when we watch an elderly couple celebrate their sixtieth wedding anniversary, holding hands and giving each other a little kiss on the lips. But oh, how the enemy hates that demonstration of love, because he knows we will look at such a relationship and begin to compare the tenderness, faithfulness, and caring we observe to our relationship with God. For God did, indeed, give us the marriage relationship, the love relationship between a man and a woman, as a picture of our relationship with Him.

Preparing a Place for Us

However, note that the Bible seems to speak mainly of our "betrothal" to God, such as in Hosea and Song of Solomon. The only time it references being married to God is when it talks about Jesus coming to take us to heaven. Apparently, the picture that Scripture gives us is that, while on earth, we are merely in a betrothal period. Jesus even alluded to this fact when He said, *"In my Father's house are many mansions* [rooms]: *if it were not so, I would have told you. I go to prepare a place for you"* (John 14:2).

In biblical times, during the betrothal period, a bridegroom would build a new room or addition to his father's house, where he would later move in with his bride. Then, one day, the bridegroom would come to take his bride from the world of her family to live in the world of his family. In the above verse, Jesus is giving us a beautiful Semitic picture of being betrothed to us by saying He is building a room onto His father's house, and when it is finished, He will come and take us, His bride, away from our present world to live in His world.

A Growing Passion

What exactly is meant by this "betrothal"? The Hebrew word translated "*betroth*" in Hosea 2:19 is *'aras* (ארס). If you look the word up in your lexicon, it will simply say that it means "to betroth." *Strong's* definition is "to engage for matrimony." We really need to look into Jewish literature and the Talmud to understand what is meant by "betrothal" if we are to make the proper comparison to our relationship with God. The word *'aras* (ארס) comes from a Semitic root found in the Sumerian language meaning "to desire." Hence, the whole idea behind a betrothal is to build a desire between a man and woman.

There is an ancient legend that when a male child is born, his soul is split in two, and half of his soul is placed by God into a female child who will one day be born. God then anoints a *shidduch* (שדח), or matchmaker, who has a prophetic gift to discern the young woman who has the other half of the male's soul. Hence the term *soulmates*.

In arranged marriages, this determination of "soulmates" was often made between two individuals who had never met each other. It was understood that there must be a period of time for the couple to learn to love one another before the marriage was consummated. Thus, we have the time of a betrothal. This is where the idea of an engagement originated. The whole idea of an engagement and an engagement ring has its roots in Judaism. I believe it is significant that this is a Jewish concept, because God is giving us a picture of our relationship with Him.

When a young couple was betrothed, traditionally, the parents were to support the young man financially so he would not have to work during this period. The length of the betrothal would vary. Generally, it was one year, but it could be more or even less. It might be one day or it might be a number of years, although I imagine the family would tire of having to support a young man for longer than a year. Once more, the idea was that during this time, the couple would begin to learn about each other and come to understand each other's minds and hearts. They would learn to love each other, that is, fall in love such that their desire and passion for each other would build to the point that the man would one day come to carry away his bride, become intimate with her, and make her his wife.

The culture had great taboos on a man touching or even looking at a woman. However, when a man was betrothed, he was granted much more liberty to touch his beloved. The couple would be allowed to go off into the wilderness and share their deepest thoughts and dreams, and they could hold hands and exchange a kiss or two, but they could go no further than that. If the man and woman did engage in sex, they were officially married. In fact, the betrothal itself begins with a wedding ceremony where the man and woman are legally married but do not yet live together or engage in marital sex.

A Love Consummated

The betrothal can be a very romantic time, a period when two lovers dream together, have the joy of learning to commit to one another, and experience the thrill of the nearness and touch of the one to whom they would one day become intimate in the deepest way. Usually, after a year of this, the bridegroom would become so 'aras (ארס), or desirous of being intimate with this woman with whom he has shared his heart, that, as we have learned, he would one night slip out of his house and take his bride away from her father's home and take her to his father's home, where they would consummate their relationship in the room he has built onto his father's house. At that time, they would be married in the full sense.

No one, not even the bride, knew when the bridegroom would reach the point of such desire that he would snatch his bride away. Everyone in the village would anxiously await that day, watch for the signs that the bridegroom was getting ready, and observe him breaking out in a cold sweat. Then, the word would get out, "It's tonight." Everyone would light a lamp and follow the groom as he went to his bride's house. Although the bride did not know the exact time, she did know the seasons, and she had a good enough idea that she would be dressed and ready when the secret was out and the bridegroom came knocking on her door.

Is that not a picture of our lives here on earth? When we accept Jesus as our Savior, we become betrothed to Him. We live the remaining days of our life in a period of engagement to Jesus, learning to love Him; spending time alone with Him; and allowing Him to hold our hand, lovingly stroke our cheek, and gently kiss us. All the while, our desire for Him grows deeper and deeper until, one day, He Himself can no longer stand to be separated from us, and He comes to snatch us away and take us to live in His Father's house in heaven.

Are you dressed and ready?

Study 27

Bonding with God

"So the people rested on the seventh day."
—Exodus 16:30

What do you think goes through God's mind when it comes time for Him to grant a miracle? Does He call in an accountant to calculate how faithful you have been in church attendance and tithing? Does He consult a marketing representative to determine your soul-winning score? If the numbers add up, you get your miracle. If not, too bad. Better luck the next time your review comes up. Is that how it works?

Winning an Elephant in a Raffle

There are many Christian books and other teachings on the theme of "How to get your miracle from God." However, I find very few "post-miracle" teachings. Not much is offered to assist you *after* you receive your blessing. Sometimes, receiving a miracle from God is like winning an elephant in a raffle. Now that you have it, what are you going to do with it?

By examining the period after a miracle is given, perhaps we can gain an understanding of miracles themselves—and when and why God grants them. If we have been seeking a miracle, it could be that it hasn't come because God knows if we did receive it, we would not handle it in a way that would be to our advantage.

I remember reading a story in a literature class about a blind man who lived during the time of Jesus. To survive, he sat on a street corner and begged for alms. One day, a woman spoke to him and they entered into a discussion. Soon, she came by every day and sat with him, and they talked about their deepest feelings. Day after day, she would describe to him the sights of the town, and before long they fell in love. Then, the blind man heard that Jesus was passing through, and as He walked by, the blind man begged Him to heal him, and Jesus did. The man received his miracle and had his sight. His first thought was to see, for the first time, this woman with whom he had fallen in love. However, when he found her, he discovered that she had been horribly disfigured from a fire when she was a child. He could not look at her, and the relationship ended.

This man sought out other women with whom to form a relationship, but he could find no other woman who touched his soul like that woman had. He would enter relationships but then end up leaving them, brokenhearted. Finally, he heard that Jesus was coming back, and when He arrived, he went to Him and begged for another miracle—that he would become blind again so he could resume his relationship with the woman who had won his heart.

There is vast storehouse of wisdom and knowledge in the mind of God that we don't know or understand. Sometimes, not receiving our miracle can be a hidden blessing because God knows what we don't know, such as how we would handle that miracle. Maybe the best thing for us—and others—would be not to receive the miracle.

The One Condition: Rest

But how should we respond when we *do* receive a miracle? Actually, for this discussion, the word *miracle* might be a little too heavy for some people, so let's just say *gift* from God. Everyone can point to something in their life and honestly say that it truly is or was a gift from God, something they can thank Him for. It might be a job, house, healthy body, spouse, child, or something else. In a prayer meeting I attended, someone held up a glass of water and said, "Lord, I thank You for this clean water to drink, for I am but dust." I didn't totally understand his point, but a cool glass of water would truly be a gift from God, especially if you lived in an area where there was no running water or fresh well to draw from.

We should be thankful for any miracle or gift from God, but our response does not stop with thankfulness alone. There are other conditions attached to miracles or gifts. Our study verse, Exodus 16:30, teaches the one condition that comes with every gift or miracle from the Lord: it is called "rest." You see, when the Israelites were living as slaves in Egypt, life might not have been a bowl of cherries, but they did have grapes, olives, cucumbers, and a variety of food. Yes, they were enslaved, but at least they had a place they could call home, knew where their next meal would come from, and had access to a local well for drawing water. Now that they were in the arid wilderness, they had no permanent home, no real shelter from the desert storms, no source of food, and no local well from which to obtain water.

The Israelites' only source for *everything* was the Lord. And, six days a week, God would open the windows of heaven and send down a bread-like substance called *manna*. Not a bad deal. They did not have to get up early in the morning to plow a field, and they did not even have to push a shopping cart through a grocery store and go through a checkout aisle. All they had to do was get up and collect their daily bread. And the price was right as well.

God gave only two conditions for this continuous miracle: for the first five days, take only what you need for one day and no more. On the sixth day, take extra for the seventh day—and *rest* on that seventh day. Do not go out and collect any manna on day seven.

Well, we know what happened. The people took extra during the week (which spoiled), and they went out to collect on the seventh day (but there was nothing to collect). Apparently, the people were afraid that God might oversleep one morning and they would have nothing to eat, so they wanted to save up for a rainy day. Of course, there would be no rainy days in a desert. Unfortunately, the people only saw the manna and their need, not the faithfulness of God to supply the manna in the first place. (See Exodus 16:1–29.)

We learn in our study verse that, after some trial and error, the people of Israel finally figured it out and "*rested*" on the seventh day. But really, how much effort was it to collect their daily manna? Was it that strenuous that they had to take a break every seventh day?

The Hebrew term translated "*rested*" is *vayishevethu* (וישבתו). It comes from the root word *shabat* (שבת), which means "to cease." Genesis 2:2 tells us that after completing the creation of the world, God "*rested*" on the seventh day. I guess all that creating must have worn poor God out! He deserved a rest. Actually, the English word *rest* can be a little misleading here. This was not a rest to regain one's strength; it was a rest in the sense of ceasing from activity. With the usage of the word in Exodus, you have a sort of play on the word *yashev* (ישב), which means "to dwell" or "to sit down." *Shabat* (שבת) has a numerical value of 702. The Hebrew word *miqoshire* (מקשר), which means "to bond," also has a numerical value of 702. Thus, this rest was not meant for catching your breath, but rather to cease from all activity so you could concentrate on one thing: *bonding with God*.

Even collecting manna might take your mind off of God and put it on temporal things. You don't bond with God by worrying or fretting over losing the gifts, or manna, He has given you. You bond with Him by thanking and praising Him for your manna. The Sabbath day is a time to worship and praise God and thank Him for His provisions throughout the week. If we worked seven days a week, we would probably not take any time at all to offer our thanksgiving to Him and to remember who it is that gives us our strength and sustenance.

Spend the Day with God

The Israelites finally figured out this principle. Rather than go looking for their daily miracle of manna on the seventh day, getting stressed out when none was to be found and assuming God was welching on His deal, they were to *rest* or *bond* with God by spending one day with Him without the interference of the daily grind.

Some people pray to win the lottery, believing that it would solve all their problems. From a natural standpoint, you would think it would. Yet, it has been reported that "lottery winners are more likely to declare bankruptcy within three to five years than the average American. What's more, studies have shown that winning the lottery does not necessarily make you happier or healthier."[6] Similarly, some people mistakenly think a certain miracle from God would solve all their problems.

The Jewish people take their Sabbath day very seriously. Perhaps they realize that this day of rest, this day of bonding with God, will accomplish more than the miracle they may desire. In fact, some rabbis teach that the Sabbath *is* their weekly miracle.

What will you do on your "miracle day" this Sunday?

---

6. Abigail Hess, "Here's Why Lottery Winners Go Broke," https://www.cnbc.com/2017/08/25/heres-why-lottery-winners-go-broke.html.

Study 28

An Abusive Husband

"And it shall be at that day, saith the Lord, *that thou shalt call me Ishi* [my husband]; *and shalt call me no more Baali* [my master]*."*
—Hosea 2:16

We have been learning that Hebrew is an emotional language. It is the language of poets and artists. Unlike with biblical Greek, you can't just go to *Strong's Concordance* and check out other possible words that might be used. Greek is a very precise language; it is the language of scientists and mathematicians. Hebrew is not that precise.

Let me give you an exaggerated example. A contemporary poet named Rod McKuen used the sun as one of his themes. In his poem "I'll Catch the Sun," he wrote that he would catch the sun and never give it back again. So, if it were dark outside, and I read his poem with a Greek mind-set, I might assume that Rod McKuen had literally caught the sun and is not giving it back. After all, the word *sun* always refers to that ball of fire in the sky, right? But with a Hebrew mind-set, I would know the sun does not necessarily mean that yellow sphere in the heavens. Instead, the sun might represent deep passion or tender emotion.

I don't think any words of prose could adequately describe a person's deep passion. That is why we need poets who can depict the depths of human emotion through metaphors and other word images. Classical

Hebrew has only 8,400 words. Extra-biblical literature gives us another 680 terms, and the Dead Sea Scrolls provide an additional 540 words or so. Still, that total falls far short of the roughly one million words found in most modern languages. Thus, much of the Old Testament is given to us in poetic form with words that can have a wide range of meanings. You need the mind-set of a poet to really be able to translate Classical Hebrew.

"My Master" or "My Husband"?

Our study verse is a good example of this. Some Bible versions will merely transliterate the original Hebrew word אישׁי as *Ishi*, and the word בעלי as *Baali* rather than translate them into English. To properly understand these words, you have to enter into Hosea's emotions—his passion and heartbreak.

As we noted in study 20, "Howling," Hosea dearly loved his wife, Gomer, even though she was continually unfaithful to him. He longed for the days of their early romance, before she ran off with another lover, when she would sing in the garden. (See verse 15.) Even Hebrew has no specific word to describe Hosea's passion for his wife, and we do not have any word in English to translate it even if Hebrew did have such a word. In the Hebrew, only a picture can be drawn—a very romantic image.

Hosea 2:16 reveals a point in the relationship between Hosea and his wife when she is calling him *Baali* (בעלי), or "my master." Whatever she does for him is out of duty and fear. *Baali* (בעלי) is really the most common word used for a husband in both Hebrew and Aramaic. This is because, in most ancient cultures, a husband was a master to his wife. Women were forced to be totally submissive to their husbands, lest they face physical punishment or even death. This is still true in many cultures in the Middle East, as we hear on the news. Yet, before being influenced by pagan cultures, the Hebrews were noted for their fair and equal treatment of women. Thus, in Hebrew and Aramaic, there are two words for husband: the more commonly used *baali* (בעלי), meaning "my master," the type of man who treated his wife abusively, and the rarely used *ishi* (אישׁי), meaning "my husband." The word *ishi* (אישׁי) has many meanings, such as "friend," "helper," or "companion." There are different usages for *baali* (בעלי), too, but they are all quite negative. *Ishi* (אישׁי) is used only in a very positive light.

In the fourth chapter of John, where Jesus was talking with the woman at the well and asking her to go home and bring back her *"husband,"* He likely used the Aramaic word *baali* (בעלי). Thus, He was asking for her husband in the sense of her "master." Here is my take on this exchange. The woman replied she had no *baali* (בעלי), or "abusive husband," and Jesus said that this was true. She had had five *baalis* (בעלי), or abusive husbands, but the one she was currently living with was not a *baali* (בעלי). She had finally found a man who treated her like a cherished wife, who loved her and cared for her. She had found an *ishi* (אישי). Yet, even after finding what she had spent her life longing to have, she discovered that she was still not satisfied. She still thirsted for *"living water"* (John 4:10). Only when she met Jesus did she find true fulfillment—and eternal life.

What Is God to You?

Hosea wanted to be an *ishi* (אישי) husband, a man who loved his wife, cared for her, and cherished her. But Gomer only saw him as a *baali* (בעלי), a master who had the power of life and death over her. She just could not see Hosea's love for her, so she performed the duties expected of a wife purely out of fear. She was too wrapped up in her adultery and guilt to believe that Hosea would overlook her unfaithfulness and betrayal.

In the same way, God longs to love us, care for us, and cherish us. Yet many Christians see Him only as a *baali* (בעלי), a master who has the power of life and death over them. Therefore, they perform all the duties they think God expects of them because they are afraid of going to hell or suffering some punishment in this life. Yet, all the time, God's heart is weeping over them, longing for them to see Him as a loving, caring Husband— an *ishi* (אישי).

In this passage, the prophet was speaking the words of God to His people. The Israelites viewed Him as a *baali* (בעלי), a master who had to be served lest they suffer severe consequences. However, I encourage you to read this passage as a poem and tap into the emotion that is being played out. You will find God pleading, like Hosea, for His bride to love Him and allow Him to be a true Husband, to be able to show His love, affection, and caring.

What is God to you? Is He a *baali* (בעלי), a "master" type of husband, who demands we follow every letter of His law lest He rain down punishment upon us and maybe even send us to hell? Are you so wrapped up in your sins or your fear of sinning and being punished that you don't see the loving Divine Husband, the *ishi* (אישי), who desires to love you, forgive you, and shower you with affection and caring?

Tragically, many people refuse to believe that God wants to be an *ishi* (אישי) to them. Instead, like Hosea's wife, they continue to treat Him like a *baali* (בעלי), an abusive husband, and in so doing, they break His heart.

Study 29

Cleave to the Lord

*"But ye that did cleave unto the Lord your God
are alive every one of you this day."*
—Deuteronomy 4:4

The context of Deuteronomy 4:4 teaches us that when a number of the Israelites died as a result of following the false god Baalpeor, other Israelites did not perish because they *"cleave*[d] *unto the Lord."* This seems to be such a wonderful promise: if we will cleave to the Lord, we will survive when others die.

However, I took a close look at this verse after reading about the earthquake in Nepal. There were Christians who died in that natural disaster. Did not Deuteronomy 4:4 apply to them? I also read about how ISIS lined up a group of Christians and beheaded them for no other reason than the fact that they were *cleaving* to God and would not deny Him.

This verse is not actually a promise at all, but rather a statement of fact. Moses is repeating a bit of history, pointing out that many of the people of Israel survived a particular incident in which twenty-four thousand of their fellow Israelites who forsook the Lord to follow the false god Baalpeor consequently died in a plague. (See Numbers 25.) There were other situations of rebellion and idolatry that might have destroyed them as well. But those who kept God's laws were not punished like those who were disobedient.

Protected by Keeping God's Law

Many of God's laws had a practical side to them that the people did not understand. For example, why should they wash their hands before eating or wash their eating utensils with hot water? They had no concept of disease-causing microbes. But they followed these seemingly meaningless and foolish practices in obedience to God. They observed good hygiene because the Lord told them to, not because they knew the science behind it as we do today. Similarly, following rigorous dietary laws kept them from contracting diseases that the other nations dealt with. And practicing strict rules concerning sexual relationships protected them from sexually transmitted diseases.

In Deuteronomy 4:4, Moses does not specifically mention the keeping of God's laws, although the surrounding verses do. In this verse, He stresses the idea of *cleaving* unto Jehovah. Many Bible translators have a real problem with this passage. The preposition *unto* is not included here. To be accurately rendered as cleaving, or clinging, *to* Jehovah, the original Hebrew would need to be *hadevaqim laYHWH* (ליהוה הדוקים), but it is actually *hadevaqim baYHWH* (ביהוה הדוקים), which is properly rendered as clinging *in* Jehovah. But of course, you do not cling *in* or *on* something; you cling *to* something. So, the translators just play with the ambiguity of the language and use the preposition *unto* or *to* rather than *in*.

However, the problem is not in the preposition but in our comprehension of the word *deveqim* (דבקים). We really cannot find a decent English word to translate this term, so it has to be explained rather than translated. The closest we can come are renderings like "cling" "hold fast," "be faithful," "remain faithful," "be loyal," and "adhere." Yet, none of these words comes close to giving us a proper understanding of *deveqim* (דבקים). Unfortunately when translating the Bible, you have to come up with only one or maybe two words at the most for rendering a Hebrew term, because there just isn't enough room to fully explain it.

Alive Forever in Christ

By using the word *deveqim* (דבקים), Moses was providing a double meaning, a literary feature that is often found in Scripture. One meaning applies to the particular time when something is experienced or record-ed, and one applies to us today. By *cleaving* to God, the people of Israel remained *chiyiyim* (חיים), or physically *"alive."* Yet *chiyiyim* (חיים) can also mean to be spiritually alive.

In Matthew 16:25, Mark 8:35, and Luke 9:24, Jesus teaches that if you want to save your life, you will lose it, but if you give up your life for His sake, you will save it. Those who died at the hands of ISIS while "clinging *in* God" may have lost their physical lives, but their spiritual lives in Jesus Christ will remain forever. No one can take away eternal life from them. As long as we "cling in God," or dwell in His heart and mind, we will never lose our eternal life. We may lose our physical life, but we all are going to lose that one day anyway, some sooner than others. However, if we *cling* or *cleave in* the heart of God, we will be *chiyiyim* (חיים), or alive forever in Jesus Christ.

Attaching Ourselves to God

But let's look further into the meaning of this word *deveqim* (דבקים). To the Jews today, *deveqim* (דבקים), which comes from the root word *deveq* (דבק), means having an attachment to God or having God always in one's mind. The Jewish concept of *devequt* (דבקות) refers to a deep, meditative state attained through prayer and Bible study. In modern Hebrew, *deveq* (דבק) is the word for *glue*. It is also a synonym for dedication toward a par-ticular goal. Yet in religious Judaism, it means attaching yourself to God in all areas of your life. In the state of *devequt* (דבקות), one enters the mind and heart of God, hears His voice, and receives direction from Him. How can we possibly put all of that into one word? And how can we use that word with the preposition *in?*

Devequt (דבקות) means unifying all aspects of your life with that of the heart and mind of God. Some would call this "mysticism." If *mysticism* is to be defined as the Jewish rabbis define it, which is seeking to unite your entire life with the heart and mind of God, always seeking to remind your-self that you are in the presence of the Lord and whatever you do, you do as unto God, then I have to confess that I am a mystic. I think many who read this word study would fit that definition of *mysticism*. *Mysticism* has just become a dirty word in Christian circles because it conjures up images of someone wearing a pointed hat with stars on it and using a crystal ball to practice the occult. That is not what I am referring to when I use the word *mysticism*. A Christian or Jewish mystic is simply one who desires to walk closely with God, who seeks His heart, and who speaks to God and to whom God speaks.

Concerning the Christians who were beheaded by ISIS, it is clear that, just before the sword fell, they were in a state of *devequt* (דבקות), for they all shouted praises to Jesus. Through their *deveqim* (דבקים), or *clinging*, to the heart and mind of God, they immediately entered a new and higher form of spiritual life. Their physical life was ended, but they continue to live.

Living in God's Presence

Devequt (דבקות) is a discipline. Orthodox Jews wear a *kippah*, also called a yarmulke or skullcap, to remind themselves that they are always in the presence of God and whatever they do, they do as unto God. Since I am not Jewish, I do not wear a *kippah* out of respect for my Jewish friends, but I do wear a baseball cap, even if I am preaching in a church. I wear it for the same reason: to serve as a reminder to myself that I am in God's presence.

As I mentioned in an earlier study, for over ten years, I have been on a journey to discover the heart and mind of God. I have recorded my journey in my books, and I continue the journey to this day, always seeking to practice *deveqim* (דבקים), or *clinging* to God. I carry no illusions that it will save my physical life; maybe it will and maybe it won't. However, I do know it is preparing me for another life, an eternal life with the Jesus whom I have grown to love more and more through the years by seeking to cling to Him. The more I seek His heart and mind, the more I understand what the apostle Paul meant when he wrote, *"For to me to live is Christ, and to die is gain"* (Philippians 1:21).

Study 30

Pour Out Your Heart to God

"Trust in him at all times; ye people, pour out your heart before him:
God is a refuge for us. Selah."
—Psalm 62:8

In 1902, Adelaide Pollard was hoping to go to Africa as a missionary, but she was unable to raise the funds needed to pay for her venture. She became greatly discouraged because she very much wanted to serve God as a missionary and had trained for it. She just could not understand why God was not blessing her efforts to serve Him in this capacity. It now appeared that she would have to head in another direction with her life. Adelaide kept her inner pain to herself, but it was wearing her out. How could God not honor such a noble request?

Then, she attended a prayer meeting where she heard an elderly woman pray, "It really doesn't matter what You do with us, Lord. Just have Your own way with our lives." God immediately led Adelaide to Jeremiah 18:6: *"O house of Israel, cannot I do with you as this potter? saith the Lord. Behold, as the clay is in the potter's hand, so are ye in mine hand, O house of Israel."*

That night, Adelaide went home and wept before the Lord. She cried out all her disappointments, discouragements, rejections, and heartbreak. Then, she began to pray. Suddenly, she found that her prayer had taken on the form of a poem. After she finished praying, she wrote out the words.

Before long, music was added to them. This prayer-poem became a classic hymn, one that I silently sang even today as a prayer to God.

I remember singing Miss Pollard's hymn when I was just a child—singing it with all my heart:

Have Thine own way, Lord!
Have Thine own way!
Thou art the Potter,
I am the clay.[7]

Melt Your Heart

Every modern English translation I read of Psalm 62:8 renders the middle phrase as *"pour out your heart."* Yet, David is telling us to *shaphak* (שְׁפָךְ) our heart to Him. The word *shaphak* (שְׁפָךְ) comes from an old Canaanite word for melting wax and pouring it into a mold. Thus, the words *"pour out"* are not a wrong translation; they are just not a complete rendering for this word. We need to *melt* and *pour out* our heart to God.

What does it mean to melt one's heart? I think Miss Pollard knew what it meant. Her heart was solid; it was fixed on going to Africa as a missionary. It was as if the desires of her heart were set in steel. That heart of steel had to be melted. Only when our heart is melted can God begin to mold it into what He really wants to do with it.

What could be more honorable than going to Africa as a missionary? Surely, God would say, "Oy, what a dedicated spirit I have. I must grant her request immediately. Rich man, I command you to give this saintly woman the funds to go to Africa." But that was not what God wanted from Miss Pollard. He gave her gifts to be used in another capacity, and only when she surrendered her heart and desires to Him did He reveal His mind and heart and show her how the gift He had given her, the ability to write poetic prayers, was her real calling.

If God had created her only to write a few hymns, even the one song "Have Thine Own Way," it would have accomplished more than she could have accomplished on the mission field in Africa. That hymn went on to

---

7. "Have Thine Own Way," 1902.

bring comfort, encouragement, and surrender to millions of Christians over the years, even to a poor soul named Chaim Bentorah. Yet Adelaide Pollard wrote over one hundred other songs and taught at a Christian and Missionary Alliance school, training future missionaries. Through her work, she prepared hundreds of others to go to the mission field.

For many Christians, life just does not go the way they hope or plan. They search their own minds and not God's mind for their purpose. Then, as they look back over the many years of their life, they can only shake their heads in despair as they consider how few things ever turned out as they had imagined. Does this describe your life? Perhaps, like Adelaide Pollard, it is time to fall down before God with all of your shattered dreams and pray what she prayed over one hundred years ago: "Have Thine own way, Lord." Allow God to melt your heart—filled with your own thoughts, desires, hopes, and plans—and pour it into His mold, so that your heart takes on His thoughts, desires, hopes, and plans.

As I continue my journey to the heart and mind of God, I know one thing I want to find when I arrive there. I want to find my heart and mind firmly planted in His—a mind and heart that have been *shaphaked* (שָׁפַךְ), melted and molded to His desires.

Experience God's Pleasure

"One thing have I desired of the Lord, that will I seek after; that I may dwell in the house of the Lord all the days of my life, to behold the beauty of the Lord, and to enquire in his temple."
—Psalm 27:4

Many people have played the game of "wishing upon a star." The idea has its origins in ancient times. At some time and place, someone saw a shooting star, and it seemed like a sign from God that He was ready to grant any request they asked for.

I believe that David wrote Psalm 72 as he relaxed on his porch one night looking up at the stars in the vast universe. While reflecting on such limitlessness, one might wonder, "If God were to grant me just one request, one wish, what would I ask for?" After all, God did later go to Solomon and say, in effect, "Ask Me for one thing, anything, and I will grant it." (See 1 Kings 3:4–15.)

David's Heart Cry

In our study verse, the Hebrew word for *"one"* is *'echath* (אחת), which is most likely from the root word *echod* (אחד). This term does mean "one," but it also seems to be a play on the word *nachath* (נחית), which signifies "to descend." Possibly, what David is saying here is, "When it comes to what

I want, it all boils down to this…," or "In the final analysis, the common denominator of all my desires is…." In other words, David is expressing that if he were granted one wish, this is what it would be.

The Hebrew word translated *"desired"* is *sha'al* (שאל), which really means "to ask." David did not just wish for or desire this circumstance, but he actually *asked* God for it. And not only did he *ask* for it, but he was also *seeking* it. The word for *"seek"* is *baqash* (בקש), which is in a piel (intensive), imperfect form. It means that he has been earnestly seeking, with all his heart, the fulfillment of his request. Thus, this is not some simple, off-the-cuff wish—it is David's heart cry.

So, what is it that he desires more than anything else? It is to *"dwell in the house of the Lord."* Many people automatically think that David is referring to heaven, but they overlook the next part: *"all the days of my life."* The Hebrew word translated *"life"* is *chi* (חי), which could mean either spiritual or physical life. However, the use of the word *yom* (יום), or *"days,"* indicates a reference to David's physical life.

In God's Presence

What, then, is *"the house of the Lord"*? David is referring to the temple, or the place where the Lord dwells. David could not hope to spend all his time in the physical temple, although he might wish to. *"The house of the Lord"* is really a Hebrew idiom for the presence of God or the heart of God. The Lord obviously does not exist only in the Holy of Holies in the temple. David is not foolish enough to believe that. He knows God is everywhere and that He is with him. The Lord had been right there by David's side when he fought Goliath. At that time, did God leave the temple to join David in battle? Of course not. David knew that. What was so special about the temple (particularly the Holy of Holies) is that this is where God opens His heart and mind to the people, where He opens His heart and mind to David.

Many people say, "I don't have to go to church this week; I can worship God at home." True enough. But as for me, I am going to church. I will get this old body out of bed, cleaned up, and semi-properly dressed up, and I will drag myself off to a church building to worship God. I could easily worship at home, but the problem is that I do many other things there, while the church sanctuary is a special place designated for the purpose of worshipping God. It is there that I can focus my full attention on the Lord and He on me, and it is there that I can enter His heart and mind. Additionally, I can be with others who also enter the heart and mind of God. I can look around and see the joy and peace on their faces and the glow of God's presence on their lives. This is a time when health issues, financial concerns, deadlines, and all the other cares I deal with during the week are put aside so I can concentrate on one thing, and one thing only— God's heart and mind. When I do, I find myself asking the same thing of God that David asked: that I might dwell in His heart and mind all my life.

Experiencing His Pleasure

Nothing else in this world can compare to entering the heart and mind of God and, like David, seeing *"the beauty of the Lord."* The Hebrew word translated *"beauty"* is *bano'am* (בנעם), which comes from the root *no'am* (נעם), meaning "delightfulness" or "pleasure." David wants to *"behold"* the pleasure of God. The Hebrew word rendered *"behold"* is *chazah* (חזה), which means "to experience something." David is saying that he wants to experience or feel the pleasure of God.

I will be honest with you: contemporary church music is not to my liking. (You may already have guessed that about me.) I get no pleasure out of it at all. With its single melody line, three guitar chords, and booming drums accompanying an "I like God" song, it all sounds the same to me and is just too loud. (Not to mention the flashing lights that accompany it!) I am one of those old timers who grew up on hymns and listened to people sing songs in four-part harmony that told a story. So, why do I go to church and participate in worship services with that type of music? For this very reason: *it is not about my own pleasure.* I can put the music I like on my iPOD anytime I want. When I go to church and sit through the playing of contemporary music, I still feel *no'am* (נעם), a delightfulness and pleasure. However, I know I am not feeling my own pleasure but rather God's pleasure, for I have entered His heart and mind in worship.

Like David, I desire to spend all the days of my life in God's heart and mind, experiencing that pleasure.

Study 32

Tuning Your Instrument

"But they harkened not, nor inclined their ear."
—Jeremiah 7:24

The context of Jeremiah 7 is that the Israelites did not "harken" to, or heed, the Word of God. For us today, the Word of God is the Bible, which pretty clearly lays out what God expects from us. For example, God's Word says, *"Thou shalt not commit adultery"* (Exodus 20:14). I don't see how that statement could be any clearer. Of course, you can play around with the word *adultery* to mean quite a few things. Jesus did say that lusting in your heart constitutes adultery. (See Matthew 5:27–28.) Moreover, there is Someone called the Holy Spirit who lives inside you, and He will make it very clear to you whether or not you have committed adultery. You will know if you have harkened to the Word of God.

So, harkening to God's Word makes sense to me, but this matter of not "inclining one's ear" has me a bit baffled. Our study verse seems to suggest that although God is speaking to us, we are not *inclining our ear* in order to hear Him. I don't know about you, but if God started to speak to me audibly out of a cloud, you can bet that I would "incline my ear," or listen, and I think you would too. Yet, quite frankly, I don't recall any time in which God's voice came out of a cloud to get my attention.

A Strong Leading

This presents the problem, "How *does* God speak to us?" There may be occasions when He would speak audibly to someone, but that is not His standard way of talking to us. Let me give you a hypothetical situation to demonstrate how we usually think God communicates with us. Let's say I feel led to pray on behalf of a certain town, and then, the next morning, I read a news story on the Internet reporting that a tornado hit that town. Well, that could very likely have been God speaking to me. Or, it might have been a coincidence.

Knowing that God is speaking to us is perhaps more like what Pastor David Wilkerson and his congregation experienced before the September 11, 2001, terrorist attacks on the Twin Towers in New York City. A couple of months before September 11, Wilkerson and the members of his church, located in Times Square, felt a strong leading in their spirits to set aside a special time of prayer for New York City. This prayer grew into a deep sense of desperation. On September 10, Wilkerson called everyone together to prepare sandwiches, and the church went to work making hundreds of sandwiches for an event they knew nothing about until the next morning. This was obviously a church that had *inclined their ear* to God. I don't think that when David Wilkerson told his congregation, "Let's stay up all night and make sandwiches," they agreed merely because they were loyal to him. Maybe they were, but I suspect that a number of people in the church had the same feeling and were really *in tune with* the heart of God so that, when their pastor suggested the idea, it came as a confirmation to many hearts.

In Tune with God's Spirit

I come to this conclusion based on my findings regarding the Hebrew word translated *"inclined"* in Jeremiah 7:24, which is *natah* (נטה). When you trace this word to its Semitic root, you find it is a musician's term, used for the tightening of the strings on a musical instrument. We call this action *tuning an instrument*. The strings of an instrument need to be tightened in order to achieve just the right tension so that when they are played, they will be *in tune* or *in harmony* with all the other instruments in the ensemble. In fact, the Hebrew word that is rendered as *"ear"* is *'azan* (אזן), which does mean "ear," but when you trace the word to its Semitic root, you find that it is also a musician's term, used for a musical instrument.

That's right—this idea of *inclining one's ear* is really a picture of tuning a musical instrument so that it is in line with the other instruments. Thus, knowing God's mind and hearing His voice is really a matter of tightening the strings of your spirit or heart so that you are in tune with God's Spirit, with His mind and heart.

In Harmony with One Another

My study partner and I recently went to a farmer's market. As she was checking out her vegetarian delights, I wandered to a corner of the market where about a dozen amateur musicians were sitting under a tent, each with a different musical instrument. There were a couple of acoustic guitars, an electric guitar, a banjo, a violin, a base fiddle, a mandolin, and other various stringed instruments. I walked up to them just as they were tuning up. For a moment, all sorts of hideous sounds came from these instruments. Then someone started to play, and suddenly, each instrument joined in, with all the musicians playing the same song in the same key, creating a harmonious sound that was absolutely beautiful. I marveled at how each musician was picking or strumming their instrument in their own way and style, but the music still blended beautifully. I could not help but think of the words *natah 'azan* (נטה אזן), *inclining one's ear*.

Similarly, Christians may have different "instruments" of theology and doctrine, and they may have their own style of worship, with some "strumming" and others "picking." Their "playing" may be formal, as with a violin; spirited, as with a banjo; or lyrical, as with a mandolin. However, if they are all in tune with God, they will be *natah 'azan* (נטה אזן), *inclining their ears*, and they will be of the same mind, the mind of God, hearing the same message from Him. God likes to listen to the beautiful music of prayer that is *natan 'azan* (נטה אזן). If, together, we harken to God's Word, we can accomplish more than we ever imagined.

Study 33

Giving Our Best

*"Out of all your gifts ye shall offer every heave offering of the L*ORD*, of all the best thereof, even the hallowed part thereof out of it."*
—Numbers 18:29

We begin this study with a quote from the Lubavitcher Rebbe, the noted rabbi of the Chabad-Lubavitch dynasty, a Hasidic orthodox Jewish movement:

> *Matnot kehunah* mean that a person dedicates the choicest portions of the yield of his material labors to a spiritual cause. In a person's own life, it means that even if the great majority of one's day is devoted to material pursuits, its best hours are devoted to Torah study and prayer. In other words, it means that a person regards the spiritual aspect of his life as "higher" than its material aspect, even when accepting that his mission in life demands that the bulk of his time, talents and resources be applied to interacting with the material world.[8]

---

8. "Parshat Korach In-Depth," From Our Sages, Chabad.org, https://www.chabad.org/parshah/in-depth/default_cdo/aid/45592/jewish/Korach-In-Depth.htm.

Offerings to the Priests

Let's consider what this quote means in light of our study verse, Numbers 18:29. The Hebrew word translated *"heave"* is an old English word meaning "to lift up." This term matches the Hebrew word *teruman* (תרומן), which signifies "a lifting up" and comes from the root word *rum* (רום)—pronounced as "room"—meaning "to be exalted" or "to be lifted up." The *tenuphah* (תנופה), or *"heave offering,"* is the portion of an offering to God that was subsequently given to the priest. The priest, in turn, would give his own heave offering to the Lord out of that gift. (See verses 25–32.)

Matnot kehunah (מתנת כהנה) literally means "the offering given to the priest." The special offerings of the Israelites were given to Aaron the high priest and his sons, and the tithes of the Israelites were given to support the Levites. The people were to give the best of their produce to the priests. This practice ended with the destruction of the temple when the priests no longer had a temple in which to serve. Unfortunately, some preachers have likened themselves to the priests of the Old Testament, saying that the laws regarding the priests apply to them. They manage to convince their congregations of this by pointing to verses like Numbers 18:29 to justify their having a material lifestyle that is much higher than the average member of their congregation. They will drive around in a new BMW while members of their church can hardly afford repairs and even gas for their fifteen-year-old Ford Focuses. That is a total misuse of this verse.

Numbers 18:29 refers specifically to the priests of the Old Testament, not to Christian pastors or preachers. The priest would offer sacrifices to God and perform other sacred duties, whereas Christian preachers expound on the Word of God in His name. Of course, the New Testament does encourage compensation for leaders in the church. As Paul wrote, *"The labourer is worthy of his reward"* (1 Timothy 5:18). The ministry of church leaders should not be taken advantage of. However, none of the early leaders of the church lived extravagant lifestyles. I remember one rabbi saying that if his congregation were to begin tithing, it would be considered a sin, as tithing was only meant for the temple and the priest, neither of which now exists. A rabbi does not consider himself a priest, and thus he is not paid to be a rabbi but rather is paid so he can devote his time to studying Torah.

Exalting the Lord

I give all this information as background so that you will understand I am not talking about giving our clergy riches. However, there is a real spiritual lesson for us here. If you read the previous chapters in Numbers, you will find that this practice of *matnot kehunah* (מתנת כהנה), particularly the giving of the holy offerings to Aaron and his sons, caused much rebellion among the people of Israel. A man named Korah, a Levite, along with other leaders, claimed that all the people were equal before God, so why did Moses and his family get such special privileges? Were they better than everyone else?

The result of this open rebellion was that these men and their families died by falling into a deep pit when God caused the earth to split open to swallow them. Two hundred and fifty of their followers were killed by fire from heaven, and another 14,700 people died in a plague the next day because of their protests over the matter. Why such drastic measures in response to something Korah had declared, which was basically true? All people are equal in God's sight. However, what Korah and the others did not realize was that the purpose of the *matnot kehunah* (מתנת כהנה) was not to exalt any person but to exalt God.

God required that people bring their *"best"* to Him. Is God so selfish that He demands the best? The Lubavitcher Rebbe explained that the purpose of the *matnot kahunah* (מתנת כהנה), giving of one's best to the priest, was not to enrich the priest but to place the spiritual part of your life on a higher level than your material life. Korah, on the other hand, only wanted to enrich and exalt himself. He did not see that the *matnot kahunah* (כהנה מתנת) was God's way of reminding us that what we have on earth is only temporal. It is that which we prepare for eternity that is most important. Thus, God demonstrated how fragile life is and how quickly it passes.

Our culture demands that we give our best to obtain fame and fortune. Yet, we find that it is not uncommon for the wealthy, those who have spent their lives doing their best to obtain fame and fortune, to become philanthropists in their latter years, giving their wealth away to charitable causes. As you grow older, you become more and more aware of your mortality, and you begin to wonder just what there is of real value in your life.

However, if you spend your life giving God your best, you will not face the regrets that others do as they approach their life's end—because you will have given your best for eternity.

No Regrets

The Hebrew word translated *"best"* in Numbers 18:29 is *chalev* (חלב). The word does mean "best," but it comes from the Semitic root for converting something into nourishment. In other words, it refers to giving what will be of benefit to other people. It is interesting that the word is built on the term *lev* (לב), which means "heart." The chet (ח) in front of *lev* (לב) indicates a bonding. When you give your best, you are bonding with the one to whom you give. Husbands will seek to give the best they can for their wives and children because they love them. When they give their family members the best they have, they bond with them, nourishing that relationship. God wants our best not because He is a selfish, "give me" God, but because He created us to be creatures who bond in relationships through giving our best.

At times, I start to become very discouraged when I reflect on the achievements of my classmates from Bible College and seminary. Some of them went on to become distinguished professors in seminaries and universities. Others have had great and successful careers as missionaries, are pastors of large churches, or are dynamic Christian workers. Some have achieved great success in business. But when I look at my life and begin to regret various decisions I have made over the years, that is when God leads me to a verse like Numbers 18:29, and I realize that all He wants from me is my best. If I can look back on my life and know I have given Him *matnot kehunah* (מתנת כהנה), my best, then I do not need to have any regrets.

The Glory of the Lord

*"So that the priests could not stand to minister because of the cloud:
for the glory of the LORD had filled the house of the LORD."*
—1 Kings 8:11

"Any sufficiently advanced technology is
indistinguishable from magic."
Arthur C. Clarke, "Clarke's third law"

As I mentioned in a previous study, the word *mysticism* is not necessarily a negative term, referring to crystal balls and tarot cards. I heard a Jewish rabbi define a Jewish mystic as one who is simply seeking a deeper relationship with God. There have been Christian mystics over the centuries who have had the same goal. In fact, most Christians who are serious about their relationship with God desire this deeper intimacy. Still, the term describes something supernatural, outside the experience of the natural world.

In 1 Kings 8:11, we read of a supernatural event—*"the priests could not stand to minister"* when the cloud appeared and the Lord's house was filled with His glory. Now, if that doesn't smack of mysticism, I don't know what does! I don't see how a relationship with God here on earth could be any deeper than that which is described in our study verse.

The Hebrew word translated *"stand"* is *'amad* (עמד), which has various definitions. It could mean "to stand," but it could also mean "to confirm," "to appoint," "to remain," "to defend," "to stand firm," "to stop," "to wait," "to be opposed," and many other possible usages. One thing is certain: something physical happened to the priests when the cloud appeared and filled God's house with His glory.

The Hebrew word rendered *"glory"* is *kavod* (כבוד), which comes from the word *kavad* (כבד), meaning "a weight." Thus, we tend to conclude that the glory of the Lord so weighted the priests down that they could not stand. However, the question needs to be asked, "Just what was this 'weight'?"

Sensing God's Mind and Heart

There is another meaning of the word *kavod* (כבוד) that is rarely used but may apply here. It is "heart." Let me give you an illustration to explain how this concept might fit. I helped to pay my way through college by working as a ventriloquist. I would often perform on a stage with a spotlight on me. The auditorium was dark, so I could not see the audience, yet I knew they were there. Even though I could not see the people, the moment I stepped onto the stage, I could "feel" them. I could tell if they were a happy audience that was ready to laugh or a quiet audience that would need some coaxing. The audience might be totally silent, but I could tell if it was friendly or hostile.

The ability to sense the attitudes of an audience is often called "animal instinct." It is really something scientific, because thoughts are electrical impulses. Animals pick up on these impulses more readily than humans, although they cannot categorize them. The emotions of fear, anger, and hostility feel pretty much the same, so if an animal picks up on fear, it will interpret it as a threat. The emotions of love and happiness are also very similar, and an animal cannot tell the difference between them either. However, it will recognize the positive feeling and be drawn to it.

As a performer, I would often first introduce myself without my wooden friend, Ralphie. I would tell a few jokes or a story, and I would use those moments in front of the audience to determine which routine I would use.

I had designed specific routines for different types of audiences, and I had to trust what I felt about a particular audience to choose the most appropriate routine.

Anyone who has performed on a stage will understand the quiet discernment of an audience I have just described. In truth, what the entertainer feels is the *kavod* (כבוד), the "glory," or the "heart and mind," of the audience. It could be called a "light feeling" or a "heavy feeling." Sometimes, in sensing the heaviness of an audience, I have actually found it difficult to move across the stage. The attitude of a particular audience would mix with my confidence or lack of confidence, my fear or lack of fear, and this combination would affect my ability to move. The "lighter" the audience, the more animated I would be.

I believe the priests in the temple felt something similar to this. They sensed God's heart and mind, His attitude. And His thoughts were so powerful that they brought the priests to their knees.

The Magnitude of God's Thoughts

Can you imagine the magnitude of the mind or thoughts of God? Those "electrical impulses," or that energy, must carry a lot of weight! Thus, to my thinking, the *kavod* (כבוד) of God, or His glory—referring to His thoughts, which are pure energy—can knock you flat!

In essence, what Arthur C. Clarke said in his "third law," found in the quotation at the beginning of this study, is that magic is only science that has yet to be discovered. I believe modern science and quantum physics explain many things we call "mystical." One day, the Large Hadron Collider (LHC), a particle accelerator developed by scientists at CERN (European Council for Nuclear Research), may actually cause two particles to strike each other at the speed of light, and the theory is that they may create a particle that will exist in two different places at the same time—what we might call "omnipresent." Whether or not they realize it, they will thus scientifically contribute evidence to God's ability to be present everywhere at the same time.

Similarly, some of what is called Jewish mysticism is only theology that Christians have yet to explore. To be sure, there is much of Jewish mysticism that I will not touch—maybe even 90 percent of it. But there is a portion of it that I feel is biblically based, and that includes a cloud that can descend upon you and weigh you down so that you drop to your knees or have to lie prostrate. Mystics might describe this as some realm of cosmic energy. Again, I call it the heart and mind of God, His thoughts, His "electrical impulses" descending, with the joy, grief, or other emotion emanating from His heart being so powerful that, when it is mixed with our own emotions, it hinders our movement or makes us unable to move at all.

Thus, I believe we can feel both the pleasure and displeasure of God. Sometimes, our sense of His displeasure is called "having a guilty conscience," but I think it is really a direct communication from God's mind to our hearts. If scientists could identify this communication as electrical energy coming straight from God, I think we could even measure it. In a vacuum, electrical energy travels at the speed of light, and, as a result, can breach the barrier between the natural and supernatural worlds. Jesus is the Light, the bridge to the supernatural world, which is a different dimension than our physical world.

In my view, this is how God lives in us: His energy passes through the space-time continuum and enters into us. The more out of sync we are with this energy from God, the more we feel His displeasure. However, the more in sync we are with Him, with the thoughts of His mind, the more we feel His pleasure.

"His Anger Was Kindled"

"And when the people complained, it displeased the LORD: and the LORD heard it; and his anger was kindled; and the fire of the LORD burnt among them, and consumed them that were in the uttermost parts of the camp. And the people cried unto Moses; and when Moses prayed unto the LORD, the fire was quenched."
—Numbers 11:1–2

"For I am the LORD, I change not;
therefore ye sons of Jacob are not consumed."
—Malachi 3:6

"There is no fear in love; but perfect love casteth out fear: because fear hath torment. He that feareth is not made perfect in love."
—1 John 4:18

Go ahead and read these three verses and explain to me how there is no contradiction between them. In Numbers, the people of God were consumed for *complaining*. We all complain. Is God so thin-skinned that He has to send fire down to consume His people for their complaints? The Hebrew word translated *"complained"* is ʾanan (אנן), which some

Hebrew scholars say refers to a complaining over hardship. In fact, the *New International Version* actually renders the word as "*complained about their hardships.*" I mean, who doesn't complain about their difficulties? And yet this response apparently just set God off such that He sent fire from heaven to consume His people.

Next, in Malachi, God has the audacity to say that He doesn't change and will *not* consume His people. But then we look at the New Testament, and we discover that "*perfect love casteth out fear.*" I would think that if fire is falling from heaven and the people are pleading with Moses to pray to the Lord to make it stop, this is an indication that God is generating some fear. Yet, if He is perfect in love, how can He create fear?

Christians have come up with a good answer to all this: we live in a different age, a different dispensation; we are now under a new covenant in Jesus Christ. God somehow got civilized by the time of the New Testament. It seems that He finally got some religion. Maybe He even got saved! Thank You, God, that You are no longer that angry, irrational Divinity of the Old Testament.

When are we Christians going to admit that some of what we say is full of contradictions and that sometimes the atheistic world is laughing at us for good reason. We make little sense when we talk about a God of love who, at the same time, sends fire down from heaven to destroy anyone who complains about some hardship. Is the mind of God really filled with vengeance, wrath, and producing fear?

Perfect Love

I recently watched a family TV drama, and you know how the creators of these programs often fashion perfect little worlds. In this episode, the family was going through some hard times and the teenage son had finally had his fill. He began to yell at his father, blaming him for all their problems. The father patiently said, "Let me explain." The son defiantly retorted, "No, I'm not going to listen to any explanation. I'm tired of your explaining." The father then reached out and hugged his son, wept with him, and said, "I understand how hard it is. I am so, so sorry." Then, of course, the son broke down and wept on his father's shoulder.

Okay, that is how such a situation would be resolved in a perfect world, but it doesn't often happen that way in family relationships. However, with *"perfect love"* in operation, it should resolve that way. In fact, I am sure it has happened that way in some families. Yet, if the above descriptions of God's response to the Israelites reflect "perfect love," then that TV depiction of a human father left God far behind in the dust when it comes to compassion and love for one's children.

Passionate Love

So, how do we explain this passage in Numbers? At the risk of sounding radical, let me just say that in 300 AD, the Christian church became an organization, and an organization needs to maintain control. You are not going to get people to attend church every Sunday and fill the coffers if you don't put a little *fear of God* in them. You know, little things like, "You don't have to go to church to be a Christian, but [ah, the old "but"] I don't see how you can be a real Christian if you do not go to church every Sunday." Or, how about this one: "You should give a tithe only out of love, but I don't see how you can be a real Christian and not tithe." There are subtle little traditions that have crept into the church to help maintain control, and of course at the root of this control is the need to have a God that you should at least be a little afraid of.

Thus, we have phrases like *"it displeased the* LORD.*"* The Hebrew word translated *"displeased"* is ra' (רע), which has a string of usages both in biblical and extra-biblical literature. "Displeasure" and "evil" are two possible meanings. So are "hurt feelings" and "wounded heart." Why don't we say that the people's murmurings "wounded the heart of God"? Well, perhaps it is because it would not create as much fear in us as saying "it displeased God" or was evil.

Next, the passage says, *"And the* LORD *heard it, and his anger was kindled."* I explained the Hebrew word for *"anger"* in an earlier study. Its root word is 'aneph (אנף), which is a term used for the snorting of a camel. Since there are many reasons why a camel will snort, why do we necessarily have to plug in the word *anger* here? Why could we not say that "God's heart was so wounded that His desire for intimacy"—one of the meanings of 'aneph (אנף)—"was 'kindled'"?

The Hebrew word translated *"kindled,"* *ba'ar* (בער), can also mean "to grow warm," "to grow hot," or "to burn." When you are emotional due to anger or a broken heart, your body grows warm as the blood flows rapidly through your veins. Why could we not say that God was so frustrated over the fact that He could not be intimate with His people due to their murmurings that He just burned with desire for intimacy?

The passage also talks about *"the fire of the* Lord." The Hebrew word rendered *"fire"* is *'ash* (אש), which could mean "fire" but could also be used as a metaphor for "passion." Why could we not say that the passionate love of the Lord was kindled? Looking further at the Hebrew word for *"kindle,"* *ba'ar* (בער), it could signify "to kindle a fire," but it is also used in extra-biblical literature to express the idea of "seeking out." Therefore, why could we not render this as, "The passionate love of God began to seek out His people and consume them"? The Hebrew term for *"consumed"* is *'akal* (אכל), which is the word for "eating." When you eat something, you ingest it; you put the food in your mouth and totally encompass it. Why could we not render this as "the passionate love of God began to seek out His people and encompass them"?

Consumed by Love

The first three verses of Numbers 11 refer to the Israelites, the people of God, but the fourth verse mentions the complaints of the "mixed multitude," the Hyksos, the pagans who had joined the Hebrews on their journey, only to find that it was not all they had anticipated. In discussing our study verses, we are focusing on the Israelites alone, and we could say that when the people murmured, God's heart was broken and He cried out for intimacy. Just like the father of the rebellious son in the TV drama, the Lord embraced the children of Israel until His fire or passion was quenched. The Hebrew word translated *"quenched"* is *shaqa'* (שקע), which does mean "to quench" but is also used to express the idea of "overflowing" and "subduing." Why can we not say that, at least in that moment, God hugged His people until He subdued them? We might translate the passage that way, but then you would have a God whom you do not need to be afraid of, and of course, how will you maintain control if that is the case?

I recently complained to God about a situation in my life, and He did not send fire down to me. I rebelled and got angry with Him, but He consumed me with His love and passion until He had subdued me, and I just loved Him in return and said, "It's okay; it really is okay." And do you know what? I still go to church and pay my tithe, and yet I am not afraid of what will happen if I don't do those things. I do them because I know God cares about me and embraces me, consuming me with His love.

An Irritant

"If any man come to me, and hate not his father, and mother, and wife, and children, and brethren, and sisters, yea, and his own life also, he cannot be my disciple."
—Luke 14:26

One time, I got into a conversation with a passenger on the disability bus who said he could not believe the Bible because of all its contradictions. I asked him to name a contradiction, and he brought up Luke 14:26, where Jesus teaches us to hate our family for His sake or we cannot be His disciple. Yet, the sixth commandment says we are to honor our parents. (See Exodus 20:12.) You can't honor someone if you hate them.

He made a good point, and if we had only the Greek to depend upon, I would be stuck trying to give an explanation like, "Jesus is speaking in some sort of metaphor or hyperbole." I would follow that with, "What Jesus meant was…" and then try to fill in the blank with something that sounded logical and spiritual. Or, I might simply say, "Well, in the Greek, it just means to love less—you are to love Jesus more than you do your family." If all else failed, I would resort to some advice from an old theology professor: "If you can't convince 'em, confuse 'em."

Are We to "Love Less"?

What concerns me is that the Greek word translated *"hate"* in Jesus's statement is *misei*, which does mean "to hate." While some lexicons may say it signifies "to love less," linguistically, I would say the lexicographers* were desperately trying to find a meaning that didn't make Jesus sound like an arrogant tyrant. Maybe there is some extra-biblical support for applying the idea of "loving less" to *misei*, but I haven't found it.

On top of that, I am not even comfortable with Jesus saying that we are to love our family with less love than we have for Him. That would imply there are degrees to love. I would much rather hear that we are to love God with a different *type* of love than we have for our family. I could handle that, but to "hate" or even "love less" doesn't seem consistent with the Jesus I have grown to love.

When I was a pastor, I saw marriages break down and even fall apart because a wife or husband neglected their spouse in favor of "service to God." Many times, for various reasons, one spouse will use their ministry as an excuse to get out of the house and away from their mate. However, there are other people who are truly torn between their love for God and their love for their mate. Take the husband who feels a real calling from God to give up a good job and go to seminary or enter the ministry. He loves the Lord and hungers to serve Him, but his wife is not ready to make that kind of sacrifice. In such a situation, is that poor soul supposed to love God more than he does his wife? That's a tough call. I'm glad that I'm not a pastor anymore!

Unrelenting Love

Discussions like this may be one of the reasons I am personally convinced that all the Gospels were originally written in Aramaic and not Greek. The Aramaic just seems to make more sense. Because Christian clergy have embraced the Greek over the Aramaic and very few have actually studied Aramaic, let alone made some application of it, I was able give my passenger on the disability bus an answer to his question that he had not heard before. My answer to his seeming contradiction brought the response, "Oh!"

You see, even if the Gospels were not originally written in Aramaic, many of the words would have had to be translated from Aramaic into Greek, as practically all scholars now believe Jesus spoke Aramaic. And the Aramaic word that is used here is *sana'* (סנא), which is not a word for "hate" but rather "a thorn" or "an irritant," like a briar that is stuck on one's leg.

The Pacific Garden Mission in Chicago had a little sign over its doorway that said, "Your mother's prayers brought you here." Many a wayward man was brought to his knees over that *sana'* (סנא), or "irritating" mother at home who was praying and weeping for her boy; that mother who stood in the gap for her child, who never wavered in her belief and trust in God. That mother's prayers and pleas for her son to turn to Jesus were a constant irritant to him. She did not love her son less than she loved God, but she was a real *sana'* (סנא) to him until he finally came to his senses and turned his life over to the Lord.

This illustration reminds me of when I used to work in a halfway house and talk with recovering drug addicts. I asked one of the residents what had turned him away from drugs to clean up his life through the power of God. He said he had a Christian wife who would "irritate him to death," telling him that she was praying for him and begging him to give his life to Jesus. She did not love him less than she loved God, but she was a *sana'* (סנא) to him. One day, he came home completely stoned and found his wife on her knees, weeping and praying to God to save him. In his drugged state, this made him so angry that he punched her in her stomach with all his strength. She lay on the floor in agony, pleading with God to forgive him. After that, every time he picked up a needle, in his mind's eye, he saw his wife lying on the floor, crying in pain, and calling out to God to save him. It was her tremendous love that finally brought him to Jesus.

Likewise, we should be "loving irritants" to our family members and others, in the sense of praying earnestly that they would return to God and develop a deeper relationship with Him. We can also be "persistent irritants" against anything in our own lives that pulls us away from the Lord, removing whatever is hindering our unity with Him. Such devotion and commitment to Christ and His purposes show that we are His disciples.

Study 37

Prostitution

"How weak is thine heart, saith the Lord God, *seeing thou doest all these things, the work of an imperious whorish woman."*
—Ezekiel 16:30

Am I missing something, or did Ezekiel just call Judah a "whore"? There are three words in Hebrew for "whore," or "prostitute," and there appears to be an order of condemnation for them. The worst is a *keleb* (כלב), which literally means "dog." This word was often used to refer to a male prostitute or a man who took on feminine characteristics or dressed like a female to solicit money from other males. I found a similar term in Ugaritic cuneiform writing that also means "dog" and "male prostitute."

Another word that is often rendered as "prostitute" is *kedeshah* (קדשה). It comes from the root word for *kodesh* (קדש), which means "to be holy" or "to be separate." As I mentioned previously, in the Astarte or Asherah cult of the Canaanites and the Qudshu cult of the Egyptians (the goddess of fertility), a woman was required at least once in her lifetime to go to the temple and sit on the sacred bench of the goddess with a crown of cords on her head and offer herself to any stranger who came along and gave a monetary offering. This woman would have a sexual relationship with the stranger and fulfill her duty to the goddess. She would then be free for the rest of her life from any further obligation, if she so chose. Some women, due to a lack of "feminine attractiveness," might sit on the bench for years before fulfilling their duty. Such women were forced into this sort of prostitution against their will.

However, there were other women who were not so opposed to the practice and fulfilled their duty many times over. A woman who did this was referred to as a *zonah* (זנה). A *zonah* (זנה) was an everyday, street-walking, for-profit prostitute. To be sure, women in those days had very few rights. Many women whose husbands divorced them or died were forced into prostitution just to survive. In Judah, Hebrew law provided for women who had lost their husbands, so there was no need to go into prostitution unless they made the choice to do so. However, often, the solution that was provided under Hebrew law was not desirable for a woman, such as being forced to live with a man who abused her or treated her like a slave. Thus, Judah had its own share of prostitutes.

Trusting in Foreign Gods

In our study verse, Judah is being compared to a *zonah* (hnz). God had provided great prosperity for His people, but as they gradually grew cold in their relationship with the Lord, He started to withdraw this prosperity. Instead of turning back to God, they began to look to other nations, particularly Assyria and Egypt, to help them maintain their affluence. When the Assyrian and Egyptian merchants passed through, they wanted to continue the worship of their pagan gods, and Judah allowed them to build shrines and places of worship in the high places.

Before long, as an act of solidarity, the people of Judah shared in this worship to help maintain their prosperity. Later, the people even told the prophet Jeremiah, a contemporary of Ezekiel, "Look, when we worshipped God, we were not prosperous, but when we offered sacrifices to the '*queen of heaven*,' we were prosperous." (See Jeremiah 44:16–18.) That is why Ezekiel pointed his finger at the people of Judah and said, "You are nothing more than *zonahs* (זנה), or prostitutes, serving whatever god will pay you the most."

Full of Themselves

The prophet said that they had a *"weak heart."* The Hebrew word translated *"weak"* is 'amelah (אמלה), which might have two possible roots. The first is 'amal (אמל), which means "weak" or "feeble." Perhaps the prophet was just saying that the hearts of the people were weak. Once their prosperity disappeared, they were desperate and sold themselves to foreign gods to maintain the status quo. Their hearts did not have the strength to endure the hardships and return to God.

The other possible root is mala' (מלא). For me, this fits the context much better because mala' (מלא) means "to be full." The people's hearts were so full of themselves that it didn't matter which god they served as long as that god paid them well enough. They were willing to make themselves zonahs (זנה), or "prostitutes," to other gods if that is what it took. As I mentioned previously, I have heard many people say, "Well, I tried Christianity, but it doesn't work." Doesn't work? Does that mean that God didn't pay them enough? I have even heard some Christians say they were giving up on God because He didn't pull them out of a certain financial difficulty or make them secure. Ezekiel had one word for people like that: zonahs (זנה). They will sell out to any god that meets their financial or security needs.

"The Lord Is My Consuming Passion"

In Psalm 23:1, David said, *"The Lord is my shepherd; I shall not want."* We have seen that the Hebrew word rendered *"shepherd"* is ra'ah (ראה), which means "a consuming passion." The Lord was David's consuming passion such that he didn't want anything else. It is similar to an artist who is passionate about his art and will sacrifice money, health, and even relationships for the sake of it.

I want to repeat some probing questions I posed earlier because they involve central issues in our relationship with the Lord: Do you love God to the point that He is your consuming passion? Or do you follow Him merely because He seems to pay you well, giving you good gifts like some sort of "sugar daddy" and keeping you out of hell? If it's the latter, then you are like a zonah (זנה), or prostitute. If God doesn't seem to come through for you, will you dump Him and embrace some other "god" that will give you what you want? If God is truly your passion, any pay or lack of pay from Him will mean nothing to you.

If you will sacrifice your finances, your security, and even your life to know God's heart and mind, then you have the right to say, as the prophet Ezekiel did, "My Lord Jehovah." (See Ezekiel 16:30.) The personal pronoun *my* may not be in your English text, but it is there in the Hebrew. I am not sure why our modern translations leave it out, rendering the term merely as "Lord God" or "Sovereign Lord." Perhaps it sounds too awkward or personal to call Him "My God." Yet David called Him *"My King, and my God"* (Psalm 5:2). The apostle Thomas made a personal declaration to Jesus after His resurrection, saying, *"My Lord and My God"* (John 20:28). If God is your passion, then your heart is strong enough to say, like Ezekiel, David, and Thomas, *"My Lord Jehovah."*

The people of Judah declared that when they worshipped the "queen of heaven," they were well-fed and prosperous. The reason was that they shared a common religion with other nations, which was good for business. In the United States, we believe in capitalism and good business. That is fine, but when we carry it over into our relationship with God and turn that into a business relationship, God sees us as nothing more than *zonahs* (זנה).

The point is that when a man lies with a prostitute, he doesn't care what is on her mind or heart, nor does the prostitute. The man gets what he wants, the woman gets paid, and that is that. Some people serve God only to get what they want. They do not care what is on His mind and heart. But God cares, and He wants us to search out His mind and heart.

How are you treating your heavenly Father?

From God, to God

"That then the LORD thy God will turn thy captivity, and have compassion upon thee, and will return and gather thee from all the nations, whither the LORD thy God hath scattered thee."
—Deuteronomy 30:3

I was reading in the Talmud this morning in Megillah 29a, and I found something very interesting about our study verse. It is so easy to miss these little gems. By way of illustration, I remember a time when I was in the hospital, recovering from surgery, and because I was in a lot of pain, the nurse handed me a morphine pill. It was about the size of a little bead or a candy sprinkle you put on a cupcake, so I said, "Hey, my pain is a whole lot bigger than this little bead." The nurse assured me that the "bead" packed a lot of wallop, and it did. It practically knocked me out!

Similarly, unless you really study the Word of God like the ancient rabbis, sages, and scholars, you will miss the little "beads" that pack a wallop. In Deuteronomy 30:3, the gem that is so easily overlooked is the word *veshab* (ואשב), meaning "and He will return." The Talmud points out that the word *veshab* (ואשב) is used here, and not *veheshib* (והשיב), which would signify "and He shall bring back." Rabbi Simon Yohai comments, "Come and see how beloved are Israel in the sight of God, in that to every place to which they were exiled, the *Shechinah* [שחינה] went with them."

Oh, the difference the absence of a hei (ה) makes! When the writer of Deuteronomy did not include the hei (ה) and simply wrote *veshab* (ואשב), he was saying that when God sent His people into exile, *He went with them.* Of course, God is omnipresent, and so He was always with them. Wherever we go, God is there. We all know that. We have understood this ever since our Sunday school teachers told us, "Now children, Jonah tried to run away from God, but you and I know we cannot run away from Him." I remember being only six years old and shaking my head up and down, saying to myself, "Gee, I am smarter than that grownup named Jonah, because I know what he did not know, and that is you cannot run away from God. He is everywhere. That Jonah is such a klutz to think he can run away from God."

Running from the Presence

What most Sunday School teachers failed to mention is that Jonah wasn't running away from God. The prophet was smart enough to know that He is everywhere and one cannot hide from Him. If we look closely at Jonah 1:3, we find that Jonah ran away from the *milipani* (מלפני), or *presence*, of God. The term *milipani* (מלפני) is in a very strange Hebraic form. The root word is *pani* (פני), denoting the face or presence of God. But *milipani* (מלפני) contains two prepositions, the mem (מ) for "from" and the lamed (ל) for "to." Literally, you would render this as "from the presence of God to the presence of God." Of course, no translator is going to render it that way because it makes no sense at all. They simply render it as running away from the presence of God.

However, this phrase actually does make sense in light of the word *veshab* (ואשב), which, as we have seen, means "and He shall return." Jonah might have thought he was running away from the presence of God, fleeing far away from the temple where the *Shechinah* (שחינה) resided—only to realize that the *Shechinah* (שחינה), too, did not reside solely in the temple.

God Is Always with Us

Every other Sunday morning, I am assigned to drive disabled persons to mass and other services at various churches in the community. It is my job to make sure my passengers make it into the church building safely without any incidents, so sometimes I actually follow them into the sanctuary. I watch as a change comes over my charges when they enter the church. They become quiet and very respectful. In some cases, if they are able, they will genuflect and make the sign of the cross before the host. They may believe, similar to Jonah, that the presence of God resides in the church and in that host on the altar. Yet they also tell me that they pray at home and sometimes even feel the presence of God there.

Perhaps there is a part of us that wants to believe God is not always present in our lives, although we know He is. When we are tempted to cheat a little on our taxes or browse a certain inappropriate site on the Web, we like to forget that God is present. Or maybe there are times when we feel we are in exile. We just don't sense the presence of God, and it seems as if He has abandoned us because He has not answered our prayers or come to our rescue. Yet, the Bible uses words such as *veshab* (וֹאשׁב), "and He will return (with us)," rather than *veheshib* (והשׁיב), "He will bring us back (will come and get us)." It uses the word *milipani* (מלפני), "from God, to God" and not just *mipani* (מפני), "from God."

Sometimes, we use terms in our Christian vocabulary that suggest God is not always with us, such as, "Let's *go to God* in prayer." We do not have to go anywhere to get to God. Another common expression I hear all the time in full-gospel churches is, "Let's *bring the presence* of the Lord here." The presence of the Lord is always here. How about saying, "Let's bring *our* presence to the Lord"? If you are not feeling the presence of God, it is not His fault, which leaves only one remaining suspect.

It takes discipline to remind yourself that you are continuously in the presence of God. As I wrote in an earlier study, Orthodox Jews wear a *kippah* or yarmulke to always remind themselves that they are in God's presence and that everything they do, they do as unto Him. I mentioned that I wear a baseball cap for the same reason. In the church I attend, I am allowed to wear my baseball cap in the sanctuary. For me, it is sign of respect for the presence of God. I am reminding myself, even in church, that I am in His presence. I recently did a live-stream teaching seminar, and even in that video, I wore my baseball cap. I feel I need to practice this discipline of *milipani* (מלפני), "from God, to God." Maybe you are always aware that you are in the presence of God. But, if not, you might want to start practicing *milipani* (מלפני) too—reminding yourself that you are continuously in the presence of God and that whatever you do, you do as unto God.

One other thing the Talmud teaches is that when the Israelites returned from captivity, God not only *returned* with them but also *rejoiced* with them. The Lord, who had joined His people in captivity, rejoiced when the time came to return home. He was just as anxious for the return as His people were! Whatever your circumstances, God is with you, and whenever you "return" from your difficulties, He will be with you and rejoice in your deliverance.

The Highest Praise

*"Let the high praises of God be in their mouth,
and a two-edged sword in their hand."*
—Psalm 149:6

During an evening service at my church, our worship leader led us in a song that spoke of the "highest praise" to God. I had to stop and really ponder that idea. I didn't think I had ever heard an explanation of exactly what "highest praise" is or how it was to be expressed. In researching this topic, I could find only one passage in Scripture that spoke of *"high praises,"* and that is our study verse, Psalm 149:6. However, not all translations render this term in the same way. Some, like the *New International Version,* just call it *"praise,"* the *Holman Christian Standard Bible* calls it *"exaltation,"* and the Septuagint uses the Greek word *ipsoseis,* which means "an act of exaltation." The word in both Aramaic and Hebrew simply means "exaltation." The term in Hebrew is *romemoth* (רוממות), from the root word *ramam* (רמם), which is in a verb form and means "to lift up" or "to place on high." We might say it means "to place someone on a pedestal." With this word, the aspect of praise is simply implied. When used as "praise," it could imply praise for the hidden and revealed knowledge of God.

What Is True Praise?

So, what exactly is "praise"? Have you ever stopped to consider what we mean by this word in English? When we "praise" someone, we are giving an expression of approval, admiration, or gratitude. Therefore, the meaning of the English word *praise* would be inappropriate for the Hebrew word *ramam* (רמם), unless we use it to express *a lifting up* of our approval and admiration of God.

Yet, when we speak of "high praise," we are talking about a praise that outranks all other praises. We are denoting ultimate praise or the greatest praise. I am not sure if this meaning is what the psalmist had in mind. Is there really a praise that is greater than any other praise? If so, how is it expressed? Is it communicated in words or in actions—or both?

When a worship leader says, "Let's give God the highest praise," they are apparently asking us to express our love and admiration for God with all our heart, soul, and mind. However, if we are not already expressing our admiration for God with all our heart, soul, and mind, are we even praising Him in the first place? I think we are back to square one. Praise is simply an expression of our love for God, and unless it comes from our hearts, it is not true praise; it is insincere or contrived.

"Being Hallelujah"

At that evening church service, after we sang the song that talked about high praise, I asked God to *show* me high praise. I looked around but saw nothing unusual, nothing that I would consider high praise. It seemed like typical praise and worship. But as our pastor gave the message, I sensed there was a point at which he left his prepared notes and started speaking "as the Spirit of God gave him utterance." (See Acts 2:4.) He went thirty minutes over his allotted time.

Now, I am a clock watcher. After all, I am a teacher, and when that closing bell rings, the class ends, no matter what point I have reached in my lecture. I have to dismiss the students and leave the room so the next professor can come in and conduct his own class. That is why, when some preachers go overtime, I start getting very restless, especially when it is a preacher who is rather full of himself and thinks you actually want to sit and listen to him talk for an extra half hour! Yet our pastor respects the clock, so when he goes overtime, I am confident he is being very sensitive to the Spirit of God, and when that happens, I lose all sense of time and recognize that it is God's Spirit who is keeping us there. This time, the pastor really got caught up in 2 Corinthians 3:18, where Paul speaks of being changed into the likeness of Jesus *"from glory to glory."* That night, I gained a new perspective of this *"glory to glory"*—and I don't think I was the only one.

There was an older woman sitting toward the front who was having a real "Pentecostal meltdown." I have no idea if she was just being bless-ed, was going through a particularly difficult time in her life, or was new to the congregation and this was her typical way "getting it down" in a service. She was whooping out praises and hallelujahs, stomping her feet, and making an absolute spectacle of herself. I could tell that some people were getting a little annoyed with her outbursts. Our pastor, likely through years of experience, or perhaps sensing the presence of God, just continued speaking as she carried on.

This woman kept repeating "Hallelujah" over and over. I began to think she *was* a bit crazy or even truly insane. But then I sensed God whis-pering to me, "Now you are witnessing the highest praise." I instantly re-membered what a worship leader had once said: the word we would use to express the highest praise is *hallelujah.* The word *hallelujah* is not even found in the Hebrew Old Testament. However, it is found in the Septuagint in Psalm 149:1 as the Greek word *allehlouia.* The word in Hebrew is *halelu* (הללו). Often, our English translations will simply render this as *hallelu-jah.* But *hallelujah* is actually a compound word, formed from *halel* (הלל), "praise," and *Jah* (יה), "God Jehovah," and it means "Praise God." The word *halel* (הלל) can signify "to shine," "to bring forth light," "to boast," or "to praise." The word is also used to denote "to make a fool of yourself," "to act like a madman," or "insanity."

We often consider a person to be a bit crazy or actually insane if they do not follow proper protocols or if they act inappropriately according to our set standards of normality. But the woman at the church service did not worry about what other people thought of her or the fact that oth-ers were looking at her. She simply opened her heart to God and let it all come out, not caring if the paramedics showed up with a net. Thus, to offer the "highest praise" is not merely to say the word *hallelujah,* but *to be* hallelujah—that is, to open up your heart and express your deep love and gratitude for God, not caring whether or not you are acting "appropriately."

When the service ended, I really sensed that the presence of God had fallen over the congregation in a soft, gentle way. I felt we had moved "from one glory to another." I do not know for sure, but I personally believe it was because one person was actually offering highest praise. One person was so caught up in the presence of God, was so into the mind of God, that she was willing to act insane to express her love for Him. And as a result, we all felt the love of God in Christ Jesus.

Might God Give Up on Us?

"Deliver me not over unto the will of mine enemies: for false witnesses are risen up against me, and such as breathe out cruelty."
—Psalm 27:12

It seems that most, if not all, of our major English translations express this plea of the psalmist in the following way: he is asking that God would not deliver him over to the will or desires of his enemies. It is a chilling thought that God might deliver us over to something really bad!

What is this "deliver over" business? When I think of the idea of delivering something, I picture an individual who has possession of something and then turns it over to someone or something else. So, it would appear from our English translations that when God takes possession of us, we don't really have the security that He will hang on to us. For whatever reason, we might do something that really annoys or angers Him, and He will decide we are too much of a handful and will "un-adopt" us, delivering us over to someone else.

Is There No Security?

For the last few years, I have been taking great comfort in just resting in the security that God has me safely wrapped in His arms and that He will never let me go, no matter what. Now I read that this psalmist, most likely David, the man after God's own heart, the man who loved God passionately, actually lived in fear that the Lord might give him up and turn him over to someone else. If David was worried about this, then maybe I should be worried too. And if I worry about it, where is all that security I was believing in?

Is there nothing in this universe that I can feel secure about? Can I not even trust God now? Do I have to perform for Him in order to be received? I am tired of performing. I am tired of being the good soldier. I just want to rest in those precious arms of Jesus, knowing that His shed blood will cover any fault or transgression I come up with.

I need that assurance. I mean, I really do try to be a good person, but then I turn right around and blow it. For example, I recently ended up being very rude to an insurance adjuster, and I had to call him back and apologize for being such a jerk. Why do I do things like that? Will God deliver me over to something bad because of it? No matter how much I promise myself I will be loving, no matter how much I beg God to give me patience with a nasty, sour, prune-faced woman who rides my disability bus, I still end up being just as nasty back at her. Will God turn me over to something dire because of that? Won't God just accept me for the fallible, sin-filled, old goat that I am, and cover more of my trespasses with the blood of His Son rather than turning me over to something terrible?

I do long for someone to accept me for what I am, faults and all. To accept me not because I am a Hebrew teacher and spend three to four hours a day studying God's Word, or because I have a PhD, or for any other fancied good traits. I want someone to just accept *me*—with all my ugliness, insecurities, faults, and failings. I long for someone who will give me credit for trying and not demand perfection from me. I "labor and am heavy laden," and I just want to go to Jesus and rest. (See Matthew 11:28.) Until I read Psalm 27:12, I felt God's acceptance. Now I worry that He is like everyone else—if I don't live up to His expectations and standards, He will toss me under the bus.

I say all this to admit that it is with extreme bias that I approach this word study. I want this verse to mean that God will *never* get so disgusted with me that He will deliver me over to the will of my enemies. So here goes. If it sounds as if I am spinning these words to say what I want them to say, I will plead guilty, and you may reject my conclusion.

Accepted Through the Blood of Jesus

The Hebrew word rendered "*deliver*" is *titteneni* (תתנני) and comes from the root word *nathan* (נתן), whose basic meaning is "to give." However, the word is in a hiphal (causative), incomplete or future form. This changes things. It means that God is not willfully giving us up—He is being forced or caused to give us up. He may have no choice. He is holy, after all, and my sinful acts just cannot coexist with Him. Additionally, since *titteneni* (תתנני) is in an incomplete or future form, it means that God has not yet done it. There is hope. He doesn't want to give us up; it is just that His holiness cannot allow us to stay. However, He has the remedy: the shed blood of His Son. All we have to do is repent and claim that blood, and He is just as happy as ever to hold on to us.

I recently saw a movie based on a true story in which a couple had taken in a foster child. They loved this young girl with all their hearts and wanted to adopt her. But the natural father refused to sign the papers to release the child for adoption. The girl was being abused by her natural father and lived in terror of her home visits with him. The foster parents fought with everything they had to keep the child away from this abusive parent. Yet, there was no legal evidence to prove the abuse. The natural father had remarried and demanded that the child be returned to him, which, according to the law, the courts had to do. Tragically, this prevented the foster parents from protecting their foster child.

The scene in the movie when the foster parents have to hand the child over to her natural father was very emotional. They were frantic and in tears as the child screamed not to be taken away. However, the natural father was holding the court papers and had every right to take her. He subsequently continued the abuse, which later was finally proven. It cost the foster parents practically everything they owned to prove this abuse and claim the child for adoption, but they were glad to pay the price.

That is a scene right out of Psalm 27:12. This Scripture does not depict a frustrated and disgusted God giving us over to our abusive enemy, but rather the devil standing there with his legal papers saying that because of our sin, he owns us. The heavenly Father, brokenhearted, is forced (hiphal) to hand us over to the devil because the enemy has the legal authority, spiritually speaking, to do so. But then, because of His death on the cross, Jesus steps in, takes the legal papers from the devil, and says, "Two thousand years ago, those sins were paid for on a cross with everything I had— My life, My very blood." The devil is forced to tear up his papers and hand us back to our heavenly Father. There is true power, "legal" power, in the blood of Jesus. If the devil lays any claim to us now that we trust in Jesus's sacrificial death and victorious resurrection on our behalf, he is simply lying.

The blood of Jesus is more than sufficient to cover our sins. Therefore, as long as I claim that blood in simple faith and repentance, I never have to worry about the devil coming along and dragging me out of my heavenly Father's arms kicking and screaming. I just snuggle closer to the Father and say to Jesus, "Would You show Your blood to that devil who is making a claim on me? I'd surely appreciate it, because I don't want to lose even a moment in the arms of my heavenly Father."

It's not that we actually need to remind the devil about the blood of Jesus; he is well aware of it and hates it. But he is a claim jumper, and we must remind *ourselves* of the rights that Jesus has over us in order to maintain our peace of mind and heart.

Study 41

Foremost on God's Mind

"He delighteth not in the strength of the horse:
he taketh not pleasure in the legs of a man."
—Psalm 147:10

I am a great fan of the old science fiction television series *Stargate*. I take particular interest in the character of Dr. Daniel Jackson, who is portrayed as a brilliant archeologist and linguist. In one episode, Dr. Jackson is discussing some ancient writings with another brilliant but secretly villainous archeologist, and he expresses interest in a Latin phrase they found on an ancient artifact. That phrase is "dominatus praeteritius mutabilitas." The evil archeologist quickly translated the words as "Conqueror of time." But Dr. Jackson immediately responded by saying, "In context, it would be more like 'Master of the uncertain past.'" The other archeologist then praised Dr. Jackson's aptitude, although it was clear he had been trying to steer our hero in the wrong direction.

The whole scene portrayed in the *Stargate* episode gives the appearance of a natural give-and-take between two experts seeking the truth. Such an exchange by experts of ancient languages is not uncommon. Similar give-and-take discussion was and is very common among Jewish rabbis as they study the Holy Scriptures, for they are experts in Hebrew and understand the difficulties of translating an ancient language. Most rabbis do not trust

English translations of the Bible because they know these renderings can be the result of one man's, or one group's, opinion.

People often ask me what a certain word *really* means in Hebrew. That is actually an unfair question. Again, maybe for Greek, it would be okay, but not for Hebrew. I would need to know the specific verse they are referring to, because although I might know the word's general usage, unless I know the context, I haven't the slightest idea what it means in that particular passage. We might refer to *Strong's Concordance* or a Hebrew dictionary to find the various usages of the word, but still not know what it really signifies in context.

God Is in Control

The King James Version renders Psalm 147:10 as, "*He delighteth not in the strength of the horse: he taketh not pleasure in the legs of a man.*" I have read a number of commentaries on this passage in which the commentators suggest that, in that day, horses were considered to be the most beautiful animals in existence, and the legs of a man that had been properly conditioned were viewed as a thing of beauty, but God does not take pleasure in such natural beauty.

I am not a brilliant linguist. However, I do challenge the renderings of three words in this verse: *yechepats* (יחפץ), from the root word *chapats* (חפץ), which is translated as "*delighteth*"; *bigeburath* (בגבורת), from the root word *gavar* (גבר), which is rendered as "*strength*"; and *yaretseh* (ירצה), from the root word *ratsah* (רצה), which is translated as "*pleasure.*"

I would suggest that, in its context, the Hebrew word for "*delight,*" *chapats* (חפץ), indicates "a bending toward" or "an inclining before." In other words, God is not saying that He doesn't delight in the strength of horses. I mean, how could He say such a thing when He created the horse's strength? Rather, He is saying that He will not bend, incline, or yield to the strength of horses. Additionally, instead of rendering the word *gavar* (גבר) as "*strength,*" I would translate it as "mastery" or "control over" horses. Finally, instead of "*pleasure,*" I would translate the word *ratsah* (רצה) as "association."

Thus, our study verse would read more like the following: "I will not yield to anyone's mastery or control over horses, and I do not associate with the strength of man's legs." Psalm 147:10 is saying that God will not yield to even the most powerful weapons on the face of the earth or the world's strongest warriors.

The context is the key to my translation. David is faced with a threat from the Assyrians, who had the most powerful army in the world. The Assyrians were considered invincible because they had the strongest and largest war chariots of any nation. They spent twenty years breeding horses that were potent and wild enough to pull these chariots, and about the same amount of time training and building the leg and arm strength of warriors to be able to control or master these horses as charioteers. David did not have the time to breed powerful horses or train warriors who had great strength in their legs to control their horses and chariots.

I am not saying that the King James Version is in error in its renderings, for indeed, the translators chose English words that match the Hebrew terms. However, there are other options to choose from. Moreover, the writers of the KJV did not have the benefits of recent archeological discoveries, which have revealed the nature of the ancient Assyrian war horses and their chariots. If they'd had access to today's knowledge, I have no doubt they would have tweaked their translations. Instead of using words that suggest God takes no pleasure in the strength of horses and man's legs, they would have used terms expressing that He will not surrender to even the most powerful weapons or the strongest warriors.

God's Thoughts Are on Us

In our twenty-first-century Western world, with rogue nations and the United States squaring off with their nuclear weapons, we have a wonderful promise that God is not at all impressed with the weapons of those rogue nations or with the might and technological superiority of the United States. He is still in control of the universe, and these weapons are no more a match for Him than the chariots and warriors of three thousand years ago. God's thoughts are on us and on bringing us into a loving relationship with Him. He can exert His will over nations and nullify their nuclear weapons any time He wants. But to exert His will on people to make them love Him, that is another matter. That He cannot and will not control. He has given us free will, and it is up to us whether we will love and serve Him. Nuclear weapons have no will of their own, but human beings do, and they are where God's focus lies. They are foremost on His mind.

Study 42

Abraham's Coffeehouse

"And Abraham planted a grove in Beersheba, and called there on the name of the Lord, the everlasting God."
—Genesis 21:33

We read in Genesis 21:33 that *"Abraham planted a grove in Beersheba."* The Hebrew word rendered *"grove"* is *'eshel* (אשל), and it actually refers to tamarisk trees, which grow wild and are small and prickly. The tamarisk is basically a bush, and Bedouins use such bushes to protect themselves from the wind. Additionally, as fuel for fire, they use the tree's bark, which gives off a lot of smoke. Bible scholars have pondered this verse for centuries. Why would Abraham plant bushes that are perfectly capable of growing wild and offer no value other than as a windbreaker and smoky fire?

Looking further at this Scripture, we see that after Abraham planted the tamarisk, he *"called there on the name of the Lord [YHWH], the everlasting God."* What does the planting of thorny bushes have to do with worshipping the Lord? Scholars have recently tried to shed new light on this matter. They found the tamarisk in Akkadian literature, where it was used for divination and for magical and medicinal purposes. It was used in the worship of the god Annunaki. The branches of the tamarisk were pictured as the bones of the gods whom Annunaki threw down to earth when they refused to work. The Akkadian word *quddus*, meaning "holy," is often associated with the tamarisk.

With this background, some scholars suggest that the planting of the tamarisk by Abraham was for the purpose of worshipping God. Pretty heady stuff. But I really hate the thought that Abraham would use a pagan symbol to worship Jehovah. Then again, Abraham was the father of the nation that would reintroduce monotheism, so we really can't slight the old boy for resorting to an ancient pagan symbol to worship the Lord. Even the ram caught in the thorns just before Abraham attempted to sacrifice Isaac could very well have been a symbol of the gods of the land of Ur, which had influenced Abraham as a child. (See Genesis 22:12–14.) The Talmud does teach that Abraham's father had made a living by manufacturing idols. Perhaps this was one way through which God purged all the idolatry out of Abraham. However, I think Scripture would have been more explicit about it if that had been the case. (The least the writer could have done was add a few more lines to explain the reason for the planting of the tamarisk trees so future generations would not spend countless hours in debate over the reason for it!)

A Vast Area with Many Rooms

Not only is there no obvious practical reason for Abraham to have planted tamarisk trees, but what is the spiritual value of even mentioning such an action? The God of the universe, our Creator, gave us only one relatively slim Book to tell us all about Himself. Why would He waste space with mysteries and other statements that don't make a bit of sense to us?

I have mentioned that I like science fiction, and frankly, to me, the Bible is like a "Tardis." The Tardis (which stands for "Time and Relative Dimension in Space") is a box a little bigger than a refrigerator that the British science fiction character Dr. Who uses as a starship. On the outside, it looks about seven feet high, four feet long, and four feet wide. However, inside, it is a vast place with so many rooms that not even Dr. Who himself has visited them all. Likewise, although the dimensions of even the largest Bibles are relatively small, I believe that when you enter the pages of God's Word, you find yourself in a vast area with so many rooms that not even the sixty-three volumes of the Talmud have visited all of them. And every verse, every word, was carefully chosen by God to reveal a message to us.

That is why I refuse to write off Genesis 21:33 as mere literary fluff that God used to fill out the pages of His Book. Our inclination would be to say, "Okay, Abraham planted tamarisk trees; that's fine" and then move on. Well, I am not moving on. I am stopping right here, and I will not leave until I have an answer as to what God is trying to tell us in this verse.

Calling on the Name of the Lord

My search takes me to a passage in the Talmud in Sotah 10a–b, seeking some answers from those who spent a lifetime studying the Word of God. Certain sages see the Hebrew word for *"grove,"* or "tamarisk," which is *'eshel* (אשל), as an acronym. Yes, they have acronyms in Hebrew. The word begins with aleph (א), which is the first letter of the word *'akila* (אכל), meaning "food," followed by shin (ש), which is the first letter of *shetvth* (שתות), signifying "drink," and lamed (ל), which is the first letter of *lewiya* (לויה), denoting "fellowship." The sages concluded that Abraham went and established a little hostel, or hotel, planting the tamarisk trees as a fence around his inn to serve as a sort of billboard sign announcing that within the grove was a place to stay. There, travelers could come and find rest, food, and companionship. But this hostel really served more like a coffeehouse with a religious theme.

The Talmud goes on to explain that the Hebrew word rendered *"called"* in Genesis 21:33 is *vayakrie* (ויכרי), which is in a hiphal (causative), imperfect (future), third person form and should be rendered, "Abraham… caused others to call (upon the name *Jehovah*)." Thus, Abraham caused God's name to be spoken by the mouths of all his guests. Roughly translated, the Talmud teaches, "After they ate and drank, they blessed him (Abraham), and Abraham said, 'Have you eaten my food? No, your food and drink were provided by Jehovah. Thank and bless Him who spoke the world into being.'"

Frankly, I prefer this explanation to the idea that Abraham set up a place to worship God using pagan symbols. I like to think Abraham was so close to the mind of God that He knew the best way to reach the pagan people was just to love them and open up a place for them to eat and fellowship, and that true worship of God is sharing His love with others. Thus, Abraham set up a mission station where he became our first missionary.

I have been so wrapped up in my praise and worship to God that I have failed to also *vayakrie* (ויכרי), or cause others to speak the name of God. We are all called to share the message of God's love and salvation. It is very easy to become one-dimensional and focus only on our own worship, needs, and problems. But when Abraham, the father of not only Judaism but also Christianity, worshipped God, he set an example for us—to share the good news as part of our praise and worship to the Lord.

Study 43

Conversion

"Repent ye therefore, and be converted [Aramaic, "surrender," "submit"], *that your sins may be blotted out, when the times of refreshing shall come from the presence of the Lord."*
—Acts 3:19

In my first pastoral experience, I served in a church that was one-fourth rank liberal, one-fourth fundamentalist, one-fourth charismatic, and one-fourth indifferent. Everyone tried to "convert" everyone else to their theological position—or lack thereof. This tense situation was about to explode the whole church into splinters when, all of a sudden, we had a visitation from the "Father of Lights" (the ancient Jewish term for *Jehovah*). It was anything like what you might expect from a revival, and yet it was everything a revival should be.

I have given a lot of thought to the idea of "conversion." For years, I have been haunted by a word I discovered in my Aramaic Bible that is rendered as *conversion* in our English Bible. I grew up in the fundamentalist church, where the main duty of the Christian was to go out and get *converts*. I was a sorry excuse for an evangelist—not that I didn't try. I went door-to-door with our "Sky Pilot" invasion; I tried the friendship evangelism of my Youth for Christ club in high school; I worked with Campus Crusade for Christ (now called "Cru") in college, sharing the "four spiritual laws" with students at the university; and I did door-to-door and street evangelism in my Practical Christian Work assignments at Moody Bible Institute.

I never got used to it. I never felt comfortable sharing my faith with others in that way, especially strangers, and I suffered extreme anxiety over my attempts at personal evangelism. I prayed that God would make me bold in sharing my faith. I dreamed of being like those spiritual giants I knew in Bible college who went out on the streets and returned with a dozen names of people they had led to the Lord. But when the Father of Lights paid a visit to the little church of my first pastorate, evangelism took on a whole new meaning for me, as did the concept of *conversion*. After that, I no longer feared evangelism.

Father of Lights

When I served in that church whose members adhered to four different theologies, I was pressured by the charismatics to speak in tongues, which I was adamantly against at that time in my life. I was pressured by the fundamentalists to go out witnessing, which I was terrified of doing. And I was pressured by the liberals to take the youth out trick-or-treating—only, instead of accepting a treat, they wanted us to encourage the people at the door to drop a monetary gift in a little box to collect donations for UNICEF. I didn't have anything against UNICEF, but I didn't see that as a church function. That left me with only the "indifferent" group to relate to!

However, if all the members of the church agreed on one thing, it was to get "converts" so we could increase our numbers and size. Nobody had a problem with getting these converts except for me, because that became my responsibility. In my writings, I never recommend books or movies to my readers, even though I mention them as illustrations or quote from them at times. However, I must make an exception, if you will forgive me. I highly recommend the movie *Father of Lights*. You can download it for free. The movie demonstrates the only way I have ever felt comfortable sharing my faith. I also recommend a book by former congressman and deputy United Nations ambassador Mark Siljander entitled *A Deadly Misunderstanding*. Siljander sees the Aramaic language as the common ground between Christianity, Islam, and Judaism, and his understanding of the Aramaic word for "conversion" is identical to the understanding that I had for years but was afraid to share. I base the following explanation on Siljander's description of the word because he does a much better job of it than I do.

You see, in the King James Version, the word *convert* appears ten times in the New Testament and five times in the Old Testament. When Peter told the people, "*Repent ye therefore, and be converted,*" the Greek word for "*converted*" is *epistrepho*, which means "to convert" or "to turn about." But Peter spoke Aramaic, and thus the word had to be translated into Greek, rendered from the Aramaic word *shalem* (שלם). This sounds a lot like *shalom* (שלם). It is from the same root and means "peace," "goodwill," and so forth, but it also has a wide range of meanings and usages. In extra-biblical literature, I found that the word *shalem* (שלם) was used to express the idea of *submission.*[9]

Conversion or Surrender?

What I hated most about personal evangelism was that I was trying to convert someone to my beliefs, my faith, my way of thinking, and my way of living. However, I was always plagued by the thought, "How do I know my way is the right way after all?" The other day, I did a study on 1 Corinthians 2:2, where the apostle Paul said that he came with "nothing more than Jesus Christ and Him crucified." I found it much easier and more natural to simply encourage someone to *shalem* (שלם), to submit or surrender to God, than to convince them to think like me.

Our society today is inundated with encouragements to *convert*. We are pressured to convert to a new toothpaste, car, diet—you name it. Everyone is trying to convert us to their way of thinking. Perhaps the least tasteful of all "conversion encouragements" are those based on religion. I have not yet read in the Bible where we are commanded to convert people to a religion.

The traditional religious language we use can obscure the true meaning of an experience with God. This whole idea of "conversion" is apparently to encourage us to change from our sinful lifestyle to a righteous life with

---

9. See Mark Siljander, *A Deadly Misunderstanding* (New York: HarperCollins, 2008), 31–33.

God. But doesn't the Bible say that salvation is by faith and not by works? (See Ephesians 2:8–9.) This is where the idea of conversion troubled me. It seemed to me this meant people were taking an active role in their own conversion, and believe me, in my years of ministry, I have dealt with many people who tried, begged, and pleaded to "convert" from their lifestyle of drug or alcohol abuse, sexual perversion, gambling, or another issue but failed miserably. In the end, we can only surrender or submit to God in faith and allow Him to change us through His Holy Spirit.

After the visitation from the Father of Lights at my first church, I went out on a pastoral call to a delinquent member of our church. She only let me into her house because I was a preacher and she felt she had to, but she told me in no uncertain terms that she was not about to be *converted*. I assured her that I had no intention of converting her. She then introduced me to her three cats, who immediately jumped up on my lap and started to purr contentedly.

The little lady stood with her mouth open and said, "My cats always run away from strangers. The fact that they came to you proves you are someone special." I told her, "My friend, if I have learned anything in these past weeks, it is that I am no one special. But I have a very special God living inside of me. I just submit to Him, and your cats do not come to me but to Him." The woman sat down and said, "I once submitted to God, but I haven't done so for many years." Before long, we were both in tears as we basked in the presence of God and she prayed a prayer of *shalem* (שלם), submission. Not *conversion*, but *submission*. The rest was left to God, who did whatever converting was necessary.

Our job is simply to submit to God and encourage others, regardless of creed, doctrine, or religion, to submit to God, too, and let Him take care of the rest.

Study 44

Furnace of Affliction

*"Behold, I have refined thee, but not with silver; I have chosen thee in
the furnace of affliction."*
—Isaiah 48:10

A reader of my blog asked me to comment on the above verse. The
really wonderful thing about writing a blog as opposed to speaking
before a live audience is that when someone asks me a question, I don't
have to come up with an immediate answer. I can spend a couple of days
researching the question first. The issue my reader brought up revolved
around the words *"chosen"* and *"affliction."*

I am particularly fascinated by the Hebrew word rendered *"chosen,"*
which is *bachar* (בחר), in the King James Version of Isaiah 48:10. The *Living
Bible* uses the word *"refined,"* the *English Standard Version* uses *"tried,"* the
New International Version and the *New American Standard Bible* use *"tested,"* and the *New Century Version* uses *"purified."* All these words are linked
by the idea of removing something that is bad. When you *test* or *try* something, you are attempting to expose the flaws or inaccuracies and leave only
the truth or what is correct. When you *refine* or *purify* something, you are
actually removing flaws.

Like the King James Version, there are a number of other translations that render *bachar* (בחר) as *"chosen,"* a term that might suggest God

specifically waits until we have been "baked in the oven" for a while before He gets around to choosing us. It is not that the English word *chosen* is wrong; it is just that we have a wider understanding of the word *bachar* (בחר), and using the term *chosen* could steer us away from its root meaning.

Choosing What Is Best

Bachar (בחר) does mean "to choose," but it is a choosing of what is the best. When it comes down to it, that is really what making a choice means: to decide what is best and then to choose it over that which is not as good. Thus, if you put all the words used by the various Bible translators together, you get the concept behind *bachar* (בחר). Unfortunately, a translator can select only one word, even though no single word can give us a complete understanding of the term. This opens up the door to what we might call "sermonizing"—in a positive sense.

During your weekly church services, hopefully, your pastor reads a portion of Scripture and then expounds on it, going into detail about its significance—preaching a sermon. That is exactly what I am doing in this book. I am preaching little sermons. I really don't translate Scripture; rather, I sermonize Scripture. I tell you what various Bible versions say and provide information about the word in the original language as I try to summarize a theme in a concise study to help you better understand what a passage of Scripture is saying so you can make personal application.

Looking further into the word *bachar* (בחר), we find it has an ancient Canaanite origin, and it is used in the Old Persian language for examining or scrutinizing something. Perhaps the best illustration of *bachar* (בחר) is that old song "Ballad of the Green Berets," which includes these words: "One hundred men we'll test today / But only three win the Green Beret." A soldier who aspires to be part of an elite group will go through a difficult training period meant to weed out those who do not have the "right stuff." Only those who qualify will be *chosen* to become a member of that elite corp.

A Good Kind of Affliction

God says that He has purified, refined, tried, and tested us; He has chosen us "*in the furnace of affliction.*" The word "*affliction*" evokes a very negative feeling. Yet, affliction is not necessarily all that bad. When I was in college, I played on the soccer team. To this day, I do not understand all the rules of soccer, but I do clearly remember that during practice, we were running, running, and then running some more. After a particularly hard workout, I overheard one of my teammates declare, "Ain't it wonderful?" I asked him, "What is so wonderful about running yourself to death?" He said, "It feels so good when you stop." He had a point. After a really rough practice, I would go back to my dorm and just lie down, basking in the joy of just resting. Never had resting felt so good. Sure, I was sore, but it was a good kind of sore.

The Hebrew word translated *"affliction"* in this verse is *oni* (עני). It comes from the root word *'anah* (ענה), which signifies a good kind of affliction. This word has a wide range of meanings, including "affliction," "depression," "trouble," "misery," and "poverty." It also means "to be humble" or "to be weak." When you trace this word to its Semitic root, you discover it has the idea of being downcast. But its use in the Old Persian is what I believe is applicable here. When a person stood before a king, they were said to *'anah* (ענה), or "bow down." They were showing their submission, or humbling themselves, before the ruler.

Our study verse was written by Isaiah during a time when the Old Persian language would have had the strongest influence on the Hebrew language. Kings in those days, as today, had a detachment of warriors surrounding them as their personal bodyguards. These were the best and most dedicated warriors of the land who would not hesitate to take an arrow for their king.

When someone entered into such direct service for the sovereign, they would surrender everything they had, their very life, on his behalf. They would go through a cycle of *bachar* (בחר) in which they would be refined, or purified, of all personal desires and agendas. Then they would be tried, or tested, to be sure they had the right skills and attitude, having no self-interest, so they could be chosen for the elite service of being the king's personal bodyguard. When a soldier completed *bachar* (בחר), he would be given the honor and privilege of standing in the king's court or by the king's bed as he slept, ready to protect his sovereign or die in the attempt.

I once heard a soldier in one of our elite special forces units respond to a question about whether he was married. He replied, "Yes, to the Constitution of the United States." This soldier had completed the full cycle of *bachar* (בחר). Additionally, I have read about the training of U.S. Navy SEALs. If a trainee feels they can no longer endure the intense program, they can ring a bell, pack up, and leave, no questions asked. Numerous trainees do end up leaving. Many are called, but few make it through the entire training without ringing that bell. A number make it to the final week, which is the worst week of the entire training period. It is there, after enduring weeks of intense, painful, agonizing training, that the largest portion of those who drop out ring the bell. They were so close to the finish, but their bodies just could not be pushed any further.

When God allows us to go through affliction, it is the good kind—the kind that will strip us of all our trust in ourselves and all our personal agendas, so the world can see that our trust is in God alone. As I write this, I reflect on five of the most difficult and painful periods of my life. Times when well-meaning Christians accused me of not trusting God, indicating that if I really trusted Him, I would not have to endure such affliction. Now I look back on those times and thank God for them. More than that, I praise and rejoice in Him for those afflictions. If it had not been for my difficulties, I would not be writing this book today. If I had not gone through the *bekur oni* (בחר עני), the "*furnace of affliction*," I would not have the love and passion for my God that I hold in my heart today. Thus, when God allows us to go through fires of affliction, what is on His mind? It is our welfare, which can only be secured by the process of those refining and purifying fires.

A Warm, Gentle Warning

"Then I beheld, and lo a likeness as the appearance of fire: from the appearance of his loins even downward, fire; and from his loins even upward, as the appearance of brightness, as the colour of amber."
—Ezekiel 8:2

There are individuals who look at the eighth chapter of Ezekiel and claim that it depicts an "alien abduction." I think something much more profound than that happened: Ezekiel was given a glimpse into the world of the Spirit and saw things that one just cannot explain in natural terms. This passage of Scripture can be very difficult to understand because it is filled with Hebraic and Aramaic idioms and metaphors. As I study Ezekiel 8 in light of the ancient Hebrew and Chaldean language and culture, I discover more depths to its meaning—and it has nothing to do with an alien abduction.

Be that as it may, books have been written, fortunes have been made, and platforms have been established by people who have used quasi-intellectual credentials to prey upon those seeking hidden knowledge of secret conspiracies by the government and governmental organizations. What amazes me is that these same people use Scripture to prove their points, even though they deny the existence of God, asserting that what we think is God is actually an extraterrestrial. They tear apart the very Scriptures that they say are totally accurate in other regards in order to support their own claims.

We hold the Bible to be accurate because of our belief in the inspiration of Scripture. However, if you deny the existence of a supernatural God, you also have to question the accuracy of the above text, which these conspiracy theorists will not do. Their whole premise is based upon the validity of the Scriptures, yet they are ignorant about ancient cultures and languages and do not understand what the passage is really saying.

Seeing Love

So, let's take a look at this passage in the light of ancient cultures, history, and languages. Ezekiel was taken into captivity by the Babylonians at the age of twenty-five. He was one of three thousand captives from the wealthy, noble class of Judah, and he settled along the Chabar River in the Babylonian territory. Although the book of Ezekiel was written in Classical Hebrew, it is filled with allusions to Chaldean culture, Aramaic expressions, and idioms. After twenty-five years in Babylon, his language and expressions would have taken on a truly Chaldean flavor, and hence we must examine this passage not only in the light of the Hebrew culture and language but also of the Chaldean.

Ezekiel began to have his visions at the age of fifty, and people from all around would travel to listen to him explain these revelations. What the prophet describes in Ezekiel 8:2 was indeed a heavenly being. However, perhaps such a vision was not as unusual as we would think. Might not today's believers, those who truly love and worship God, see something similar? We cannot be sure what Ezekiel saw, because the prophet could only try to explain in natural terms what was supernatural. No human words can adequately explain the supernatural, so we must resort to metaphors and other poetic devices. For example, in Genesis 49:14, when the writer says that Issachar is a *"strong donkey"* (NKJV), he is not saying that Issachar is a literal horselike creature with bulging muscles; he is merely trying to set a natural picture to an abstract concept. Ezekiel is doing something similar here.

Note that the prophet talks about *"a likeness as the appearance of fire: from the appearance of his loins even downward, fire."* The Hebrew word translated *"likeness"* is *demuth* (דמות), from the root word *damah* (דמה), which means to be similar but in a quiet way. Using the word *damah* (דמה), Ezekiel is employing a richly poetic word, both in Hebrew and Aramaic, which incorporates not only a natural picture but also a sensation, meaning that he is trying to express what he feels: the supernatural being that he could not describe in natural terms radiated warmth and comfort. Additionally, in using the Hebrew word *'ash* (אש), or *"fire,"* he was indicating that this was not a threatening, out-of-control fire that would consume him, but rather one that brought this warmth and comfort.

The Hebrew word rendered *"appearance"* is *kemareh* (כמראה). It is from the root word *ra'ah* (ראה), which means "to see," but it is also rooted in the word *kemar* (כמר), which means "to kindle a fire for warmth" and can signify "love and compassion." This is another beautifully poetic word for describing something that causes you to feel love, compassion, and warmth. Literally, it means "to see love."

If you could draw a picture of love, what would it look like? I can imagine Ezekiel sitting around a campfire with a group of twenty-first-century, Western, cultured Christians who had somehow traveled back in time to the prophet's day and are listening to him describe his experience. If Ezekiel could speak modern English, he would say, "What I saw was warmth, compassion, and love." Then, he might add, "Have you ever seen warmth, compassion, and love?"

"As the Look of God"

Ezekiel says something rather strange with his phrase *"the appearance of brightness."* The Hebrew term for *"brightness,"* *zohar* (זהר), is a wonderful word. It is a common Jewish name that means "aglow" or, in its verbal root form, "to glow and radiate." This term is used for someone who has access to deep, hidden knowledge and secrets—secrets that bear a warning but not a threat. The combination of *kemareh* (כמראה), *"appearance,"* with *zohar* (זהר), "aglow," would form an Aramaic idiom used to express "a warm, gentle warning."

Then we have the Hebrew word translated *"colour of amber,"* which is *chasmal* (חשמל) and can mean "the color of amber," "the color of copper," "gleaming metal," "glowing metal," or "glitter." Moreover, this word can also signify "aglow." But here is the kicker: the word *chasmal* (חשמל) is an Aramaic idiom common along the Chebar River region that means "as the look of God."

Thus, what Ezekiel saw evoked a feeling of warmth, love, and compassion. The vision was so awesome that it looked like God or what he could imagine God would look like.

Have you ever met another Christian who was just *chasmal* (חשמל), or aglow, with the presence of God? Maybe the individual was not physically beautiful, but the *chasmal* (חשמל), or the look of God, was so great upon them that you did not see their physical appearance because you were blinded by the love of God reflected there. Someone has said, "We are the only Jesus that some people will ever see." I think there have been times when, in the countenance of another Christian, I have seen something of what Ezekiel saw. How about you?

Study 46

Praising in Dance

"Let them praise his name in the dance: let them sing praises unto him with the timbrel and harp."
—Psalm 149:3

H ave you ever gone through a period of time when you felt like old Job? When one messenger after another kept coming to your door with more bad news? In Shakespeare's *Hamlet*, when Claudius receives a string of bad news, he cries out, "When sorrows come, they come not single spies, but in battalions."[10]

Thanking God for a Bad Day?

There is a story in Jewish literature about a famous rabbi who encouraged his students to praise God even for a bad day. One student asked, "Master, if God only gives good things, then He will surely not give us a bad day. How then should we praise Him for something He did not give to us?" The rabbi scratched his head and admitted that he had no answer to that question. But he said that a man in the next village by the name of Ben Yohanan could answer his question.

---

10. Harold Jenkins, ed., *Hamlet*, The Arden Shakespeare, Richard Proudfoot, Ann Thompson, and David Scott Kastan, gen. eds. (London: Thomas Learning, 2003), Act 4, Scene 5, lines 78–79.

The next day, the students journeyed to the village to seek out Ben Yohanan, learning from the other villagers that he spent practically all his waking hours studying Torah. The students found him in the poorest section of town, living in a one-room shack that had only a table, a chair, a stool, and a cot. Yohanan was too ill to work and lived on a very small pension that barely kept him alive.

When they knocked on Yohanan's door, he joyfully called to invite them in, apologizing for not getting up because he had injured his leg the prior day. He also apologized that he had nothing more to offer them than bread and water, but the students assured him they were not hungry. When Yohanan asked why such bright young men would honor him with a visit, one explained that their rabbi had sent them to him to answer a question he could not answer. Ben Yohanan asked the rabbi's name, and when he heard it, he exclaimed, "Why, he is one of the most learned rabbis in the region. How is it that I can answer a question he could not? But go ahead and ask." So, they repeated their question: "If God only gives good things and we are to praise him for all things, how can we praise Him for a bad day?" With that, Ben Yohanan broke out laughing and said, "Your rabbi has certainly made a mistake in sending you to me to answer that question. I could not possibly know the answer, for you see, I have never had a bad day."

Indeed, how can we have a bad day when each day that we have here on earth is another opportunity to sing and dance and praise the Lord? Each day is a new opportunity to study His Word and learn something new. Each day is a fresh opportunity to enter the mind and heart of God and experience the depths of His love.

Twirling in the Joy of the Lord

The literal meaning of the first part of Psalm 149:3 is, "They shall praise His name in from the dance." The Hebrew word translated "*dance*" is *bemacheval* (במחול). This term comes from the Semitic root *cheval* (חול), which means "to spin around in a circle" or "to twirl." Yesterday, I watched a small child run from her mother and then stop and begin to spin around in a circle out of pure joy. There is something pleasurable about spinning around in a circle. People pay a small fortune at Six Flags, Disneyland, or other amusement parks for such an experience.

The word *cheval* (חול), "to spin around in a circle," is spelled chet (ח), vav (ו), lamed (ל). One rabbi pointed out that the chet (ח) equals eight, and when put on its side, it is the symbol of infinity. Thus, the word indicates that this is a dance that connects you to the infinite nature of God. Even more telling is that the word *cheval* (חול) has a numerical value of twenty-six, which is the same numerical value of God's name *YHWH* (יהוה). The Hebrew word rendered *"praise"* is *halel* (הלל). As I mentioned earlier, this is the word from which *hallelujah* is derived. We learned that *halel* (הלל) does mean "to praise," but in its Semitic root, it means "to act madly" or "to act foolishly." Seriously, this comes straight from the likes of Georg Fohrer's *Hebrew and Aramaic Dictionary of the Old Testament*. Esoterically, the double lamed (לל) in *halel* (הלל) indicates a movement toward the heart of God. It also indicates two uplifted hands.

The idea here is not so much the act of spinning around physically, but rather spinning and weaving yourself around God by *haleling* (הלל), or praising, His name in the form of a *cheval* (חול), or dance, that is meant to bind you with God. The more you spin, the tighter the binding becomes. In fact, in ancient times, children used to spin around in circle when they worshipped God. David *chevaled* (חול), or spun around in a circle, before the ark of the covenant such that his wife rebuked him for *haleling* (הלל), or acting foolishly, in a way she thought undignified for a king. But David had entered into full worship. (See 2 Samuel 6:16–22.)

Many years ago, I heard a talk by Richard Wurmbrand, who spent many years in a communist prison for his faith. He said that other such prisoners who were put into solitary confinement would spin around in circle out of pure joy, praising God. Their sorrows also "came in battalions," yet they had learned the biblical secret to finding joy in the midst of trouble, and they became just like little children without a care in the world as they twirled and praised God.

Some days, it seems as if you have nothing left in life. The enemy appears to have come in and taken everything of value from you. Often, when sorrows come to my door one after another, I find myself tossing and turning in bed at night, wondering why God has allowed all these things to come upon me, or why He does not give me at least one little blessing. Other people who seem to be less devoted to God give wonderful testimonies about how He provided them with a new house or car, while I struggle to pay a tax bill or even renew my subscription to an archaeological journal. My faith is so shaken, I really begin to question whether God is a God of love, a God who cares—or even if there is a God at all. At those times, I just get out of bed and go to the center of my apartment and begin to spin around in a circle. Can you imagine a sixty-four-year-old man spinning around like a little child? I start praising God, and before long, I am praising Him out of pure joy, wearing myself out, so that I just collapse into a sound sleep!

A Heart Filled with Faith and the Holy Spirit

The second phrase in this verse, *"Let them sing praises unto him with the timbrel and harp,"* literally reads, "In a tambourine and a harp they shall make melody." I can't think of two instruments that are more incompatible than a tambourine and a harp. But they were commonly played together at banquets and festive occasions. The timbrel, or tambourine, was symbolic of victory.

The Talmud teaches that the Levitical harp players in both the first and second temple were to sing a melody that no one else was permitted to learn. The melodies were passed down from father to son until the destruction of the second temple. Since that time, those melodies have been hidden. The Hebrew word translated *"harp"* is *kinor* (כנר), spelled kap (כ), nun (נ), resh (ר). These letters and their order represent filling one's heart with faith and the Holy Spirit. The word for *"praises"* here is *zamar* (זמר), which literally means "to cut" or "to divide." It is in a piel, (intensive) form, which gives the idea of dividing into rhythmical numbers or the formation of melodies. The connotation of the harp and praise or melody is to make music that comes from a heart filled with faith and the Holy Spirit. These would be new melodies, hidden melodies.

Thus, the primary idea behind Psalm 149:3 is more than singing and dancing to the tune of the harp and the tambourine. It is spinning and weaving yourself around God, binding yourself to Him so that the melodies you sing come from a heart filled with faith and the Holy Spirit.

Study 47

"I Am He"

"As soon then as he had said unto them, I am he, they went backward, and fell to the ground."
—John 18:6

The beginning of John 18 is a very curious passage. Those who came to arrest Jesus were a combination of Roman soldiers and Jewish officials. I always wondered why Jesus had to ask who they were coming for and then identify Himself. (See John 18:1–5.) The Bible makes it very clear that Jesus knew they had come for Him. He could easily have stepped forward and said, "I'm here. Let's go." Also, why did Judas identify Jesus with a kiss?

Historically, it was not uncommon for a heretic to be arrested and tried before the Sanhedrin. Also, if he had loyal followers, it was not unusual for one of those followers to identify himself as the teacher to prevent his master from being arrested. Then their master would have a chance to escape and be safely hidden away when the deception was finally discovered. With Jesus so willing to give Himself up, perhaps it created suspicion among those arresting Him that someone was trying to take His place; thus, it took an eyewitness to make the identification, which was Judas with his kiss.

What is more puzzling is that when Jesus first said, "I am he," the soldiers and officials fell to the ground. I have read numerous commentaries on this incident, and each one has a different theory, ranging from Jesus's captors being so surprised that He had admitted to His identity that they stepped backward, falling over each other, to the idea that some supernatural event caused them to fall to the ground.

I doubt I can answer a question that has been asked for over two thousand years. Scholars more intelligent than I am have struggled with this issue but come to no agreement as to the reason the captors all fell. However, I do have one idea that I believe may be close to the answer.

The Holy Name

In Greek, the phrase translated "I am he" is *ego eimi*, which simply means "I am." This is a pretty standard expression, with nothing unique about it. However, Jesus did not originally utter His response in Greek. When identifying Himself, He may have spoken the holy name of God *YHWH* (יהוה) in Aramaic. I find it very curious that "I am" in Aramaic, *ana* (אנא), is repeated twice as *dana ana* (דנא אנא), the first time with a daleth (ד), which is the preposition *that* in Aramaic. Thus, Jesus literally said, "I am that I am."

The Jews who came to arrest Jesus might have recognized that He was saying *YHWH* (יהוה) in Aramaic. For someone to utter that sacred name, even in a different dialect, could have so startled the Jews that they stepped back and stumbled over each other. The Aramaic word for *"went backward"* is *bestra* (בצר) and contains the idea of moving backward to protect oneself. Could it be that, at this moment, there was a blinding heavenly light or the appearance of angels with drawn swords? I think the text would have said so if that had occurred. More likely, the Jewish officials might have stepped away to avoid hearing the sacred name of God. The Jews were not only fearful to speak the holy Name, but also to hear it. All this, of course, is pure speculation on my part, merely some ponderings.

Everything Is Under His Control

However, of this one thing we can be sure: Jesus voluntarily gave Himself up to be arrested and crucified. In ancient times, if a leader or master was taken forcibly, his followers would have fought to the death to protect him. However, if the master or leader willingly allowed himself to be taken, it would be the obligation of the followers to scatter and separate, lest they be caught together and accused of scheming some plot or lest they actually be overhead discussing their master, and everything they said be used against him. This leads me to believe that the disciples didn't scatter because they were cowards; they did so to protect their beloved Master.

Thus, Jesus made it very clear that He was giving Himself up of His own accord; otherwise, there would have been quite a brawl. Except for Peter impetuously drawing a sword and striking the ear of an official's servant, whom Jesus healed (see John 18:10–11; Luke 22:49–51), the disciples did the thing that was expected of them, and that was to scatter and wait out the trial. If their scattering was an act of cowardice, why did John and perhaps other disciples appear at the cross? (See John 19:26–27.) Surely, they would have stayed hidden during the execution lest they be next. But the very fact that the execution was taking place meant that the disciples could no longer say anything that would harm their Master; He was already receiving the death sentence.

If there is any lesson in all this, I believe it is the continuing message that Jesus gave to His disciples and to us: He has everything under control. Simply uttering His name can dramatically change a situation. When we are in a difficult place, it may not seem that way. Like Peter, we may want to step forward with our own "sword" to change the tide of our circumstances. But Jesus reminds us that He is the great *dana ana* (אנא דנא), the "I Am" (Exodus 3:14), the King over all.

Sins as Scarlet

*"Come now, and let us reason together, saith the L*ORD*: though your
sins be as scarlet, they shall be as white as snow; though they be red
like crimson, they shall be as wool."*
—Isaiah 1:18

Isaiah 1:18 is one of those popular verses among Christians that we hear
all the time. However, every time I hear or read it, I wonder, "Why does
God call sins 'as scarlet'? Scarlet is the color of blood, and it is the blood of
Jesus that *removes* our sin, so why would sin be equated with that color?"

Frankly, I just don't like assigning a color to sin. In Bible college, I
worked briefly with a Christian organization, and they had what was called
the "Wordless Book," with five colors representing different aspects of the
gospel message. The color black was used for sin, and I was supposed to
present the book to a group of inner-city children with dark complexions,
saying that the color black represented evil and that God would forgive and
cleanse them, making them white. My refusal to use the Wordless Book,
or at least the color black for sin, created a falling out between the organization's director and me. I would have failed my Practical Christian Work
(PCW) assignment had not the director of the PCW department for the
college expressed similar shock over the use of the color black for sin. I
understand that the organization has long since corrected this politically

incorrect designation. Yet, I wondered why they had chosen black in the first place when Scripture, at least in Isaiah 1:18, chose the color scarlet for sin.

I don't think the ancient Middle East had the potential misunderstandings about the use of color that we do in our culture, so it is doubtful God was trying to be politically correct in using red to represent sin. So the question stands, "Why *scarlet?*"

An Unusual Insect

For one thing, people in ancient times were not as used to color as we are. Today, for the most part, we live in a colorful world, and we have turned color into a real science, creating more and more shades. People in ancient times were usually awed when they saw bright colors, because they did not see them very often. Their surroundings were mostly desert brown, with some greenery. However, the appearance of a brightly colored flower, animal, or even insect created quite a stir and even a sense of worship toward the Creator.

Thus, scarlet, as a bright color, would have been rarely seen in ancient times. The Hebrew word translated *"scarlet"* in our study verse is *kashanim* (כשנם), from the root word *shani* (שׁני), which is a word for a particular insect. The *ka* (כ) in front of the word is a preposition meaning "like" or "as," so it would literally read, "Though your sins be like an insect...." Well, that makes as much sense to us as the word *scarlet*. However, translators are correct to use *scarlet* because the people of that day were very familiar with this unusual insect, and they could not help but observe it and wonder about it. You see, this insect would attach itself to a tree to bear its young, and when it died and dried up, it would turn a bright scarlet.

New Spiritual Life and Beauty

The United States Congress recently passed a budget with billions of dollars in defense spending. The allocation was pretty bipartisan, not only because defense is a major priority with our country, but also because it creates jobs. There are probably few people in the nation who have not heard of the Army, Navy, Air Force, and Marines. Most of us are familiar with terms like *nuclear weapons, ICBM missiles, tanks, aircraft carriers,* and even *F-15s.* When you think about it, we probably know quite a bit about our national defense, and there are numerous families in this country that have a friend or relative who is in the military or working on a defense project in a civilian capacity.

My point is that just as everyone today knows what a nuclear weapon is, everyone in Israel knew what *"scarlet"* referred to. Many people were employed to gather those little insects. Once the creatures died, dried out, and began to decay, becoming scarlet in color, they were collected, crushed, and turned into a red dye. This dye was applied to the clothing of royalty and the wealthy or elite of society. When an individual wearing scarlet approached, you know they were a person of great importance.

Thus, when someone heard the word *shani* (שני), or *scarlet,* they would immediately think of a dead, decaying insect. Then, they would quickly associate their sin with something dead and rotting that choked the spiritual life out of them. However, they would also recognize that, in the right hands, something dead could be transformed into something beautiful. God was saying that even though our sins make our spirits as dead as that scarlet insect, He can restore us to new spiritual life and beauty.

Forgiveness for Sins—Whether Obvious or Secret

There is an additional connotation to *scarlet* that can help us further understand the meaning of Isaiah 1:18. The other day, I was reviewing some of the notes I had gathered for my doctoral dissertation, and I found a notation about the uniform of the Assyrian army. The Assyrians were the Israelites' greatest enemies during the time of Isaiah. In fact, after years of warfare, they eventually conquered Israel. Most likely, everyone living in Israel had heard stories of the battles between the two nations, and one thing they would have discussed was the uniform of the charioteers.

You may remember from an earlier study that Assyria had the greatest and most powerful horses to pull their chariots, which were unmatched by any other nation in the world. The Assyrians spent twenty years breeding horses capable of pulling these chariots. Each chariot was manned by three warriors: one to drive the chariot and the other two to shoot arrows at the enemy. The chariots would lead the charge during battle, racing as closely as possible to the enemy lines, where the archers would release their arrows. Then, the chariots would circle around for another attack.

My cousin is married to a Vietnam veteran who served with the "Spotlight" unit. I had never heard of this outfit before, but the men who belonged to it had to be some brave warriors. They drove a jeep at night with a spotlight attached, and when enemy movement was detected, one of the soldiers would mount the spotlight and flash it on the area where the enemy was hiding so our infantry would know where to shoot. This assignment was so dangerous that the soldier who mounted the spotlight might as well have said, "Hey, everyone hiding in the bushes! Here I am—take your best shot!"

That experience was similar to what it would have been like to be a member of the chariot brigade. You were wide open and vulnerable to the enemy forces, and the opposing army would let loose all of its arrows on you. Casualties were quite high, but one arrow did not usually bring a warrior down—these were tough soldiers. However, they would still bleed when hit. Consequently, they wore a scarlet-colored uniform to conceal the blood from their wounds. The soldiers in the opposing army might shake their heads, wondering if they were actually fighting against a god, exclaiming, "Hey, that guy has half a dozen arrows in him, and he is not even bleeding!"

Thus, scarlet also became known as a camouflage, a means of keeping the extent of your injuries concealed from onlookers. To me, this means that when God describes our destructive sins as being scarlet, He is saying that these sins are not always the obvious ones; they also include those that are concealed—our secret sins. Yet, even our hidden sins can be cleansed by Jesus's blood.

I find it very interesting that the writer of Isaiah carried along the warrior motif. The root of the Hebrew word translated as "*sins*" is *chata'* (חטא), which is an archer's term for "missing the mark or target." Those ancient charioteers would have had an even shorter lifespan if they had been unskilled archers and kept missing their targets. With reference to our sins, God has made provision for us in Christ so that, instead of continuing to miss the mark, we can be forgiven, receive His Spirit, and learn to love Him wholeheartedly as we stay on target with His Word.

The Accuser

> *"Then Satan answered the LORD, and said: Doth Job fear God for nought? Hast not thou made an hedge about him, and about his house, and about all that he hath on every side? thou hast blessed the work of his hands, and his substance is increased in the land."*
> —Job 1:9–10

Few things drive me to distraction faster than to listen to a discussion or teaching on the book of Job and then hear a concluding remark such as this: "But remember, God restored Job with twice as much as he had before." It makes it seem like if we go through a trial, we can be sure God will restore us twofold. The part about Job's restoration is actually an epilogue; it is not the moral of the story. The moral is found at the beginning of the book, in Job 1:9–10, not at the end.

Job's motivation for serving God wasn't that he was well paid by the Lord. To say that the message of the book of Job is that God will restore you financially and otherwise if you endure your suffering will only confirm the challenge in the story that was laid out by the enemy. Besides, did God resurrect Job's children, bring his trusted servants back to life, and erase Mrs. Job's grief over the loss of her sons and daughters? Job would trust God whether he was restored or not. That is the lesson of the book.

Serving God is no guarantee of material or physical restoration. The only guarantee is that we will be rewarded spiritually with the peace and presence of the Lord.

A Destructive Role

In the original Hebrew, the challenge concerning Job is laid out before God by a created spiritual being called *hasatan* (השטן), with the *ha* (ה) designating the definite article "the." The Greek Septuagint uses the word *diabolos*, which also includes a definite article, *hos*. Placing the definite article before a noun would suggest that it is not a proper noun or a name, but rather a description. Based on this, I'm not sure why translators insist on giving the enemy a proper name. It would appear that the writer of the book of Job did not intend to honor this being with an actual name. Translators, however, drop the article from the word and then transliterate it from the Hebrew, turning it into the proper name *Satan*.

In Hebrew, *hasatan* (השטן) simply means "the adversary." In Greek, the word *diabolos* simply means "a false accuser" or "a slanderer." However, the Semitic root word of *hasatan* (השטן) is *sata'*, which carries the idea of "sweeping away as by a flood of hate or persecution," or "sweeping away someone to cause them to go astray," "to scatter," or "to control."

If we were to give a name to the enemy, it would be *sata'*. As *sata'*, he is both accuser and executioner, while the name *hasatan* (השטן) limits his destructive role to that of an accuser. The enemy is called *hasatan* (השטן) in this passage to express the specific role he is playing here. Though it is not his only role, it is one of his most powerful ones.

The Enemy's Strategy

The enemy's accusation seemed to be well-founded. In Job 1:4, we learn that Job's sons "*feasted*" and invited their sisters to join in on their feasts. The Hebrew word that is rendered "*feasted*" is *misata'* (משתה). This is an obvious play on the word *sata'*. The "t" in *misata'* (משתה) is a taw (ת) rather than a teth (ט), yet the words are pronounced the same. The mem (מ) in front of *sata'* for *misata'* (משתה) would indicate an excess. The word itself means to eat and drink to excess or to become drunken. The mem (מ) indicates a flooding of destructive passion.

Job's sons and daughters were not using their father's wealth and prosperity to help humankind or further God's kingdom. They were using it to fill their own passions. They themselves did not offer any sacrifices for sins they may have committed; it was Job who had to offer the sacrifices. Note, too, that Job did not offer the sacrifices to express his love and devotion to God; he offered them in hopes that he could atone for the sins of his children and thus allow God to keep His hand of protection on them. (See Job 1:5.) Yet, due to the sins of Job's children, God could not keep His hand of protection on them to shield them from this *hasatan* (השטן), or accuser.

An accuser is one who points out the wrong of another and demands a punishment. This is such a fitting title for our chief enemy because he is the one chomping at the bit to carry out the execution. I found that the word *satan* in extra-biblical literature is actually used for an executioner. So, the enemy is setting himself up here as both accuser and executioner.

When Job said, *"The thing which I greatly feared is come upon me"* (Job 3:25), what "came upon him" was the loss of his children. He probably knew that one day his sons and daughters would have to pay the piper if they continued to sin against God. I can hear this *hasatan* (השטן) whisper in his ear, "It's entirely your fault, Job, old boy. You did not train your kids well to worship God, and now He can no longer protect them from me."

The enemy hoped to use a similar tactic to defeat Job, seeking to bring him to the point of cursing God. Yet, *hasatan* (השטן) could not look at the depths of Job's heart like God could. Thus, he thought he could destroy Job with his accusations. If the loss of his children would not break him, then the loss of all his wealth, in addition to extreme mental torment— helped along by Job's friends—should do the job. I imagine the accuser saying, "Job, think about it. Your children died and your wealth is gone because it was being used for excessive feasting and drunkenness. You're to blame, Job. You sinned, and you made God angry. Job, you are a bad person."

Defeating the Accuser

The enemy uses the same strategy today. We have a need, so we go to God to make our request, and what happens? The accuser steps up to the plate and says, "Well, well, just who do you think you are? Do you really expect God to hear your prayer when you have such lust, greed, intolerance, selfishness [you fill in the blank] in your heart? Do you really expect God to hear your prayer when you have been such a bad Christian?" In response, we scratch our heads and say, "You know, he's right." And he is—except for one thing. It is called the blood of Jesus Christ.

We allow the enemy to accuse us, but God knows us better than we know ourselves. If we could look into God's mind, we would see that He longs for us not to be filled with guilt and remorse, but rather to let His Son, who paid for all our mistakes, cover that guilt and remorse with His blood. When we receive God's forgiveness through Christ, we can turn around and point our finger at this accuser, this *hasatan* (השׂטן), and say, "Accuser and executioner, you are a deceiver; you are filling me with lies about what is going on in God's mind and heart. But because of the blood of Jesus Christ, I am no longer guilty of the things you accuse me of. I can make my requests known to God, and He will hear me."

The enemy hates to be reminded of the blood of Jesus because it exposes him for the liar that he is. It completely defeats any accusation he has against us. When the blood of Jesus Christ is applied to us, the enemy can no longer be *hasatan* (השׂטן). And we don't have to honor him with a proper name. We need to believe what the Scriptures teach us about the mind of God—that He loves us and stands ready to forgive us and free us from our guilt. If we know the mind of God, then the enemy cannot fill us with his lies and defeat us.

Study 50

A Song of Victory

"The LORD is my strength and song, and is become my salvation."
—Psalm 118:14

Years ago, I used to sing a little chorus based on this verse. My spirit was always quickened when I heard the words "the Lord is my song." Until recently, I never really stopped to consider what those words meant or why my spirit rejoiced when I heard that the Lord is my song. I am beginning to learn that my spirit seems to understand things long before my mind does. Frequently, my study of Scripture in the original languages allows my flesh to catch up with my spirit.

I often say that my studies in Hebrew are not revelational as much as confirmational. Many people who read my word studies do not tell me that I have given them any new revelation, but that the studies confirm what they have long believed in their spirits but could never really find any solid support for in Scripture. I usually find that scriptural support in the Hebrew. Thus, I approached the above verse knowing that the Spirit of God was trying to tell my spirit something and that in studying it in the Hebrew, I might learn what that was.

A Pruning Hook

My first step was to identify the Hebrew word for *"song"* using an interlinear Bible I found online. I discovered that there are many words for "song" in Hebrew, but the word translated *"song"* in this verse comes from the root word *zamar* (זמר). I then went to the *Brown-Driver-Briggs Hebrew and English Lexicon* (BDB), where I found an absolutely fascinating history of the word *zamar* (זמר) as I traced it through its Semitic origins. It means "a pruning hook."

Next, I spent some time on the Internet researching the history of the pruning hook. I found out that the meaning of the original word gradually evolved to signify a song because the pruning hook is shaped like a scythe. The curved blade was mounted on a pole for the purpose of cutting away the dead wood and branches of a tree. (Today's pruning instruments have changed little from ancient times.) Eventually, the pruning hook became a weapon used by Persian soldiers to pull enemy combatants off their horses.

You may be wondering what all this has to do with *song*. In my research, I discovered that a skilled farmer would swing his pruning instrument back and forth from branches to branches, and this would create sort of a rhythmic, whistling noise. Since the object of pruning is to cut away the bad and leave the good, this word came to be used to express a song of triumph, victory, and salvation from one's foes. Thus, *"the LORD is my strength and song"* of victory. This is a song declaring that the Lord has removed all the bad things from my life and left only that which is good, and He brings me to victory.

What Is Most Important?

Let us now study the word *zamar* (זמר) letter by letter. This method is solely to aid us in our mediation on the word; it is not a linguistic tool. By studying the letters, we will find something even more profound. The word *zamar* (זמר) is spelled zayin (ז), mem (מ), resh (ר). The zayin (ז) looks like a sword and does indeed signify a sword or weapon. The sages used to say that the zayin (ז) cuts away all that is really unimportant to us and leaves only that which is important. Thus, this *"song"* is a song of what is most essential to us. The psalmist is saying that his song is God; it is God who is most important in his life. The zayin (ז) cuts or prunes away all that is unimportant so that he can see what is important—the Lord.

So, what is this song that expresses what is vital to us? The next letter, mem (מ), represents water. It also represents the revealed knowledge of God. When you dive into the open sea, water completely surrounds you. Therefore, when you sing this song, it surrounds you with the revealed knowledge of God. This is not your traditional victory or fight song like "On Wisconsin." It is a song that speaks of God and His love, and in singing this song, you become completely surrounded by the presence of God, who is revealing Himself to you.

The last letter in *zamar* (זמר) is resh (ר), which comes to us with the convicting power of the Holy Spirit. It speaks of the Spirit's role in enlightening us to the things that need to be cut away or pruned from our lives so that we can see what is most important. Thus, the resh (ר) is about repentance, about turning away from our sins and whatever else keeps us from seeing what is really important to us, the chief of which is God.

When we sing this *zamar* (זמר), we are singing a song that surrounds us with the knowledge of God. When we see only Him, through repentance, we throw off all that keeps us from Him, and the "zayin" cuts it out of us, pruning us and leaving only our love for God.

God Alone

To conclude this study, let's look at the numerical value of *zamar* (זמר). The zayin (ז) equals 7, the mem (מ) equals 40, and the resh (ר) equals 200. The total value of the word *zamar* (זמר) is 247. The Hebrew word *mazaqaq* (מזקק) also has a numerical value of 247. As I mentioned in earlier studies, the sages teach that if two Hebrew words have the same numerical value, the Spirit of God may show you a relationship between them that will be of significant spiritual value. *Mazaqaq* (מזקק) means "to refine." When I sing or listen to a *zamar* (זמר), which for me is often a song of praise and worship, the Lord is performing a refining process in me, stripping or pruning away all that dross—everything that separates me from Him. And in my praise and worship, in my *zamar* (זמר), I am left with Him alone.

Study 51

God Is Jealous

*"For thou shalt worship no other god: for the LORD, whose name is
Jealous, is a jealous God."*
—Exodus 34:14

*"O beware, my lord, of jealousy! It is the green-eyed monster
which doth mock the meat it feeds on."*
—Shakespeare, *Othello*[11]

In Shakespeare's play *Othello*, the protagonist's servant, Iago, sought to
destroy his master by planting a seed of jealousy in his heart. Iago placed
a handkerchief belonging to Othello's wife, Desdemona, in the room of
Cassio, Othello's lieutenant. It was just a little thing, yet Iago knew that
"trifles light as air are to the jealous confirmations strong as proofs of holy
writ."[12] Just the thought that Desdemona was having an affair with his
trusted servant threw Othello into such a rage that he ended up murdering
his wife.

---

11. E. A. J. Honigmann, ed., *Othello*, The Arden Shakespeare, Richard Proudfoot, Ann
Thompson, and David Scott Kastan, gen. eds. (London: Thomas Learning, 2006), Act 3,
Scene 3, lines 167–169.
12. Ibid., lines 325–327.

Misdirected Passion

Actually, jealousy was generally considered a noble emotion to the Renaissance man. It showed how deeply he felt toward someone. To be jealous was a good thing because it demonstrated you were so passionate toward someone or something that, to defend your passion or honor, you would challenge someone to a duel and be willing to die over the matter. Such a passionate person was to be honored and trusted. Today, of course, we see this mind-set and behavior as misdirected passion.

In another play, *Hamlet*, Shakespeare challenges the notion that this type of jealousy is a noble emotion. Hamlet tells his close friend Horatio, "Give me that man that is not passion's slave, and I will wear him in my heart's core, ay, in my heart of heart, as I do thee."[13] Here the playwright takes a potshot at the conventions of his day. He is countering the idea that such an imprudent person is to be honored and respected by expressing that if we are to trust another person with the very center of our heart, it is best not to do so with someone who is a slave to his passion. The concept of jealousy started to lose its positive connotation about the time of Shakespeare, from which it evolved to mean something entirely negative today.

Shakespeare warned against the destructive nature of jealousy, and yet our study verse says that God's *"name is jealous,"* and He *"is a jealous God."* Does that somehow make Shakespeare more noble than God? The emotion of jealousy has resulted in murder and other wrongdoing known as "crimes of passion." Movie and television dramas are filled with plotlines featuring such crimes. Jealousy also causes much pain and terror among people. For example, women find themselves being stalked by jealous lovers, constantly living in fear for their lives. The courts are filled with divorce cases of wives and husbands seeking to exact revenge through high alimony settlements and child custody rights against spouses whose behavior caused them to be jealous.

What could jealousy possibly have to do with God, who is love? My study partner told me about a famous woman on television who said that when she heard God was a jealous God, it ended her belief in the God of

13. Jenkins, ed., *Hamlet*, Act 3, Scene 2, lines 71–74.

the Bible. She believes in a type of God, but not the deity described in the Scriptures. Actually, I don't blame her for feeling that way based on her understanding of this verse. Much of her career was built on interviewing people whose lives were destroyed by jealousy.

A Protective Jealousy

I would have a problem believing in a jealous God, too, if His jealousy were like what is described above. One definition of the English word *jealousy* is "jealous resentment against a rival, a person enjoying success or advantage." Our modern definition of jealousy is rooted in the idea of resentment. However, in our study verse, the Hebrew word translated "*jealous*," *quanna* (קנא), has a very different meaning.

There are actually two Hebrew words for jealousy: *quana* (קנא) and *quanna* (קנא). Both come from the same root, but there is a big difference between them. *Quana* (קנא) is a jealousy of envy and rage. This is the type of jealousy that caused Othello to become caught between the jaws of affection and anxiety, eventually leading to a tragic end. In contrast, *quanna* (קנא) is a protective jealousy. The word is sometimes translated as "zealous." Both of these words are rooted in an expression of deep passion. The Semitic root of *quanna* (קנא) is used to denote someone who experiences such deep emotion that their face turns red.

Today, to translate *quanna* (קנא) as *jealousy* is archaic because we no longer see this emotion as a badge of honor. Probably the best translation would be *passion*, in a purely noble or admirable sense. In English, the concept of passion still has a positive association. For example, it is passion that motivates someone to perform at their best. It is passion that causes a man to lay down his life to protect his wife and children. It is passion that drives a person to sacrifice everything for a worthy cause. And it is because of God's passion for us that He desires to give us the very best. This is the same passion that caused Jesus to sacrifice His life on our behalf.

"*For thou shalt worship no other god: for the* Lord, *whose name is Jealous, is a jealous God.*" What do you think motivates people to worship various false gods? I don't believe it is out of any real love or passion for their god. It is for the purpose of obtaining something for their personal and, often, selfish benefit. Presentations of offerings and expressions of praise and worship are given with the hope of winning such favor with the god that their prayer, wish, or desire will be granted.

God stands ready to grant our requests, but only if they are really a benefit to us at this time. He alone has a full perspective on our lives. And if He does grant them, it will be with no strings attached, unlike the case with false gods. God will grant the requests of His children out of love and passion, not because we "pay" Him with praise and worship.

An Everlasting Love

Thus, God's jealousy of us is a protective jealousy, and it is a jealousy that reacts against our worshipping something that will give us less that He can give. His heart is wounded if we worship another god, just as a wife's heart is deeply wounded and grieved if her husband adores another woman. What God has to offer is far greater than anything any other "god" has to offer. So, yes, God is a "jealous" God—not with the selfish type of jealousy, *quana* (קנא), but with the protective type, *quanna* (קנא). He says to us, "*Yea, I have loved thee with an everlasting love: therefore with lovingkindness have I drawn thee*" (Jeremiah 31:3).

"Forget Not All His Benefits"

"Bless the LORD, O my soul, and forget not all his benefits."
—Psalm 103:2

To be very honest, sometimes it is really hard to bless the Lord. The old soul can get knocked down, dragged out, and stomped upon, and the last thing it wants to do is praise God. It would just like to crawl under "yon rock from whence it came," lick its wounds, and feel sorry for itself.

Although they can't be certain, many commentators tend to think this was David's situation in Psalm 103. His soul was really beaten up. For one thing, his best friend had betrayed him. Even worse, his own son had plotted to overthrow him and had even succeeded in sending David fleeing from his throne, escaping with just a few trusted servants and followers into the wilderness. If all that wasn't bad enough, some Benjamite, a relative of the former king, Saul, started throwing rocks at him. (See 2 Samuel 15–16.)

David understood what it is like to have a tormented soul. It is really hard to grab hold of your soul and command it to praise the Lord when everything within you is suffering. Yet, David knew how to respond: he commanded his soul to remember all of God's *benefits.* Other translations say "His kind deeds," "all His rewards," or "all the good things He has done." The majority, however, stay with "benefits."

In our culture, when we hear the word *benefits*, we immediately think of employment benefits, such as health insurance, 401k retirement plans, and paid time off. Such benefits are not directly connected with the type of work employees do. They are incentives that employers give to recruit new personnel and keep current workers on board and happy. Yet, as I expressed in an earlier study, I didn't sign on with God for His "benefits." I signed on because He loved me and I wanted to love Him. That is why, for myself, I need to find a different English word than *benefits* to express the idea in Psalm 103:2.

God's Lovingkindness

The Hebrew word rendered *"benefits"* is *gimmel* (גמל), like the Hebrew letter that represents a camel. What does a camel have to do with benefits? In ancient times, a camel was a key to survival in the desert. *Gimmel* (גמל) has its origins in the Phoenician language and means "stopping," "weaning," "going without," and "repaying in like kind." It is used for a camel because of the animal's ability to go without food and water for a long time. The service of a camel will increase with the care that is given to it. It other words, if you take care of your camel, he will take care of you; he will "repay you in like kind."

Another meaning signified by the letter gimmel is "lovingkindness." This is an acceptable rendering of the word *gimmel* (גמל), and it is one I would choose when translating it. The letter itself is a picture of a man running to offer assistance to someone. Again, this is where I have a problem plugging in the word *benefits* for *gimmel* (גמל). As I mentioned earlier, employers give benefits to their employees as an incentive. They don't usually give them because they are filled with "lovingkindness" for those who work for them. Some may, but that is not the main motivation in providing them. They want something in return: a good day's work from their employees. If they don't receive this on a consistent basis, the employees can kiss their jobs—and those benefits—goodbye.

Nonetheless, if someone demonstrates lovingkindness, it will be chock-full of benefits. Only, these benefits will come from a heart of love and not a sense of obligation. Thus, in Psalm 103:2, David is saying, "And do not forget all of God's *lovingkindness.*"

Recently, the woman who directs the food pantry at my church told the congregation about a fifteen-year-old girl who came to volunteer one day. She had never seen this teenager before, so, after the work day ended, she asked her why she had come to help. The girl explained that when she was a small child, her father had had an accident on the job and become paralyzed. When she was ten years old, he passed away, leaving her mother alone to raise fourteen children. The mother developed health problems, including heart issues and a neck condition that left her paralyzed on one side.

This fifteen-year-old had faced amazing hardships growing up. Then, shortly before she volunteered at the food pantry, her best friend committed suicide. This traumatized her so much that she could not get out of bed for two weeks. Yet during this time of deep depression and despair, she remembered how, when she was a child, her aunt had taken her to the church to help out in the food pantry, and she remembered the love she felt there. So, she called the church and volunteered. The day she was scheduled to work, her ride fell through. However, she was determined to assist in the food pantry to help others in unfortunate situations, so she walked to the church—a half-hour trek.

In the midst of her despair, this young teenager thought about the benefits, or the lovingkindness, of God. And like the *gimmel* (גמל), she sought to return that kindness. As a result, God is healing her soul. If a girl living in the midst of circumstances that, to quote Thomas Paine, would "try men's souls" can turn to the lovingkindness of God and seek to return that lovingkindness, can't we do the same? We have the ability to begin the healing process of our souls today if we will do what David and this young teenager did and reach out for God's *gimmel* (גמל).

Healing for the Soul

Just this past week, there were events in my life that dragged my soul through the *"miry clay"* (Psalm 40:2). Yesterday, I met a couple who praised me for my writings and told me how much they were blessed by my work. Yet even that affirmation did not pull me out of the mud. In fact, I felt worse than ever—I felt like a big hypocrite. I cried out to the Lord, "Oh,

God, I am such a hypocrite. I don't deserve these good things. I am so sorry I failed You."

In the evening, I was going over my mailing list when I ran across the names of a husband and wife who ministered together as a team in the Chicago area. They had taken one of my Hebrew classes, but I had not spoken with them in three years. Oddly, I had their phone number tucked away, so I gave them a call to see how things were going, with the idea that we might reconnect. Sadly, I learned that the husband had passed away. My soul cried out for this widow who was left alone, struggling to keep the ministry going that she and her husband had started. This afternoon, I paid her a visit, and we shared together about the *gimmel* (גמל), the *benefits* or the *lovingkindness*, of God. Do you know what happened? I could actually feel my soul begin a healing process once again. As I reflected on the mind of God, which is filled with such lovingkindness, I repented of selfishness and a failure to recognize the *gimmel* (גמל) of God.

Is your soul battered and beaten down? Don't forget His *gimmel* (גמל), or His lovingkindness. Does your praise and worship seem insincere? Then do what David did: pick up your soul by the collar, slam it against the wall, and command it to think on all the *gimmel*s (גמל), or acts of lovingkindness, you have received from the Lord. What is going through God's mind is not your failures and your faults, but only His mercy, forgiveness, and *gimmel* (גמל)—His lovingkindness.

Study 53

He Will Not Slumber

"Behold, he that keepeth Israel shall neither slumber nor sleep."
—Psalm 121:4

Many years ago, I taught school in Arlington, Virginia, a county that borders Washington, D.C. I lived in a private room in a house with three other borders. One of them was an engineer working on the new rapid transit system for the District of Columbia, the second worked for the CIA (I never saw much of him, as he was always out of the country on "business"), and the third worked for the Secret Service in the White House. Whenever the Secret Service agent was off duty, he was usually sleeping. I asked him if he ever got drowsy while on duty guarding the White House, and he looked at me as if I had just sworn at him. Then, he replied, "If you were responsible for the life of the most important and powerful man in the world, would you get drowsy?" I had to think about that one. Being a teacher, I knew that if I did not keep my classes interesting, I would hear a wide variety of snoring coming from the students—and sometimes I did!

No matter how tired you become, if you are involved in an activity that is stimulating or absorbing, you will, under most circumstances, be able to overcome your drowsiness. At one point in my life, I worked a couple of jobs, and there was a time when I went more than forty hours without sleep but never once became drowsy because I was active the whole time. I also know what it is like to consistently get eight to ten hours of sleep and then sit in a boring classroom struggling to stay awake while dreaming of going back to my room to take a nap.

Asleep on the Job?

Some time ago, I worked the midnight shift as a security guard for a high-rise apartment building. At one point, I was very tired and fighting sleepiness. As I caught myself dosing, I began to think about the Secret Service agent's words: "If you were responsible for the life of the most important and powerful man in the world, would you get drowsy?" I was guarding a building filled with newscasters, soap opera actors, athletes, lawyers, physicians, and others. These were ordinary people who had achieved the ultimate success in their chosen fields, just as the president in the White House had achieved the ultimate success in politics. However, at the apartment building, while there might have been the possibility of a break-in, no one was gunning for the news anchor at Channel 9 or a soap opera character. Because there was practically zero threat, I found myself getting drowsy. But if my supervisor had given me notice that the newscaster had received a death threat due to an investigative news report she had given, and I was to be on alert for an armed assassin, I don't think I would have gotten very drowsy on that job!

This brings us to our study verse. On the surface, the fact that God neither slumbers nor sleeps for Israel indicates that He takes His job and the ongoing threat against those whom He deeply loves very seriously. The Hebrew word translated "*keepeth*" is *shamer* (שמר), which means "to guard" or "to watch over." The One who *guards* Israel will neither *slumber* nor *sleep*. The New Testament makes it clear that Gentiles who love God are brought under the umbrella of Israel. So, the One who guards Israel is guarding us. Again, this is a Guard who takes His job so seriously that He will always remain alert.

God's Attention Is Never Diverted from Us

The Hebrew word for "*slumber*" is *num* (נום), which means "to be drowsy" or "to sleep"—but to sleep lightly, such that you are easily awakened. Examining this word's built-in commentary, we discover that it is spelled nun (נ), vav (ו), (final form**) mem (ם). The nun (נ) suggests that the slumber comes from being blocked off or having your attention diverted. As I pass through the valleys of life, I know God is not sleeping, but sometimes I wonder if His attention is diverted from me, and in that moment, the enemy could jump in and get his grubby hands on me. This is not so, according to the word *num* (נום). The nun (נ) tells me that His attention is never diverted, even for a moment.

Next, the vav (ו) denotes a hook, or a dependency upon someone or something. Thus, the vav (ו) represents our connection to God from earth to heaven, from the flesh to the spiritual. If God never *nums* (נום), or slumbers, then He will never allow His connection with us to be severed by any distraction or diversion.

Finally—and I love this—the word for *"slumber"* ends with a mem (ם). The mem's "shadow," or negative connotation, depicts a drowning in destructive passion. God will never allow any destructive passion to separate us from His watch. No matter what God thinks or feels about our lifestyle or sins, that will not influence His watchful care over us.

In 1981, President Ronald Reagan was shot in an attempted assassination. When he was taken into the operating room, he looked up at his surgeons and said, "I hope you guys are Republicans." The surgeon replied something like, "Mr. President, right now, we are all Republicans." One time, I asked my Secret Service housemate if being a Republican had any effect on his guarding a president who was a Democrat. Did I ever regret asking that question, even as a joke! He let me know in no uncertain terms that politics had absolutely no bearing on his duties. This is exactly what the mem (ם) tells us: no sin or anything else we do will have a bearing on God's attentive care on our behalf.

I might fall deeply into sin, but because I have been cleansed by the blood of His Son Jesus Christ, God will still not *num* (נום), slumber, or let His attention be distracted from me. He will not sever His connection with me, nor will He allow my sin to affect His watchful care over me. After all, I have a big advantage with my divine Bodyguard that a president does not have with his bodyguards, who may disagree with his politics: my

Bodyguard died on the cross for any sins or adverse "politics" I might hold to. Come to think of it, a president, regardless of his politics, does have the same Bodyguard, if he wants Him. That mem (מ) belongs to him just as much as it does to me. All he has to do is ask for it.

By the way, *num* (נום) is in a jussive form here. This makes the word permissive, meaning that God will not allow Himself to slumber. Slumber sometimes sneaks up on us when we are doing a vital job. It may sneak up on a pilot flying a plane, a soldier on guard duty, or even a mother with her baby. But God will not permit that to happen on His watch. It will just never happen.

God Becomes Our Praise

"But thou art holy, O thou that inhabitest the praises of Israel."
—Psalm 22:3 (KJV)

"You are enthroned as the Holy One; you are the praise of Israel."
—Psalm 22:3 (NIV84)

"But thou dwellest in the holy place, the praise of Israel."
—Psalm 22:3 (DRA)

"And Thou [art] holy, Sitting—the Praise of Israel."
—Psalm 22:3 (YLT)

Psalm 22:3 in the King James Version is a favorite verse among those who seek a deeper worship of God. It is quoted during worship services in many churches. As believers feel the warm presence of God, someone is bound to say, "The Lord inhabits the praises of His people." This statement indicates that when we praise God, He steps into the middle of our worship session and, like a sponge, soaks it all up, and that this somehow empowers Him or induces Him to perform miracles. At least, that is how I always pictured it. Our praises are like fuel, and as soon as God reaches a certain level of "praise fuel," He is off and running with the miracles.

Actually, I believe the majority of Christians could not identify where this statement about the Lord "inhabiting the praises of His people" is found in the Bible. Most likely, few have ever looked up the verse to make sure it is being quoted correctly, and even fewer have ever really studied the verse. Tragically, fewer still have ever looked into the depths of this verse for its deeper treasure.

I am convinced that even with all the Bibles people own or that are available to them in this nation, and with all the Bible teachings they have access to through books, the broadcast media, the Internet, and their own churches, most Christians remain biblically illiterate. Many read books *about* the Bible but never really read the Bible itself. Generally, people are content to believe that if the preachers quote a verse or passage, then it must be found in the Bible exactly as they quote it.

Before World War II, the average person rarely traveled one hundred miles from the place they were born. Christian radio was in its infancy, there were significantly fewer Christian books than there are today, and the Christian bookstore boom was decades away. There were no TVs, DVDs, CDs, or Internet streaming. The sum of a person's knowledge of the Bible was from Sunday morning sermons, Sunday School lessons, and messages from occasional visiting evangelists. Although we live in an age of mass communications where much more information is accessible, this approach of merely accepting a preacher's take on a passage hasn't really changed much.

On top of this, with all the various types of media available, many Bible preachers and teachers are scrambling to come up with new and different spiritual concepts to keep or gain an audience. They struggle to present something that people have not already heard. Then, someone happens to come up with a really catchy phrase, such as "The Lord inhabits the praises of His people," and suddenly it goes viral. Songs are written about it, preachers repeat the theme on radio and television, and before long, many local pastors are repeating it from the pulpit. It quickly filters down to home Bible studies where people begin saying, "The Lord inhabits the praise of His people" as if they were on the cutting edge of this worship business. Soon everyone is talking about it, but they most likely heard it from someone who heard it from someone who heard it from someone....

Again, no one really opens their Bibles to study the original verse, and as a result, people just skim the surface of this portion of Scripture and never find the rich and beautiful picture found in it.

God Opens His Mind and Heart to Us

There are a number of translations of Psalm 22:3, all of which give their own perspective on it. As you can see from the various renderings at the beginning of this study, there is a difference of opinion over the proper syntax in this verse. Does God inhabit the praises of His people, or is *He* the praises of His people? Actually, our knowledge of Hebrew syntax has increased tremendously since the King James Version was translated, and most modern translations reflect the latter idea.

Nevertheless, of the hundreds of times I have heard this verse quoted, I don't think I have ever heard it quoted correctly. It does not say "His people"; it says *"Israel."* This difference is important because it reveals the context. The background is that David is in the midst of a great national crisis. He is calling out to God, and the nations are laughing at him for trusting in the Lord rather than in human strength. We must also not lose sight of the fact that this psalm prophesies of the coming of Jesus, and Jesus is the praise of Israel, as I will shortly discuss.

Additionally, these passages have a special meaning for us individually. When David says that God "sits" or is "enthroned" in Israel, it is a reference to the temple or tabernacle where the ark of the covenant resided. The Hebrew word here is *yesav* (ישׁב), which means "to inhabit," "to settle," "to sit," and similar terms. In its Semitic root, it is a picture of the place where a king would sit to delegate his power, will, knowledge, and rule. The Bible is clear that God is omnipresent; He is everywhere. However, it was in Israel where the *Shechinah* (שׁחינה) glory rested.

Today, our bodies are the temple of God. (See 1 Corinthians 3:16.) As believers who have received Jesus as our Savior, God always inhabits our praises. Of course, He inhabits us when we don't praise, as well. He has said He will never leave us or forsake us. (See, for example, Hebrews 13:5.) If God dwells within us, this means that His very mind and heart dwell within us. Our praise and worship do not summon Him, but they do open up His mind and heart to us. And when that happens, we experience that "warm and fuzzy" feeling.

A devoted husband and wife can feel close to one another even when they are separated geographically. However, when they are together and hold each other, with their minds upon one another and not upon the events of the world, then they, too, feel that warm, fuzzy feeling. Why? It is a time when each is sharing their deepest thoughts, their mind and heart, with their beloved.

I once had a student who got married during summer break. In the fall, when I asked him what married life was like, he said, "When things are not going right at work and I come home feeling discouraged, my wife puts her arms around me, we share the events of the day together—the good and the bad—and then she says, 'It's okay.' You know what? It *is* okay."

God is always with us because He dwells within us. When we praise and worship Him, we let Him hug us as we share our cares with Him. Then, He whispers to us, "It's okay." And you know what? It is okay. Based upon my personal experience with this, I have a little problem when a worship leader encourages us to praise the Lord for the reason that "He inhabits our praise." I just can't believe I am using my praise to summon the presence of God. My praise is the *result* of His habitation within my heart.

Devoting Our Lives to God

Note carefully how Psalm 22:3 begins in the King James Version: "*Thou art holy.*" The Hebrew word translated "*holy*" is qodesh (קְדֹשׁ), which means to be separate and sacred. However, it is also the word used for a sacred prostitute, one who is devoted to prostitution in honor of idols. The Rahab mentioned in the book of Joshua was such a prostitute. I have seen enough Hollywood movies to know that the authorities don't have much respect for street prostitutes. In fact, they will kick their door down and come marching in without an invite. However, when the king of Jericho got word that Rahab might be sheltering Hebrew spies, he sent messengers who knocked at her door and politely asked about the spies. She openly admitted that the men had been in her house. Then, Rahab told the messengers some bold-faced lies: she said that she hadn't known who the men were and that they had already left the city. If the officials hurried, they could catch up with them. In reality, after changing her allegiance to the God of the Hebrews, Rahab had hidden the spies and provided for their escape, asking them to spare her and her family when the city fell to the Israelites.

The king's messengers appeared to show surprising respect for Rahab, and they believed her big lies without so much as a question. This seems to indicate she was more than just a street prostitute or the owner of a brothel. She was apparently a woman of some influence. In fact, historical evidence shows that she was most likely a priestess or high priestess living in the elite section of the city. As a high priestess, she would offer herself sexually as a holy or sacred prostitute of the goddess whom the people worshipped. This intimate relationship was intended as an act of worship in order to draw close to the goddess with the hope of winning some favor with her.

Thus, *qodesh* (קדשׁ), or "holy," means more than just the idea of separate and sacred; it signifies a separation to devote one's life to a deity. In our case, we devote our lives to the one true God, Jehovah. And this is what Rahab ended up doing. The spies from Israel granted her request, and she and her family were spared to join God's people in the promised land. Furthermore, Rahab eventually became the ancestor of King David.

For the above reasons, I cannot help but see Psalm 22:3 as a messianic reference to Christ, giving a picture of Jesus as *qodesh* (קדשׁ), or *holy*. Spiritually, He is the One with whom we are intimate, and in that intimacy, we are drawn closer to the Father. Accordingly, when Jesus dwells within us, *He becomes our praise*. The Lord is "the Praise of Chaim Bentorah" and "the Praise of [insert your name]." The root word for the Hebrew word translated *"praises"* is *halal* (הלל), which means "to shine." When we say "Hallelujah," or "Praise the Lord," we are also saying, "Lord, shine in us. Let the world see You and not us."

So we come full circle. Yes, the Lord does inhabit the praises of His people. However, what this means is that, when we praise and worship Him, sharing His mind and heart, the world can see God—His light and His power—in us.

Study 55

In All Our Heart

*"But if from thence thou shalt seek the L*ORD *thy God, thou shalt find
him, if thou seek him with all thy heart and with all thy soul."*
—Deuteronomy 4:29

My study partner pointed out that Orthodox Jews render the preposition *"with all thy heart"* as **"in** all thy heart." That is curious. Does it really make a difference if you render the preposition as *in* instead of *with*?

I had never really looked closely at Deuteronomy 4:29, although I used this verse all the time. In the phrase *"with all thy heart and with all thy soul,"* the preposition *with* is not really there in the Hebrew. In front of the words translated as *"all"* is the letter beth (ב). Beth (ב) is normally rendered as "in" or "on." It is not unheard of to render a beth (ב) as "with," and the ambiguous nature of the Hebrew language will allow you to do that. However, normally, you would use the word *amam* (אממ) if you wanted to say "with." Still, every English translation I have read uses "with." Yet, the Jews, the people of the Old Testament and the guardians and masters of the Hebrew language, tend to use "in" rather than "with." What should we do with this information?

Searching our Heart and Soul

As I read the verse again, I found that using the word "in" tends to fit much better than "with." Just between God, you, and me, "with" just does not seem right. To render this as *"with all thy heart"* would seem to imply that you are searching for God outside of your heart—in nature, in sermons, in pictures, and so forth. Yet, to say we search for Him "in" all our heart would mean that our search occurs in our very own heart, where God resides.

My study partner also pointed out that there are many rooms to our heart. When we search for God in each one of these rooms, we acknowledge that He occupies all of them. Note, too, that we must search for Him "in all our soul." If we go through a financial, health, or personal crisis, we often experience anxiety and fear. In such situations, we must search our heart and soul to find God, because He is there, in control, working in every event of our lives. He is in all our situations. Rather than sit back and moan and groan about our lives, we must visit the rooms in our heart and the areas in our soul and find God there.

When the Israelites were in the wilderness for forty years, they faced many trials. They were hungry and thirsty. They endured brutal desert storms and other hardships. They contended with hostile armies. In these situations, they had a choice: they could sit around and bellyache about their circumstances or they could search for God *in* all their hearts and *in* all their souls. In that way, they would find God *in* the midst of all their hardships. Unfortunately, most of the time, the majority of the Israelites chose to complain.

I believe what God is saying in Deuteronomy 4:29 is that when we go through personal trials and hardships—and when we hear in the news about terrible happenings like carjackings and mass shootings and wonder if something like that will happen to us—we begin to question why God isn't doing anything to stop these tragedies. Why is He silent? It is during those times when we should look at our heart and soul very carefully, and we will find God right there, working away at whatever project He has going on within us.

Our heart is like the Dan Ryan Expressway in Chicago—it is always under construction. Most of the time, I have no idea what type of work is being done on the expressway. Sometimes, two of four lanes are closed, although I don't see any construction workers there. For no apparent reason,

I find myself moving at a snail's pace in bumper-to-bumper traffic. But, of course, there is a reason for the lanes being shut down; there is always a reason. Similarly, you know God is in your heart, but you sure don't see any work going on. It might seem as if your world is crashing down around you, prompting you to scream, "God, where are You?" Once again, at such times, you need to search your heart. You may find God in your recreation room or study room, doing some renovations. To you, it might seem like your world is falling apart, but God is just doing some remodeling.

When Pharaoh questioned Moses about why he should free God's people from slavery, he asked, *"Who is the LORD, that I should obey his voice to let Israel go? I know not the LORD, neither will I let Israel go"* (Exodus 5:2). Pharaoh knew all about the Hebrew God, but when he said that he didn't *"know"* Jehovah, he used the word *yada'* (ידע), which indicated that he had no relationship with Jehovah, so why should he obey Him? Moses and Aaron's reply is interesting: *"The God of the Hebrews hath met with us"* (Exodus 5:3). The Hebrew word translated *"met"* is *qara* (קרא), which means "to call out." But the next word is *alenu* (עלינו), which denotes "within us" not "with us." Moses and Aaron's response was that God Jehovah is not a God whom we worship in order to get things. He is a God who lives inside us and is a vital part of our lives.

Many Christians talk about how God did not dwell within people during Old Testament times, and how Jews do not believe God dwells with them. They point out that God did not live within people until Jesus breathed on His disciples to receive the Holy Spirit, and the Spirit descended at Pentecost. Although I understand what they are saying, I have to ask the following questions: Why do we have a Hebrew word like *alenu* (עלינו), which seems to indicate that God dwelled within Moses and Aaron? Why do the Orthodox Jews say *"in* all our heart" rather than *"with* all our heart"? And why do our translators insist on using the word *with*? Perhaps the Jews believe God lives within human beings more than we Christians do.

God's Got Our Backs

Returning to the incident with old Pharaoh, when he said that he didn't know the Lord, he was essentially saying, "My gods give me the sun, food, and wealth. What has your God ever done for me?" Pharaoh served his gods because they paid him well. Moses's answer was, "Jehovah 'calls out' within us—He lives *within* His people. Do your gods live within you, Pharaoh? Hmmm?" As I've expressed in studies throughout this book, serving God Jehovah is not about getting things. It is about Him living inside of us. It is about God being involved in every event and circumstance of our lives. Our God is with us every moment, every second, of every day.

Therefore, the major difference between our God and the other "gods" in this world is that our God lives inside our hearts. He is not a God off in the distance who grants us little favors if we behave and give Him offerings. He lives in us and through us, and in all things that happen in our lives, big or small, He is playing an active role. Even if our ship sinks, He is right there treading water with us. I find many Christians living as if God were like some pagan deity, dwelling at a distance. But rest assured, no matter what, He's got our backs!

> *For from Him and through Him and to Him are all things. To Him be the glory forever. Amen.* (Romans 11:36 NASB)

Study 56

Consumed

"For we are consumed by thine anger,
and by thy wrath are we troubled."
—Psalm 90:7

In the above verse, it would seem that the psalmist is bemoaning the fact that life is short, and the reason for it is that man is consumed by the anger and wrath of God. In reading the first six verses of this psalm, however, I really don't get the idea of melancholy due to the shortness of life. In fact, I really believe this is a very upbeat passage, even though, the way it is translated, it makes it sound as if we live our lives under the watch of an angry, wrathful God.

My study partner pointed out that the Hebrew word rendered *"consumed"* could come from two possible roots. It is written in the text as *kalinu* (כלינו), with the third person plural pronominal ending *nu* (נו). This leaves the question as to whether the root word is *kalal* (כלל) or *kalah* (כלה). Most translators agree that the root word is *kalah* (כלה), which has a wide range of meanings. It could mean "consume," but in its Semitic origins, it has the idea of "completion" or "to bring to an end." It could also mean "to destroy," "to ruin," "to waste," or "to cause to vanish." Additionally, it can refer to the kidneys or the secret parts of one's body. Furthermore, it is the word for a bride, with the idea that when a man takes a bride, he is bringing an end to his life as a single person and beginning a new life joined with another. Thus, *kalah* (כלה) can also signify an intimate, loving relationship.

What about the other possible origin of *kalinu* (כלינו)? The root word *kalal* (כלל) refers to the whole or fullness of something, to become complete or finished. As the old saying goes, "A man is not complete until he has a mate; then he is finished." (Hopefully, you will understand that *finished* here affirms that completeness!)

A Longing for Intimacy

My study partner decided to incorporate the many possible meanings for *kalah* (כלה). She considered first the idea of looking at this passage through the eyes of a bride—in other words, through the eyes of one who has a loving, intimate relationship with God—and this will be the focus of our study.

From a bride's perspective, it is difficult to render the Hebrew word whose root is *'aneph* (אנף) as "*anger*." Even if we do, we see it in a much different light. Because of the love a bride has for her bridegroom, she is constantly in a state of stress or agitation over the possibility of offending her beloved. This causes the "kidneys," or inner parts, of her body to be upset. As we have discussed in previous studies, the word *'aneph* (אנף) does not have to mean "anger." It is merely an expression of great emotion. We have seen that the Semitic root of *'aneph* (אנף) comes from the snorting of a camel. A camel can snort when it is angry, frustrated, grieving, or in heat (that is, desirous of an intimate relationship).

Therefore, we would not be incorrect to read this verse as, "We are consumed by Your desire for intimacy." Here we have a beautiful, and rather nontraditional, picture from Psalm 90. It does not depict the psalmist bemoaning the fact that his life has been shortened because of God's anger. Rather, it portrays him viewing life's brevity as merely a short betrothal period in which to await the wedding and consummation of the marriage in heaven, where the bride will enter the house of the Bridegroom's Father to live there forever. This period of waiting for the consummation (which occurs at life's end) is creating an anxiousness in the *kalah* (כלה), or bride, and this anxiousness is only aroused by the bridegroom's *'aneph* (אנף), or longing for intimacy.

This perspective follows nicely into the next phrase, which is translated, *"By thy wrath are we troubled."* There are many possible renderings for the word *chemah* (חמה) beyond just "wrath," as explained in study 6, "A Lover's Quarrel?" *Chemah* (חמה) is derived from the Semitic root word *yacham* (יחם), which means "to be feverish" or "to be hot," in the sense of sexual arousal. That would go hand in hand with one of the root meanings of *'aneph* (אנף), a longing for intimacy.

We could then read this verse as the following: "I am consumed by Your desire for intimacy, and Your feverish desire for such an intimacy is troubling." The Hebrew word translated *"troubled,"* is *bahal* (בהל), which means "to make haste," "to be alarmed," or "to be in a hurry." Thus, we could interpret this passage in a more positive light. Rather than *"by thy wrath are we troubled,"* it would be, "By Your feverish passion for intimacy, we are in a hurry (to consummate our marriage)."

Consummation of the Marriage

In study 26, "Betrothed to Jesus," we talked about the betrothal period in ancient Hebrew culture. The couple were joined in marriage, and many times, it was during the marriage ceremony that they were first introduced. That is why, although they were married, there was an "engagement" period of about a year in which they did not have any sexual relationship. During that year, the bridegroom did not work at a vocation but was busy building an addition onto his father's house, as well as spending as much time as possible with his bride. They would go off alone and share their desires and longings with one another. They would dream of a future together, and after a year, the sexual tension between the two would grow until the groom could not stand to be separated from his bride any longer. Everyone around knew the bridegroom was getting *bahal* (בהל), feverish, and they anxiously awaited the night when the bridegroom would go to the house of his betrothed, snatch her away, and take her to his father's house.

Of course, the whole community had been waiting for this moment, and so they followed the groom on his way to the bride's house. They had prepared a big festival to enjoy the occasion while the bride and groom went off alone to consummate the marriage. There was even a big celebration like a toast when it was announced that the marriage had been consummated.

Looking at our study verse and indeed the whole of Psalm 90 through the eyes of a *kalah* (כלה), we can see a picture of a bride during her betrothal period, representing a believer during their time on earth, anxiously awaiting the consummation of their union with Jesus. It is but a short time, a short wait. The days of our life are numbered (see Psalm 90:12), the consummation of our marriage with Jesus is fast approaching, and we feel *kalal* (כלל), or a longing to be complete in Him. We experience *yacham* (יחם)—a passion to enter the house of the Father forever.

Study 57

Power

> *"Who knoweth the power of thine anger?*
> *even according to thy fear, so is thy wrath."*
> —Psalm 90:11

As in the previous study from Psalm 90, we will consider the above verse through the eyes of a new bride and will again render the word *'aneph* (אנף), translated as *"anger,"* as a desire for intimacy. Thus, we would read this verse as, "Who knows the power of Your desire for intimacy?"

The word rendered *"knoweth"* is *yada'* (ידע), which we have learned is an intimate knowing. My study partner studied this word using the meaning behind its letters to aid in her meditation. She found that the yod (י) represents the Spirit of God, the daleth (ד) signifies a doorway, and the ayin (ע) denotes the eyes of God. Thus, the Spirit of God opens a doorway for us to see through His eyes. Only through God's eyes are we able to view the power or strength of His desire to be intimate with us.

The Power of God's Desire

People spend their lives attempting to win favor with God, trying to be reassured that they are good enough to go to heaven. Yet they fail to realize that God wants them a million times more than they want Him. He sent His Son to earth to die for us, to provide a means by which we could be purified to be His bride. He has already proposed to us, and all we have to do is to say yes. Can we even fathom such a desire or the power of that desire?

The Hebrew word translated *"power"* in Psalm 90:11 is *'oz* (עז). The first letter is ayin (ע), representing spiritual seeing and insight, and the second is zayin (ז), signifying a weapon. Having spiritual insight into the power or strength of God's desire for intimacy with us is a potent weapon when doubt enters our lives. If we only had *'oz* (עז), the weapon of insight into God's desire for intimacy with us, we would never need to fear, because we would know that God will truly protect us, lead us, and guide us to our future home with Him.

The word *'oz* (עז) comes from the root word *'ozaz* (עזז), among whose meanings is "strengthen (oneself)" and "be strong." *'Ozaz* (עזז) is also the root word for the name *Uzziah* (עזיהו). King Uzziah became ruler of Judah at the age of sixteen and reigned between 783–742 BC. His reign was one of the most prosperous besides that of Jehoshaphat since the reign of Solomon. He conquered the Philistines and the Arabians and received tribute from the Ammonites. He was a powerful, strong *ozaz* (עזז) ruler; hence his name *Uzziah* (עזיהו), meaning "Jehovah is my strength." King Uzziah knew the power or strength of the *'aneph* (אנף) of God. We could say this means either the power of God's anger or the power of His desire for intimacy. I believe it is in keeping with the passionate love of God to say it is the power of His desire for intimacy.

An Outpouring of Love

The phrase *"even according to thy fear"* can be very puzzling if we think of fear in our modern sense, which is a concern for one's safety and well-being. Yet the Hebrew word translated *"fear"* is *yara'* (ירא), which comes from the same root as the word *Torah*, meaning "law" or "instruction." *Yara'* (ירא) is also used in the sense of showing respect and reverence. Thus, Psalm 90:11 might read, "Who can be intimate with the power of or insight into God's desire for intimacy with us, according to our reverence for the Word of God and His wrath?"

We should note that the Hebrew word translated *"wrath"* here is different from that rendered *"wrath"* in verse 7 in our previous study. In this verse, it is the word *'ebrah* (עברה), which signifies an outpouring or overflowing. Only the translator's interpretation of the context leads to using the word *"wrath."* In the context that I see here, I would use the word *overwhelming* or *outpouring.* Therefore, we could read this as, "Who can be intimate with the power of or insight into God's desire for intimacy with us, according to our reverence for the Word of God and His outpouring (of love)?"

When we have this insight into God's powerful love for us, we are enabled to fulfill His purposes and plans for our lives—and He establishes the work of our hands. (See Psalm 90:12–17.)

Rejoice with Trembling

"Serve the LORD with fear, and rejoice with trembling."
—Psalm 2:11

If we take this verse out of context, what we have is a dire warning that we must serve God out of fear that He might harm us, and then, even if there is rejoicing, we must do so as we tremble with fear.

I once saw a picture of Jesus holding hands with a group of children as they danced in a circle together. If I had to choose one word to describe that picture, it would be *joy*. Many Christians seem to picture God as a grumpy old man, sitting on a throne in the sky, with bolts of lightning in His hands that He tosses down on His misbehaving children. Yet, Scripture paints a different picture of Him—He is a God of joy who loves to rejoice with His children.

When Christians come together to praise and worship God with singing and dancing, I can't believe that God is looking down from heaven and saying, "Hey, angels, get a load of this. That old Charlie, I didn't put an ounce of rhythm in his body, but there he is, trying to dance. What a sight!" I like to think He is right there with old Charlie dancing the night away. I believe God is the life of the party. He laughs, He sings, and He loves to give everyone a hug. I mean, even an old Aspie like me enjoys His hugs. His embraces are filled with joy, which He loves to share.

Hebrew Words for "Joy"

There are over fifteen words in Hebrew for "rejoice" or "joy." How many words do we have in English for this emotion? Perhaps only one or two other words that express a similar idea. Yet, as I stated previously, whatever is important in a culture is reflected in its language. Perhaps joy is just not very important in our culture.

Here are some of the Hebrew words for "joy" or "rejoice" that reflect various types of joy:

- *simchah* (שמחה): the joy of the Lord

- *samach* (שׂנח): joy in performing religious ceremony

- *shamerch* (שמדח): joy that is expressed outwardly

- *sus* (שׂוש): an inward feeling of joy, not expressed

- *sachaq* (שׂחק): joy that comes from playing

- *tsahal* (צהל): joy in the success of someone else

- *alats* (עלץ): joy in victory

- *chadah* (חדה): the renewal of joy

- *masos* (משׂוש): joy in being with friends or family

- *ranah* (רנה): shouting for joy

- *gil* (גיל): joy expressed by spinning around in a circle

In Psalm 2:11, where it says we are to *"rejoice with trembling,"* which word for "rejoice" or "joy" does the psalmist use? It is *gil* (גיל). I believe the author of this psalm was David, who seemed to love spinning around in a circle. (See, for example, 2 Samuel 6:14, where the Hebrew word for *"danced"* indicates "to whirl.")

Actually, the word *gil* (גיל) is also used to denote "generations." It suggests the idea of "moving around in a circle": the young become old, and the old die off as the next generation of young people take over, and then that generation becomes old, and the cycle continues. Perhaps David is saying we should approach old age with trembling? I don't think so.

In the Presence of Awesome Beauty

The Hebrew word translated "trembling" is *bire'adah* (ברעדה). The Semitic origin of the term is the word *ra* (ר). In Hebrew, there are about ten different words with a Semitic root of *ra* (ר), which is the basic word for "evil." However, *ra* (ר) does not necessarily have to signify something bad. The Semitic concept of this word is an outside influence that causes us to react in a certain way in which we have little or no control over our actions.

The particular *ra* [ר] word connected with *bire'adah* (ברעדה) is *ra'ad* (רעד). It does, indeed, mean "to tremble," but this trembling is the result of being in awe. The source of the awe could be either positive or negative. For example, we might be in awe of the strength and power of an invading army. But the word in Psalm 2:11 is in a feminine form. The sages suggest that this is a trembling that occurs when a person is in the presence of something with awesome beauty. It is so beautiful that you actually begin to quake in response.

The best illustration I can think of for *"rejoice with trembling"* is the opening scene of the movie The *Sound of Music*, where actress Julie Andrews, playing Maria, sings the opening score while spinning around on the top of an Austrian mountain. I believe this is similar to what David did when he was a shepherd alone with his sheep. I imagine him so taken with the beauty of God's creation that he would spin around in the midst of that beauty, praising the Lord.

Shall We Dance?

Let's now turn to the context of Psalm 2:11. David is speaking to kings and judges. (See verse 10.) He is addressing leaders, people who have great responsibility, just as a pastor has great responsibility for the well-being of the members of his congregation. David is saying to these leaders, "*Serve the* LORD *with fear."* The Hebrew word translated "*fear*" is *yara'* (ירא), which signifies a fear for the welfare of someone or something other than yourself. In other words, serve the Lord with the reverent fear that you might do something that would offend Him or wound His heart. Yet, while you are concentrating on protecting God's heart, take time to go to the mountains alone and bask in the beauty of His creation; just spin around like a little child, praising Him.

Julie Andrews' character in *The Sound of Music* was always getting into trouble with the convent because she would neglect her religious duties to go off to the mountains and *"rejoice with trembling."* Many Christians are very good at fulfilling the first part of this verse: they fear God. In fact, they exhaust themselves in performing their religious duties in order to protect the heart of God and bring joy and pleasure to Him. However, they totally overlook the message of the second part of the verse, which instructs them to *"rejoice with trembling."* They never think about going off alone into God's creation, absorbing the awe and beauty of what He has made, and then just spinning around like a little child, rejoicing and dancing with Him. You should know that God desires dance partners—and you don't have to worry about stepping on His toes!

Too many of us are great Cinderellas, spending all our time serving others and scrubbing the cinders off the walls and floors while our Prince is standing at the door, saying, "Forget trying to clean all that soot for a while. Come over to My palace and let's dance!" Of course, Jesus wants us to bring the message of His love and the cleansing power of His blood to other people. But He also wants us to put down our "scrubbing tools" and take a little time to just dance with Him. Our dancing and rejoicing with Jesus in the beauty of His creation brings just as much joy to Him— perhaps more—as the work we do for Him.

Study 59

Kiss the Son

"Kiss the Son, lest he be angry, and ye perish from the way,
when his wrath is kindled but a little.
Blessed are all they that put their trust in him."
—Psalm 2:12

Most Christians automatically assume that *"the Son"* is a reference to Jesus. In fact, most modern English translations of the Bible render the word *bar* (בר) as *"Son,"* with a capital S. The only English translation I found that does not render this word as "Son" is the JPS Tanakh 1917, the Jewish translation, for obvious reasons.

However, here is the problem with the common translation. In Hebrew, the word for "son" is *ben* (בן). Only in Aramaic is the word *bar* (בר) used as son. This passage was written in Hebrew, so why suddenly insert an Aramaic word? It is true that Aramaic words do occasionally show up in the Hebrew text as borrowed terms, but I see no reason to insert an Aramaic meaning in this case. In fact, the context becomes really confusing when we say that *bar* (בר) is an Aramaic word in this passage and we translate it as "Son." The flow is much clearer if we consider *bar* (בר) to be a Hebrew word, the meaning of which is "purity."

In all fairness, using the word "Son" and capitalizing it to imply a reference to Jesus has some basis. For one thing, although there is no superscription attributing this psalm to David as its author, Acts 4:24–26 suggests that it was written by him. This would follow the teaching of the Talmud in Sukkah 52a that the Messiah would descend from the line of David.

Genesis Rabbah, a commentary by ancient Jewish rabbis, teaches in 44:8 that there were three persons who were bidden by God to ask Him for something: The first was Solomon, who was instructed to request what he wanted God to give him. (See 1 Kings 3:4–15.) The second was Ahaz, who was invited to ask for a sign. (See Isaiah 7:1–14.) And the third was the Messiah, to whom God says, "*Ask of me, and I shall give thee the heathen for thine inheritance, and the uttermost parts of the earth for thy possession*" (Psalm 2:8).

Thus, even Jewish tradition teaches this psalm in a messianic context. On this basis, Christians may legitimately assume that the word *bar* (בר) is Aramaic and correctly render it as "Son" with a capital S, implying that we are to kiss the Son of God—Jesus.

I'm okay with this interpretation, except the idea that Jesus will become angry with us and we will perish if we don't kiss Him is a little unnerving to me. Our salvation has nothing to do with "kissing" Jesus. Additionally, Jesus threatening us to submit to Him doesn't fit His character.

Offering Submission and Loyalty

The Hebrew word translated "*kiss*" is *nashaq* (נשׁק), which is derived from an old Akkadian word that signifies a voluntary joining together or a desire to be joined together. The rendering of the word as "kiss" in Hebrew is really a later, postexilic use of *nashaq* (נשׁק), which carried the idea of joining two lips together or putting the lips to a cheek. Kissing was and is a romantic gesture as well as a gesture of submission and loyalty, such as a subject would give to a sovereign. Sometimes, it is both.

At the end of a wedding ceremony, the preacher tells the groom, "You may now kiss the bride." Note that he does not tell the bride to kiss the groom, or simply tell the couple they may kiss one another. The preacher is telling the groom that he will submit and be loyal to his bride. Even though the groom will be given the headship of the family, he is still promising his bride that he will submit to her feelings, to the cry of her heart, and will protect those feelings by being loyal to her. He is promising to give her and the desires of her heart priority in any decision he makes.

Thus, *"kiss the Son"* may mean to submit to Jesus and be loyal to Him. I am great with that interpretation, too, except I don't like the idea that God has to follow up this comment with a threat: *"lest...ye perish."* When a groom is told to kiss his bride, there is no threat associated with that. He is submitting to the feelings of her heart out of love, not out of the fear of some threat.

Expressing a Passion and Desire for Jesus

Let's return to the fact that *"kiss"* is a postexilic rendering of *nashaq* (נשׁק), because it leads to a difficulty. If the New Testament attributes Psalm 2 to David, then the use of *nashaq* (נשׁק) as "kiss" postdates David's time. Thus, we should revert to the original use of the word, which is a voluntary joining together. The word *nashaq* (נשׁק) is in a piel (intensive), imperative (command) form. My study partner expressed it as "setting ablaze your desire to know Him." If we follow this with the word "Son," it pretty well follows the traditional interpretation of "kiss the Son" as a sign of both submission and love. Since "kiss" is in an intensive form, it would indicate a kiss of desire. Thus, this is not a command to kiss in order to show respect and submission, but rather a command to express your passion and desire for Jesus.

Having Pure Motives of Love

Then we have the problem of the word *"Son."* Do we really accept *bar* (בר) as an Aramaic word for "son," or do we use the Hebrew meaning of "purity"? I think purity fits the context just as well or better. We are commanded to kiss God, or to embrace or desire purity in our relationship with Him. Not only does this fit the context, but it also presents a fundamental motivation for all Christians. Is our motivation to follow and serve Jesus based upon a threat, or is it based upon our desire to know Him in purity, with pure motives of love?

God's Distress over Our Impure Motives

Next, if we accept the traditional rendering of 'aneph (אנף) as anger, then the next phrase, "*lest he be angry, and ye perish from the way,*" does not go with the idea of using bar (בר) as "purity." But from previous studies, we know that the word 'aneph (אנף) does not have to be rendered as "anger." Our modern concept of anger essentially refers to a manifestation of inward fears, which is something we cannot assign to God, because He has no fears. My study partner insists we should say "righteous anger" here. In other words, we need to assign an adjective to the word *anger* to explain what type of anger we are dealing with.

The simple fact is that we have no equivalent word in the English language for 'aneph (אנף). My study partner and I agreed that, in this context, the best rendering for 'aneph (אנף), which simply indicates a strong emotional response, would be *distraught*. This is not a perfect rendering of 'aneph (אנף) here, but it is the best we can come up with. The word brings in the emotions of grief, disappointment, and sadness, a proper rendering for 'aneph (אנף).

The idea is that we are to embrace, with passion, purity in our relationship with God—having no personal agendas other than to just love Him. If we "love" Him like some gold digger wanting to gain material blessings or personal honor, it will grieve God's heart, just as it would grieve the heart of a wealthy woman to discover her fiancé is courting her only for her money and not out of genuine love.

If we seek God for personal gain—to become rich and receive other material benefits—then we using God for our own personal desires, and we would be in danger of "*perish[ing] from the way.*" The Hebrew word for "perish" is 'abad (אבד), which means "to be destroyed," "to be exterminated," or just "to vanish." God would be distraught if our motives were not pure because we would be in danger or wandering down a path into an abyss.

The Refining Fires of God's Passion

That next part is a little more difficult to understand: "*when his wrath is kindled but a little.*" We could use Revelation 3:18 as a parallel verse: "*I counsel thee to buy of me gold tried in the fire, that thou mayest be rich; and white raiment, that thou mayest be clothed, and that the shame of thy nakedness do not appear; and anoint thine eyes with eyesalve, that thou mayest see." In Greek, the word translated "gold" is *chrysion*, which is pure gold, refined to be of monetary value. The point is that when God refines us by fire so that we can be of true value, all our personal desires and wants burn away, enabling us to desire God purely out of a heart of love.

Thus, the phrase "*when his wrath is kindled but a little*" would suggest the same idea. Just a small portion of His "wrath" will burn away the impurities in our heart. The root of the Hebrew word translated as "*wrath*" is again *'aneph* (אנף). Thus, instead of *wrath*, I would use *passion*. Just a small portion of His passion for us will burn away the impurities that separate us from Him.

By saying that *'aneph* (אנף) does not refer to anger or wrath but rather to God's passionate love for us, I know I am trying to put a positive spin on something that is traditionally read in a negative context. That may be the case. However, look at how this verse ends: "*Blessed are all they that put their trust in him.*" The first part of the verse apparently implies that if we do not kiss Jesus or show respect and honor for Him, then we will perish in the abyss because it will kindle His wrath. Consequently, after being threatened and intimated, I am now to be blessed by putting my trust in a deity who has bullied me with anger, wrath, and punishment? I think I am more blessed by submitting to a God who passionately loves me and is grieved that, by not loving Him in purity, I have placed myself on a path of destruction. To me, that really expresses the heart of David, a heart that was truly in love with God.

Study 60

"It Is I"

"Therefore my people shall know my name: therefore they shall know in that day that I am he that doth speak: behold, it is I."
—Isaiah 52:6

"What's in a name? That which we call a rose by any other word [name] would smell as sweet."[14]

There is something special about the rendering *"Behold, it is I"* in Isaiah 52:6. Every time I read this phrase, I experience a thrill, a quickening in my heart. Yet, in the past, I wondered why those words were even included because they seemed redundant. The declaration made little sense to me. This verse is speaking of a future event in which God's name will be known, and then there is the interjection *hinei* (הני), which can be translated either as *"Behold, it is I"* or *"Surely, it is I."* If God's people will already know that it is He, why does He need to add that explanation? However, after my many years of searching for the heart and mind of God, I long to hear those words from the lips of the One I have learned to love with all my heart. I don't mind the repetition!

---

14. Brian Gibbons, ed., *Romeo and Juliet*, The Arden Shakespeare, Richard Proudfoot, Ann Thompson, and David Scott Kastan, gen. eds. (London: Thomas Learning, 2003), Act 2, Scene 2, lines 43–44.

The Bodleian manuscripts, which are the Old Testament manuscripts housed in the Bodleian Library at Oxford University, contain the words "I am YHWH" rather than *hinei* (הני). This would seem to fit the verse much better because then God is not saying "*Behold, it is I*," but rather "I am Jehovah." The word *YHWH* (יהוה) has an unusual form to it and literally means "I was, I am, and I will be." It would further be appropriate because the verse centers on the name of God and knowing His name. But I have grown to love seeing the word *hinei* (הני) because it makes it so much more personal to hear "It is I" than "I am Jehovah." Let me explain.

Intimate with God and His Reputation

In Isaiah 53:6, the Hebrew word translated *"name"* is *shem* (שׁם) and means "a reputation, what a person is." The word for *"know"* is *yada* (ידע), referring to intimate knowing. In this context, to know is to be *intimate with the reputation behind this name*. Thus, the verse could be read as, "Therefore, My people will become intimate with Me," or "Therefore, My people will become intimate with My reputation." Both mean essentially the same thing: we will become intimate with God, His plans, and His desires, and we will seek to carry them out.

Not long ago, I marked the tenth year of my journey to discover the heart and mind of God. At the end of my workday, I locked up my disability bus and then took a walk through a park across the road where I could be alone with God. He and I talked about the past ten years of the journey. That week, I had been reviewing the many hundreds of devotionals or word studies I had written over those years while I was searching for information for a new book. As I reviewed them, I could see that each year, with each word study, I grew a little bit closer to God's heart and mind, and I marveled over the fact that I was still getting closer. I am convinced that I will spend eternity gaining a deeper understanding of the heart and mind of God.

This study on "It is I" is one I completed four years ago, but I have revised it because, at that time, I had barely scratched the surface of my understanding of it. During those four years, I have felt the warmth of God's light and the comfort of His arms. I can almost hear the soothing sounds of His voice. His Word, the Bible, is becoming more and more precious to me. As the hymn says, "The things of earth"—the world's honors,

recognitions, and accomplishments, as well as the pursuit of financial security—are all becoming "strangely dim."[15] I know I am getting closer to
God's heart and mind because the rewards of this natural world that used
to matter are gradually losing their value to me. Some people whom I know
don't understand my change of priorities.

That evening in the park, as I walked and talked with the Lord, I wanted to reach out and touch Him, to pass through a portal into His presence.
Yet, I could sense God say, "You still do not *know* [*yada* (ידע)] My name."
Knowing His name is more than just understanding its meaning. It is having an intimate relationship with that name. God desires that we love Him
with all our heart, soul, and mind.

*"Jesus said unto him, Thou shalt love the Lord thy God with all thy heart,
and with all thy soul, and with all thy mind. This is the first and great commandment"* (Matthew 22:37–38). In study 11, "Thou Shalt Love," we asked
the question of why God makes loving Him a command. It is because
learning to love is a daily process that has to be maintained. It starts as just
a seed and then begins to grow. A seed must be cared for, watered, and fed,
or its growth will cease. I mentioned previously that each morning, every
orthodox Jewish male recites the first commandment as a reminder that
his greatest mission on this earth is to grow in his love for God.

"Your Journey Has Only Begun"

On my own journey, I have learned that I will never come to a complete understanding of the heart and mind of God. It will take an eternity.
Every time I weep and rejoice over the presence of God's love, thinking I
have finally concluded my journey, I hear a little voice that whispers, "Your
journey has only begun. There is more, so much more."

In the Twenty-third Psalm, David said, *"Surely goodness and mercy shall
follow me all the days of my life: and I will dwell in the house of the* LORD
for ever" (verse 6). The Hebrew word translated *"house"* here is *byith* (בית),
which simply means "a dwelling place." Some commentators say David is
referring to the tabernacle, which was the place of God's habitation during

---

15. Helen H. Lemmel, "O Soul, Are You Weary and Troubled?" ("Turn Your Eyes Upon
Jesus"), 1922.

that time. But the tabernacle—and even the temples that were built later—did not last "forever." David is talking about eternity as well as his present state in the flesh. We automatically assume David is referring to heaven, but what is heaven? In our natural state, we cannot comprehend what the spirit world is like. Thus, we have to find something in the natural realm to compare it to, and so we compare it to a celestial city with mansions.

As I grow closer to the heart and mind of God, I find that I am drawn to an obscure use of the word *byith* (בית), or dwelling place. In extra-biblical literature, I found *byith* (בית) used to denote a dwelling place of light. Jesus said that He is *"the light of the world"* (John 8:12; 9:5). He is an all-encompassing light, a light with no boundaries.

Ten years ago, when I began my journey, I had a dream about a light. I cannot describe it; I cannot even comprehend it. Yet, it was so beautiful, so peaceful, so restful, that when I woke up, I tried to go back to sleep so I could continue dreaming of that light. Alas, the dream never returned. Even today, I wonder if perhaps that dream was God commissioning me on this journey to discover His heart and mind.

I am convinced that the Father's house, or *byith* (בית), is that light, a light with no boundaries or end. When I pass from this earth, I will do what my dream did not allow me to do, and that is to *enter into* the vastness of that wonderful, indescribable light. I will enter into the mind and heart of God and really *yada'* (ידע), know Him, be intimate with Him. I will dwell in His heart and mind forever. I need no mansion, no streets of gold, no pearly gates—not even visits from loved ones who have gone before me. All I long for is to dwell in that light, to dwell in God's heart and mind, and experience ever greater depths of intimacy with Him, depths of intimacy that will continue forever. I will spend eternity doing what I have been doing for the last decade: discovering new and amazing things about God's heart and mind, which are like a well that will never run dry. Yes, it will never run dry throughout eternity!

But when I finally enter into that light, the first thing I long to hear—what I wake up each morning with my heart aching to hear, what I have a burning anticipation to hear—is that word *hinei* (הני), "It is I." I want to hear the voice of the One dearest to my heart and live in His presence forever.

Select Glossary

Akkadian: the language of the Assyrians.

Aramaic: A sister language of Hebrew that has many dialects. Hebrew essentially became a dead language during the time of the Babylonian captivity circa 597 BC. The Hebrew of the Jews was blended into the Aramaic, which was the language of the Babylonians. Then, when the exiled Jews returned to Palestine, Aramaic became their national language, with Classical Hebrew remaining only as a ceremonial language. Various dialects of Aramaic were in use during Jesus' day. Most likely, Jesus spoke the Northern, or Old Galilean, dialect, which was very idiomatic, while those in Jerusalem spoke the Southern dialect that was more formal. (See also Classical Hebrew.)

Classical Hebrew: Classical Hebrew is the language in which the Old Testament was written. Also known as biblical Hebrew, it is an archaic form of the Hebrew language that existed as a spoken language until the time of the Jews' captivity by Babylon, circa 597 BC, after which it was blended with and replaced by the Aramaic language. Many scholars believe that Classical Hebrew essentially became a dead language at this time and that, by the first century AD, it existed only as a ceremonial language. Although Modern Hebrew developed from Classical Hebrew, the two forms have many differences.

cuneiform: One of several of the earliest known systems of writing in which the scribes used a blunt reed as a stylus, pushing the reed into a soft, clay tablet to make a wedge-shaped mark. Many Semitic languages used this form of writing, including the Akkadian, the Sumerian, the Hittite, the Ugaritic, and the Old Persian languages. (See also **Ugaritic.**)

Dead Sea Scrolls: Also known as the Qumran Caves Scrolls, the Dead Sea Scrolls are a collection of 981 different texts discovered between 1946 and 1956 in eleven caves near the ancient settlement at Khirbet Qumran in the West Bank, a few miles from the shore of the Dead Sea and thirteen miles east of Jerusalem. The collection has proven to be of great religious and linguistic significance, as it includes the second-oldest known surviving manuscripts of works that were included in the Hebrew Bible. Fragments of every book in the Old Testament, with the exception of Esther, have been identified in the scrolls. The Isaiah scroll is relatively intact and is one thousand years older than any previously known copy of the book. The collection also contains prophecies by Ezekiel, Jeremiah, and Daniel, as well as psalms attributed to King David and to Joshua, that are not found in the Hebrew Bible. Also found in the scrolls but not in the Hebrew Bible are the last words of Joseph, Judah, Levi, Naphtali, and Amram, who was the father of Moses. Most important, the Dead Sea Scrolls predate the Masoretic text, thus shedding new light on the accuracy of that text, which is the basis for most English Bible translations and is the standard text used in Bible colleges and seminaries. (See also **Masoretes.**)

final form: Also known as a *sofit letter.* Five of the twenty-two letters of the Hebrew alphabet are formed differently when they appear as the last letter of a word. In the original Hebrew text, there were no spaces between words. The reader could know only from his personal knowledge where one word ended and where the next word began. However, five letters did have a different appearance when they were found at the end of a word, indicating that the next letter was the first letter of a new word. These five letters are the following: kap (כ), with a final form of (ך); mem (מ), with a final form of (ם); nun (נ), with a final form of (ן);

pe (פ), with a final form of (ף); and sade (צ), with a final form of (ץ). (See also **Hebrew alphabet**.)

Gematria: A practice in which Orthodox rabbis, using the numerical value of a Hebrew word, would seek to find a relationship between it and other Hebrew words that shared the same numerical value. This method is not to be confused with numerology, which places a mystical meaning on numbers. It was simply a teaching tool to guide one into a deeper understanding of the Scriptures. (See also **numerical value**.)

Greek: The Greek of the New Testament is called Koine Greek and was the universal language of people living in the Eastern Mediterranean region under the Roman Empire.

Hebrew: See **Classical Hebrew**.

Hebrew alphabet: The Hebrew alphabet consists of twenty-two consonants. Four of these letters—aleph (א), hei (ה), vav (ו), and yod (י)—are also used interchangeably as vowels. Writing in Hebrew is read from right to left. (See also **Classical Hebrew**.)

hiphal: A verbal form expressing a causative action, as in "I will cause my voice to be heard."

idiom: An idiom is a language, dialect, or style of speaking peculiar to a people.

imperative: A verbal form expressing a command or a supplication, as in "Hear my voice, O Lord."

lexicographer: A compiler and/or writer of ancient words and their meanings that are included in a lexicon.

lexicon: A wordbook, or dictionary, of an ancient, dead language, such as Latin, ancient Greek, or Classical Hebrew.

Masoretes: A group of Jewish scribe scholars who worked between the sixth century and the tenth century AD. They were responsible for compiling a system of pronunciational and grammatical guides in the form of diacritical notes on the external form of the biblical text in an attempt to establish an authoritative fix on the pronunciation of the Hebrew Bible, as well as on paragraph and verse divisions. At this time, the Jews were scattered throughout the world, and Hebrew had become essentially a dead language, surviving only with ceremonial usage. With six centuries of Jews living in foreign nations and learning to speak many different languages, there was a fear that the original pronunciation of the Hebrew language would be lost without some indication of vowels in the written text. The Masoretes took it upon themselves to add these vowels, which are still widely used today. The resulting Masoretic text of the Old Testament is the standard Hebrew Bible used in today's Bible colleges and seminaries and among Bible translators.

niphal: A verb that denotes a passive or reflexive voice, as in "My voice was heard by me."

numerical value: This term refers to a quasi-decimal numbering system using the letters of the Hebrew alphabet in which every word is assigned a numerical value. For instance, the word for "weeping" in Hebrew is *baki* (בכי). Beth (ב) represents the number 2, kap (כ) represents the number 20, and yod (י) represents the number 10. Since the total of these three numbers is 32, the numerical value of the word *baki* (בכי) is 32. Some Orthodox Jews, in order to express a spiritual truth, sought to find relationships between Hebrew words that have the same numerical value. For instance, the word for "heart" is *lev* (לב). Lamed (ל) is the number 30, and beth (ב) is the number 2. So, the word for "heart," *lev* (לב), has a numerical value of 32, the same value as the word for "weeping," *baki* (בכי). The Orthodox rabbis would use this numerical equivalency to illustrate that all weeping comes from the heart. (See also **Gematria** and **Orthodox Jews**.)

Orthodox Jews: "Judaism that adheres to the Torah and Talmud as interpreted in an authoritative rabbinic law code and applies their principles and regulations to modern living." (*Merriam-Webster's 11th Collegiate Dictionary*, s.v., "Orthodox Judaism.")

piel: A verbal form showing intensity, as in "My voice was profoundly heard."

play on words: A play on words, or a wordplay, is the use of a single word to bear two meanings in the same context. There are numerous wordplays in the Hebrew Bible. For instance, in Genesis 1:1, we find the first play on words: *"In the beginning God created...."* The word *"beginning"* is translated from the Hebrew *bereshit* (בראשית), and the word *"created"* is translated from *bara'* (ברא). When God constructed the story of creation, He twice used the same three letters (ברא) that form the root word of the verb "to create," which is so crucial to the entire story.

Semitic root: All Semitic languages have root words. Among these Semitic languages are the Akkadian language; the Assyrian language; the Aramaic language, which was the language of the Babylonians; the Persian language, from which present-day Arabic developed; the Canaanite language; and the Phoenician language. These languages are interrelated through words whose roots are common among the Semitic languages. For this reason, we can often gain insight into a Hebrew word by examining its origins in other Semitic tongues.

Septuagint: The Septuagint is also known as the Greek Old Testament. It is a translation of the Hebrew Bible into Koine Greek, or an Egyptian Greek. It derives its name (often identified by the Roman numerals LXX) from the seventy Jewish scholars who completed the translation circa the second century BC. The Septuagint is often quoted in the New Testament, particularly by the apostle Paul in his letters. The story behind the Septuagint centers on Ptolemy II, who was king of Ptolemaic Egypt from about 283–246 BC. He was the promoter of the Library of Alexandria and reigned during the height of the literary splendor of the Alexandrian court. Greek literature from that time reflects quotations from Jewish law, and possibly from this Jewish influence, as well as from the fact that the Hebrew language was quickly becoming extinct, Ptolemy commissioned seventy Jewish scholars to translate the Old Testament into Koine Greek. It is believed by many (although it is disputed among some scholars who consider it legend) that these seventy scholars were forbidden to consult with each other during the translation process and that when they concluded their translations, all seventy were in perfect agreement. Recent discoveries from the Dead Sea Scrolls have shown that the Septuagint carries a higher degree of accuracy than the Masoretic text.

syntax: This term refers to the arrangement of words to form a sentence. In English, much depends upon word order, but in the Hebrew language, the order of the words is not as important. For example, in English we say, *"In the beginning, God created...the earth"* (Genesis 1:1). We know by the placement of the verb *"created"* that God created the earth—not that the earth created God. However, in the Hebrew, this meaning isn't as apparent by the word order; therefore, the Hebrew word designating *"the earth"* is preceded by an *'eth* (אֵת), which is not an actual word but rather a symbol for a direct object, indicating that God is doing the action, and the earth is the direct object receiving the action. Some people have argued that Hebrew has no set rule of syntax, so that we must depend upon the context alone to determine the word order. However, most scholars disagree with that theory.

Talmud: A collection derived from oral tradition and commentaries, consisting of the Mishnah (oral laws) and Gemara (commentaries). There are two editions of the Talmud. One was produced in Palestine around AD 400. The other, which is the most commonly used, was produced in Babylonia around AD 500 and is written in Tannaitic (Mishnaic) Hebrew and Aramaic.

Torah: The word *Torah* is sometimes used for the first five books of the Tanach, or Old Testament, known as the Pentateuch. Other times, it refers to the Old Testament as a whole. The term is also used to refer to the parchment scroll on which the Pentateuch is written, or even to denote the entire body of Jewish religious literature and teaching contained in the Old Testament and the Talmud. Like many words in Hebrew, the meaning changes according to the context in which it is used.

Ugaritic: A Northwest Semitic language that was rediscovered in 1928 in the ruined city of Ugarit, Syria, which was destroyed circa 1180–1170

BC. It is one of the oldest phonetically-based languages written in a cuneiform abjab (alphabet without vowels) on clay tablets, and was used around the fifteenth century BC. It is also the oldest example of the family of West Semitic scripts that was used for the Phoenician, Hebrew, and Aramaic languages. Its grammatical features are highly similar to that of the Hebrew grammar. The Ugaritic language has been used by scholars of the Hebrew Bible to clarify biblical Hebrew texts. (See also Aramaic, cuneiform, and Classical Hebrew.)

Index of Hebrew, Greek, and Aramaic Terms

The following are the meanings of Hebrew letters and words, and Greek and Aramaic words, for primary terms found in *Hebrew Word Study: Exploring the Mind of God*. Please see Author's Note at the beginning of this book for an explanation of Hebrew vowel and apostrophe use in this volume.

Hebrew Letters

ayin (ע): denotes the eyes of God; represents spiritual seeing and insight [Study 57]

chet (ח): has a numerical value of eight, and when put on its side, is the symbol of infinity [Study 46]

daleth (ד): signifies a doorway [Study 57]

gimmel (ג): signifies being surrounded by the passionate love of God or lovingkindness [Study 16; Study 52]; denotes a camel; is a picture of a man running to offer assistance to someone [Study 52]

lamed (double) (לל): pictures uplifted arms or hands [Study 20; Study 46]; indicates a movement toward the heart of God [Study 46] mem (מ): represents water [Study 16; Study 50]; represents the womb; signifies the process of birthing something new [Study 16]; represents the revealed knowledge of God [Study 50]; the mem's "shadow," or negative connotation, depicts a drowning in destructive passion [Study 53]

nun (נ): signifies being blocked off or having your attention diverted [Study 53]

resh (ר): denotes a mini-Rosh Hashanah, mini-New Year, or new beginning [Study 16]; represents the convicting power of the Holy Spirit and repentance [Study 50]

vav (ו): denotes a hook, or a dependency upon someone or something [Study 53]

yod (י): signifies one's attention directed to God [Study 20]; denotes the Spirit of God [Study 57]

zayin (ז); signifies a sword or weapon [Study 50; Study 57]

Hebrew Words

'abad (אבד): to perish; to be destroyed; to be exterminated; to vanish [Study 59]

'achar (אחר): end; after; behind; tarry; continue [Study 23]

'agav (עגב): love, in the sense of our colloquial expression "making love"; selfish love or lust [Study 15]

'ahal (בהל): to be troubled; to make haste; to be alarmed; to be in a hurry [Study 56]

ahav (אהב): love [Study 11; Study 15]

'akal (אכל): consumed; eating; encompassing [Study 35]

'akazari (אכזרי): fiercely protective; comes from the root word *kazar* (כזר), meaning "to be valiant, daring, and courageous" [Study 24] 'al (על): upon; over [Study 21]

alenu (עלינו); with us; within us [Study 55]

'amad (עמד): to stand; to confirm; to appoint; to remain; to defend; to stand firm; to stop; to wait; to be opposed [Study 34]

'amelah (אמלה): weak; possibly "full of oneself," from the root *mala'* (מלא), meaning "to be full" [Study 37]

'anag (ענג): delicate; a princess who is spoiled and pampered [Study 22]

'anan (אנן): to complain about hardship [Study 35]

'aneph (אנף): an expression of great emotion that could reflect anger, frustration, desire (especially for intimacy), passion, grief, and many other possibilities, including "distraught"; word originated from the snorting of a camel [Preface; Study 24; Study 35; Study 56; Study 57; Study 59]

'aras (ארס): to betroth; to engage for matrimony; comes from a Semitic root found in the Sumerian language meaning "to desire" [Study 26]

'ash (אש): fire [Study 35; Study 45]; passion [Study 35]; warmth and comfort [Study 45]

'azan (אזן): ear; in its Semitic root, a term for a musical instrument [Study 32]

baali (בעלי): "my master" [Study 28]

ba'ar (בער); to kindle; to grow warm; to grow hot; to burn; used in extra-biblical literature to express the idea of "seeking out" [Study 35]

bachar (בחר): to chose (what is the best); to refine; to try; to test; to purify; used in the Old Persian language for examining or scrutinizing something [Study 44]

bano'am (בנעם); beauty; comes from the root *no'am* (נעם), meaning "delightfulness" or "pleasure" [Study 31]

bar (בר): purity [Study 59]

baraku (ברכו): to bless; to make happy; to praise; in a piel, imperative form, it is an intense command [Study 14]

baqash (בקש): to seek (earnestly) [Study 31]

bemacheval (במחול): dance; from the Semitic root *cheval* (חול), which means "to spin around in a circle" or "to twirl" [Study 46]

besimchah (בסמחה): joy; to be joyful [Study 5]

bigeburath (בגבורת): strength; from the root word *gavar* (גבר), indicating "mastery" or "control over" [Study 41]

bire'adah (ברעדה): trembling, in the sense of being in awe (positive or negative) [Study 58]

byith (בית): a physical or spiritual house, such as in "house of prayer" [Study 2; Study 60]; a dwelling place of light [Study 60]

chalev (חלב): best; from the Semitic root for converting something into nourishment; refers to giving what will be of benefit to other people [Study 33]

chamed (חמד): covet; pleasant; pleasing; beautiful; nice to look at; desirable; to be excited; to be hot; the idea of intimacy or totally possessing or consuming something; modern Hebrew form *chamudi* (חמדי) means "my precious one" [Study 9]

chaphats (חפץ): delight; represents one's will; signifies that which brings pleasure [Study 3]

charash (חרש): rest; in hiphal (causative) form, it includes the concepts of fabricating, enchanting, ploughing, or engraving, with the basic idea of producing something; to be "enchanted "or "bewitched"; signifies an obsession (Study 5)

charon (חרון): fierce; anger; wrath; displeasure; passionate determination; in its Semitic root, has the idea of a raging fire [Study 24] *chasmal* (חשמל): the color of amber; the color of copper; gleaming metal; glowing metal; glitter; aglow; also an Aramaic idiom meaning "as the look of God" [Study 45]

chatah (חטה): sins; sinners; an archer's term for "missing the target" [Study 6; Study 24]

chazah (חזה): to behold; to experience something [Study 31]

chazaq (חזק): to be hardened; to be stubborn [Study 18]

chemah (חמה): fury; passionate love; from the root *yacham* (יחם), a term used for sexual excitement [Study 6]; wrath [Study 56]

cheval (חול): to spin around in a circle; to twirl [Study 46]

chi (חי): physical or spiritual life [Study 31]

chimadeti (חמדתי): rooted in the Hebrew word for "covet," *chamed* (חמד): delight; great delight; desire; rapture [Study 9]

chiyiyim (חיים): physically or spiritually alive [Study 29]

demuth (דמות): likeness; from the root word *damah* (דמה), meaning to be similar but in a quiet way [Study 45]

deveqim (דבקים): cleave; cling; hold fast; be faithful; remain faithful; be loyal; adhere; related to *devequt* (דבקות), or unifying all aspects of your life with that of the heart and mind of God [Study 29]

'ebrah (עברה) wrath; overwhelming; overflowing [Study 24; Study 57]

'echath (אחת): one; most likely from the root word *echod* (אחד), which is related to a word signifying "to descend" [Study 31]

'eshel (אשל): grove; tamarisk trees; the Akkadian word *quddus*, meaning "holy," is often associated with the tamarisk; *'eshel* (אשל) is considered by some sages to be an acronym signifying "food," "drink," and "fellowship" [Study 42]

gadal (גדל): joy; great and mighty [Study 5]

gamar (גמר): to perfect; to bring to an end; to bring to completion [Study 16]

gil (גיל): joy, as expressed by spinning around in a circle; generations [Study 58]

gimmel (גמל): benefits; lovingkindness; has its origins in the Phoenician language and means "stopping," "weaning," "going without," and "repaying in like kind." It is used for a camel because of the animal's ability to go without food and water for a long time and for the animal's reciprocal service to people [Study 52]

hagah (הגה): to meditate: to moan; to growl; to utter; to muse; to devise; to plot; to roar; to imagine; may be related to the word *'aqah* (קה), meaning "encircle" or "surround" [Study 4]

halel (הלל): to praise; to shine [Study 39; Study 46; Study 54]; to bring forth light; to boast; used to denote "to make a fool of yourself," "to act like a madman," or "insanity" [Study 39; Study 46]

hasatan (השטן): "the adversary"; its Semitic root word is *sata'*, which carries the idea of "sweeping away as by a flood of hate or persecution," or "sweeping away someone to cause them to go astray," "to scatter," or "to control" [Study 49]

hinei (הני): "*Behold, it is I*"; "Surely, it is I" [Study 60]

ishi (אישי): "my husband"; friend; helper; companion [Study 28]

Jah (יה): God Jehovah [Study 39]

kalah (כלה): to consume; to destroy; to ruin; to waste; to cause to vanish; in its Semitic origins, it has the idea of "completion" or "to bring to an end." The word can also refer to the kidneys, the secret parts of one's body, a bride, or an intimate, loving relationship [Study 56]

kalal (כלל): to become complete or finished [Study 56]

kap (כ): after; like; as [Study 13]

kavas (כבס): cup; stork or pelican; nurturing love [Study 12]

kavod (כבוד): glory; heart; from the word *kavad* (כבד), meaning "a weight" [Study 34]

kemareh (כמראה): appearance; from the root word *ra'ah* (ראה), which means "to see"; also rooted in the word *kemar* (כמר), which means "to kindle a fire for warmth" and can signify "love and compassion" [Study 45]

kinor (כנר): harp [Study 46]

koach (כוח): strength; human strength and/or power, either physical or intellectual [Study 14]

lenisheveri (לנשברי), from the root word *shavar* (שבר): broken [Study 7]

lev (לב): heart [Study 7]

levav (לבב): heart [Study 13]

machashabah (מחשבה): thoughts; from the root word *chashab* (חשב), meaning "plans, purpose, thoughts, and imagination" (Study 1)

magid (מגד): to declare; to look into one's eyes when saying something (Study 1)

Matnot kehunah (מתנת כהנה): "the offering given to the priest" [Study 33]

mazaqaq (מזקק): to refine [Study 50]

melek'an (מלכן): angels; king; royalty; ruler; kingly messenger; teacher; prophet; anyone who takes on a leadership role to deliver a message or proclamation [Study 14]

milipani (מלפני): presence [Study 38]

miqodeshi (מקדש): sanctuary; literally, "my place of separation" or "my place of holiness" [Study 23]

misata' (משתה): feasted; to eat and drink to excess or to become drunken; the mem (מ) indicates a flooding of destructive passion, and there is a play on the word *sata'* (see entry for *hasatan*) [Study 49] *nagash* (נגש): come near; contains the idea of drawing near or approaching with an offering, a present, or a request [Study 10]

nashaq (נשק): to kiss; an act of submission; an expression of love and passion; carries the idea of joining two lips together or putting the lips to a cheek; derived from an old Akkadian word that signifies a voluntary joining together or a desire to be joined together [Study 59]

nashem (נשם): breath of life; natural breath [Study 17]

natah (נטה): to incline; in its Semitic root, to tune an instrument [Study 32]

na'veh (נאוה): comely; beautiful; from the root word *na'ah* (נאה), meaning "to dwell" or "to sit" [Study 22]

nebim (נבם): prophet [Study 23]

num (נום): to slumber; to be drowsy; to sleep—lightly, such that you are easily awakened [Study 53]

oni (עני): affliction; comes from the root word *'anah* (ענה), which signifies a good kind of affliction and can also mean "to be humble" or "to be weak"; in the Old Persian, *'anah* (ענה) means "to bow down" [Study 44]

'oz (עז): power; comes from the root word *'ozaz* (עזז), among whose meanings is "strengthen (oneself)" and "be strong"; *'ozaz* (עז) is also the root word for the name *Uzziah* (עזיהו) [Study 57]

palal (פלל): root word for prayer; in its Semitic root, it refers to the notch in a tent peg (Study 2)

qara (קרא); to meet (with); to call out [Study 55]

qarah (קרה): contrary; casual; to meet without prior intent; an accomodating arrangement; a marriage of convenience; the word's origins lie in the concept of a structure whose roof is connected to its walls by beams [Study 6]

qari (קרי): from the root word *qarah* (קרה) (see *qarah*) [Study 6] *qavar* (קור): mighty; strong or powerful to help or rescue another person [Study 5]

qodesh (קדש): holy; separate; sacred; signifies a separation to devote one's life to a deity [Study 54]

quana (קנא): a jealousy of envy and rage [Study 51]

quanna (קנא): a protective jealousy; zealous; passion [Study 51]

ra' (רע): to be displeased; displeasure; evil; hurt feelings; wounded heart [Study 35]

ra'ah (ראה): a seer [Study 23]

ra'ah (רעה): shepherd; evil [Study 8]; a consuming passion [Study 37]

racham (רחם): love; lovingkindness; a very personal and individualized blessing; strength; protection; assurances; guidance; consolation; support; spiritual gifts; the gift of faith; repentance and forgiveness; persistence; fortitude; cheerfulness [Preface]; a deeply affectionate and romantic love [Study 15; Study 21]; to pity; to have compassion on; tender and compassionate; tender mercies; to have mercy upon [Preface; Study 21]

ranan (רנן): singing; a celebration or jubilation [Study 5]

romemoth (רוממות): high praises; exaltation; from the root word *ramam* (רמם), meaning "to lift up" or "to place on high" [Study 39]

ruch (רוח): spirit; Spirit of God; breath; wind [Study 17]

Ruch Kodesh (רוח קדש): Holy Spirit [Study 17]

sala' (סלע): solid rock; a boulder [Study 19]

secho (שחו): thought; thoughts of love and intimacy (Study 1)

sha'al (שאל): to desire; to ask [Study 31]

shachah (שחה): to worship [Study 1]

shamad (שמד): to destroy; to exterminate; in its Semitic origins, to bring to a conclusion; closure; ending [Study 24]

shamer (שמר): to keep; to guard; to watch over [Study 53]

shani (שני): scarlet; a word for an insect that turns bright scarlet after it dies and dries up [Study 48]

shaphak (שפך): melt and pour out [Study 30]

shaqa' (שקע): to quench; can express the idea of "overflowing" and "subduing" [Study 35]

shavar (שבר): a breakthrough [Study 7]

shem (שם): name; a reputation; what a person is [Study 60]

shema (שמע): to hear; to comprehend [Study 11]

sod (סוד): secret; the mysteries of God; the mind and heart of God [Study 8]

sur (סור): to rebel; to withdraw [Study 20]

sus (סוס): rejoice; a pure form of joy that is not at the expense of others (Study 5)

tarash (תרש): solid rock; a boulder [Study 19]

tenuphah (תנופה): heave offering [Study 33]

teshuqah (תשקה): desire; from the root word *shuwq* (שוק), which signifies a longing and reaching out (Study 9)

titteneni (תתנני): to deliver; from the root word *nathan* (נתן), whose basic meaning is "to give" [Study 40]

torah (תורה): law; first five books of the Bible (Study 3)

tselutha (צלותא): prayer; intercessory prayer (Study 2)

tsom (צוֹם): fastings; in its Semitic form, the Aramaic and Hebrew word *tsom* (צוֹם) has the idea of submitting the very necessities of one's life in order to receive some knowledge [Study 2]

tsur (צוּר): a rocky cliff; a rocky wall; the wall of a mountain; from the Akkadian language, the idea of designing, forming, sculpturing, or carving in or on rocks [Study 19]

vayakrie (וַיִּכְרִי): to call [Study 42]

vayishevethu (וַיִּשְׁבְּתוּ): rested; comes from the root word *shabat* (שׁבת), meaning "to cease"; to bond [Study 27]

veshab (וָאָשֻׁב): to return [Study 38]

yada' (ידע): to know; a sexual relationship with the emphasis on knowing someone intimately [Study 15]; knowledge, in terms of relationships; intimacy [Study 25; Study 55; Study 57; Study 60]

yalal (ילל): to howl; to wail [Study 20]

yara' (ירע): fear; also used in the sense of showing respect and reverence; comes from the same root as the word *Torah*, meaning "law" or "instruction" [Study 57; Study 58]

yare' (ירא): fear; reverence and respect [Study 8]

yaretseh (ירצה): pleasure; from the root word *ratsah* (רצה), indicating "association" [Study 41]

yasar (יסר): to chastise; to influence toward a goal; instruction; correction [Study 6]

yechepats (יחפץ): to delight; from the root word *chapats* (חפץ), which indicates "a bending toward" or "an inclining before" [Study 41]

yesav (ישׁב): to be enthroned; to inhabit; to settle; to sit; in its Semitic root, it is a picture of the place where a king would sit to delegate his power, will, knowledge, and rule [Study 54]

YHWH (יהוה): Jehovah [Study 29; Study 42; Study 46; Study 47; Study 60]

yom (יום): days [Study 31]

zamar (זמר): praises; literally means to cut or to divide; in a piel form, it gives the idea of dividing into rhythmical numbers or the formation of melodies [Study 46]; a pruning hook [Study 50]

zohar (זהר): brightness; aglow; in its verbal root form, to glow and radiate [Study 45]

zonah (זנה): an "everyday," for-profit prostitute [Study 37]

Aramaic Words

ana: "I am" [Study 47]

'avar: to pass; overwhelming [Study 12]

bar: Son [Study 59]

bestra: go backward; contains the idea of moving backward to protect oneself [Study 46]

chekam: to know, in an intimate sense [Preface]

dana ana: "I am that I am" [Study 47]

kamar: sorrowful; to burn; to kindle; used to signify a burning love or compassion [Study 12]

kasa: cup; to ask [Study 12]

kia: such as; as though [Study 13]

ruch: spirit; spirit of God; breath; wind [Aramaic, Study 17]

sana' : a thorn or an irritant, like a briar that is stuck on one's leg [Study 36]

segad: to worship; an "air kiss" [Study 17]

shalem: peace; goodwill; in extra-biblical literature, used to express the idea of submission [Study 43]

sharara: truth; to be tightly bound together, like strands of fabric tightly bound with each other to form a rope [Study 17]

shekev: "if possible"; "if this happens" [Study 12]

Greek Words

agape: unconditional love [Study 11]

agapos: love [Study 11]

brabeueto: peace; to arbitrate; to umpire [Preface]

chrysion: pure gold, refined to be of monetary value [Study 59]

de'esesin: prayer; petition; intercessory prayers (Study 2)

diabolos: a false accuser; a slanderer [Study 49]

egno, from the word *ginosko*: to know, in an intimate sense [Preface]

ego eimi: "I am" [Study 47]

epistrepho: to convert; to turn about [Study 43]

koinonia: communion by intimate participation [Study 9]

misei: to hate [Study 36]

parelthato: to pass; to avert; to avoid; to pass over [Study 12]

pneuma: spirit; Spirit of God; breath; wind [Study 17]

proskyneo: to worship; to throw a kiss [Study 17]

taka: according to [Study 13]

English Keywords and Key Phrases for Hebrew, Greek, and Aramaic Terms

(Please refer to the specific entries above for word meanings.)

according to: *taka* [Greek; Study 13]

accuser: *diabolos* [Greek; Study 49]

adversary, the: *hasatan* (השטן) [Hebrew; Study 49]

affliction: *oni* (עני) [Hebrew; Study 44]

after: *kap* (כ) [Hebrew; Study 13]

aglow: *zohar* (זהר) [Hebrew; Study 45]

amber, color of: *chasmal* (חשמל) [Hebrew; Study 45]

angels: *melek'an* (מלכן) [Hebrew; Study 14]

anger: *'aneph* (אנף) [Hebrew; Preface; Study 24; Study 35; Study 56; Study 57; Study 59]

appearance: *kemareh* (כמראה): [Hebrew; Study 45]

as: *kap* (כ) [Hebrew; Study 13]

as though: *kia* [Aramaic; Study 13]

backward (go): *bestra* [Aramaic; Study 46]

beautiful: *na'veh* (נאוה) [Hebrew; Study 22]

beauty: *bano'am* (בנעם) [Hebrew; Study 31]

behold: *chazah* (חזה) [Hebrew; Study 31]

"Behold, it is I": *hinei* (הני) [Study 60]

benefits: *gimmel* (גמל) [Hebrew; Study 52]

best: *chalev* (חלב) [Hebrew; Study 33]

betroth: *'aras* (ארס) [Hebrew; Study 26]

bless: *baraku* (ברכו) [Hebrew; Study 14]

breakthrough: *shavar* (שבר) [Hebrew; Study 7]

breath: *nashem* (נשם) (natural breath) [Hebrew; Study 17]

breath: *pneuma* (spirit; Spirit of God; breath; wind) [Greek; Study 17]

breath: *ruch* (רוח) (spirit; Spirit of God; breath; wind) [Hebrew; Study 17]

breath: *rucha* (spirit; Spirit of God; breath; wind) [Aramaic; Study 17]

bride: *kalah* (כלה) [Hebrew; Study 56]

brightness: *zohar* (זהר) [Hebrew; Study 45]

broken: *lenisheveri* (לנשברי) [Hebrew; Study 7]

call: *vayakrie* (ויכרי) [Hebrew; Study 42]

chastise: *yasar* (יסר) [Hebrew; Study 6]

cleave: *deveqim* (דבקים) [Hebrew; Study 29]

closure: *shamad* (שמד) [Hebrew; Study 24]

come near: *nagash* (נגש) [Hebrew; Study 10]

comely: *na'veh* (נאוה) [Hebrew; Study 22]

compassion (to show): *racham* (רחם) [Hebrew; Study 20]

complain: *'anan* (אנן) [Hebrew; Study 35]

complete: *kalah* (כלה) [Hebrew; Study 56]

complete: *kalal* (כלל) [Hebrew: Study 56]

consume: *'akal* (אכל) [Hebrew; Study 35]

consume: *kalah* (כלה) [Hebrew; Study 56]

English Keywords and Key Phrases for Hebrew, Greek, and Aramaic Terms

(Please refer to the specific entries above for word meanings.)

betroth: *'aras* (ארס) [Hebrew; Study 26]

bless: *baraku* (ברכו) [Hebrew; Study 14]

breakthrough: *shavar* (שבר) [Hebrew; Study 7]

breath: *nashem* (נשם) (natural breath) [Hebrew; Study 17]

breath: *pneuma* (spirit; Spirit of God; breath; wind) [Greek; Study 17]

breath: *ruch* (רוח) (spirit; Spirit of God; breath; wind) [Hebrew; Study 17]

breath: *rucha* (spirit; Spirit of God; breath; wind) [Aramaic; Study 17]

bride: *kalah* (כלה) [Hebrew; Study 56]

brightness: *zohar* (זהר) [Hebrew; Study 45]

broken: *lenisheveri* (לנשברי) [Hebrew; Study 7]

call: *vayakrie* (ויכרי) [Hebrew; Study 42]

chastise: *yasar* (יסר) [Hebrew; Study 6]

cleave: *deveqim* (דבקים) [Hebrew; Study 29]

closure: *shamad* (שמד) [Hebrew; Study 24]

come near: *nagash* (נגש) [Hebrew; Study 10]

comely: *na'veh* (נאוה) [Hebrew; Study 22]

compassion (to show): *racham* (רחם) [Hebrew; Study 20]

complain: *'anan* (אנן) [Hebrew; Study 35]

complete: *kalah* (כלה) [Hebrew; Study 56]

complete: *kalal* (כלל) [Hebrew: Study 56]

consume: *'akal* (אכל) [Hebrew; Study 35]

consume: *kalah* (כלה) [Hebrew; Study 56]

enthrone: *yesav* (ישׁב) [Hebrew; Study 54]

evil: *ra'ah* (רעה) [Hebrew; Study 8]

exaltation: *romemoth* (רוממות) [Hebrew; Study 39]

fastings: *tsom* (צום) [Hebrew and Aramaic; Study 2]

fear: *yara'* (ירע) [Hebrew; Study 57; Study 58]

fear: *yare'* (ירא) [Hebrew; Study 8]

feasted: *misata'* (משׁתה) [Hebrew; Study 49]

fierce: *charon* (חרון) [Hebrew; Study 24]

fiercely protective: *'akazari* (אכזרי) [Study 24]

fire: *'ash* (אשׁ) [Hebrew; Study 35; Study 45]

fury: *chemah* (חמה) [Hebrew; Study 6]

generations: *gil* (גיל) [Hebrew; Study 58]

God Jehovah: *Jah* (יה) [Hebrew; Study 39]

gold, (pure): *chrysion* [Greek; Study 59]

hardened: *chazaq* (חזק) [Hebrew; Study 18]

harp: *kinor* (כנר) [Hebrew; Study 46]

hate: *misei* [Greek; Study 36]

hear: *shema* (שׁמע) [Hebrew; Study 11]

heart: *lev* (לב) [Hebrew; Study 7]

heart: *levav* (לבב) [Hebrew; Study 13]

heave offering: *tenuphah* (תנופה) [Hebrew; Study 33]

high praises: *romemoth* (רוממות) [Hebrew; Study 39]

know: *chekam* (in an intimate sense) [Aramaic; Preface]

know: *egno,* from the word *ginosko* (in an intimate sense) [Greek; Preface]

know: *yada'* (ידע) (in an intimate sense) [Study 15; Study 25; Study 55; Study 57; Study 60]

law: *torah* (תורה) [Hebrew; Study 3]

life: *chi* (חי) [Hebrew; Study 31]

like (preposition): *kap* (כ) [Hebrew; Study 13]

likeness: *demuth* (דמות) [Hebrew; Study 45]

love: *agape; agapos* [(unconditional love) Greek; Study 11]

love: *'agav* (עגב) (selfish love) [Study 15]

love: *ahav* (אהב) (general word for love) [Hebrew, Study 11; Study 15]

love: *chemah* (חמח) (passionate love) [Hebrew; Study 6; Study 56]

love: (various meanings, including a deeply affectionate and romantic love and tender mercies): *racham* (רחם) [Hebrew; Study 15]

lovingkindness: *gimmel* (גמל): [Hebrew; Study 52]

master: *baali* (בעלי) [Hebrew; Study 28]

meditate: *hagah* (הגה) [Hebrew; Study 4]

meet (with): *qara* (קרא) [Hebrew; Study 55]

melt: *shaphak* (שפך) [Hebrew; Study 30]

mercy (to show): *racham* (רחם) [Hebrew; Study 20]

mighty: *qavar* (קור) [Hebrew; Study 5]

missing the mark: *chatah* (חטה) [Hebrew; Study 24]

name: *shem* (שם) [Hebrew; Study 60]

prophet: *nebim* (נבם) [Hebrew; Study 23]

prostitute: *zonah* (זנה) [Hebrew; Study 37]

pruning hook: *zamar* (זמר) [Hebrew; Study 50]

purity: *bar* (בר) [Hebrew; Study 59]

quench: *haqa'* (שקע) [Hebrew; Study 35]

rebel: *sur* (סור) [Hebrew; Study 20]

refine: *mazaqaq* (מזקק) [Hebrew; Study 50]

rejoice: *sus* (סוס) [Hebrew; Study 5]

rest: *charash* (חרש) [Hebrew; Study 5]

rested: *vayishevethu* (וישבתו) [Hebrew; Study 27]

return: *veshab* (ואשב) [Hebrew; Study 38]

reverence: *yara'* (ירע) [Hebrew; Study 57; Study 58]

rock: *sala'* (סלע) [Hebrew; Study 18]

rock: *tarash* (תרש) [Hebrew; Study 18]

rocky cliff or wall: *tsur* (צור) [Hebrew; Study 19]

rule over: *mashal* (משל) [Hebrew; Study 9]

scarlet: *shani* (שני) [Hebrew; Study 48]

secret: *sod* (סוד) [Hebrew; Study 8]

seek: *baqash* (בקש) [Hebrew; Study 31]

seer: *ra'ah* (ראה) [Hebrew: Study 23]

shepherd: *ra'ah,* (רעה) [Hebrew; Study 8]

singing: *ranan* (רנן) [Hebrew; Study 5]

thorn: *sana'* [Aramaic; Study 36]

thought: *secho* (שׂחו) [Hebrew; Study 1]

thoughts: *machashabah* (מחשבה) [Hebrew: Study 1]

trembling: *bire'adah* (ברעדה) [Hebrew; Study 58]

troubled: *'ahal* (בהל) [Hebrew; Study 56]

truth: *sharara* [Aramaic; Study 17]

twirl: *cheval* (חול) [Hebrew; Study 46]

umpire, to: *brabeueto* [Greek; Preface]

upon: *'al* (על) [Hebrew; Study 21]

warmth: *'ash* (אש) [Hebrew; Study 45]

weak: *'amelah* (אמלה) [Hebrew; Study 37]

wind: *pneuma* [Greek; Study 17]

wind: *ruch* (רוח) [Hebrew: Study 17]

wind: *rucha* [Aramaic; Study 17]

withdraw: *sur* (סור) [Hebrew; Study 20]

worship: *proskyneo* [Greek; Study 17]

worship: *segad* [Aramaic; Study 17]

worship: *shachah* (שחה) [Hebrew; Study 1]

wounded heart: *ra'* (רע) [Hebrew; Study 35]

wrath: *chemah* (חמח) [Hebrew; Study 56]

wrath: *'ebrah* (עברה) [Hebrew; Study 24; Study 57]

About the Authors

Chaim Bentorah teaches biblical Hebrew, Aramaic, and Greek to lay teachers and pastors in the metro Chicago area through Chaim Bentorah Ministries. He also speaks to church and parachurch groups about the nature and means of studying the Old Testament in the original Hebrew. His books combine a devotional emphasis with scriptural studies into the deeper meanings of Hebrew words.

Chaim and his study partner, Laura Bertone, write daily word studies on their blog at www.chaimbentorah.com. They are also the copastors of a cyber Messianic church through their subscription All Access online at HebrewWordStudy.com, on which they conduct twelve-week classes in basic Hebrew, a weekly Monday evening Bible translation class, and a Sabbath Torah study on Saturday mornings that follows the Parshah (Weekly Torah Portion).

Chaim Bentorah has a bachelor of arts degree in Jewish Studies from Moody Bible Institute, a master's degree in Old Testament and Hebrew from Denver Seminary, and a PhD in Biblical Archaeology. All of his Hebrew professors in college and graduate school were involved in the translation of the *New International Version* of the Bible. In their classes, he learned of the inner workings involved in the translation process. In graduate school, he and another student studied advanced Hebrew under Dr. Earl S. Kalland, who was on the executive committee for the translation work of the *New International*. It was this committee that made the final decisions on the particular renderings used in the original *NIV* translation.

Having done his undergraduate work in Jewish Studies, Chaim was interested in the role of Jewish literature in biblical translation. Professor Kalland encouraged him to seek out an orthodox rabbi and discuss the translation process from a Jewish perspective. From this experience, he discovered many things about the Hebrew language that he had not learned in his years of Hebrew studies in a Christian environment. Later, from his contact with Jewish rabbis and his studies in the Talmud, the Mishnah, and other works of Jewish literature, as well as his studies in the Semitic languages, Chaim began doing Hebrew word studies as devotionals and sending them out by e-mail to former students whom he had taught in his thirteen years as an instructor in Hebrew and Old Testament at World Harvest Bible College, as well as those he taught through Chaim Bentorah Ministries. After self-publishing several books of Hebrew word studies and related topics, Chaim chose ninety word studies to create *Hebrew Word Study: Revealing the Heart of God*, which was his first book with Whitaker House. This was followed by *Journey into Silence*, an account of his experiences on three silent retreats and the word studies he did on them. Chaim believes that if we take the time to study the Hebrew language, we can see the true beauty of God's Word and come to know God and His heart in a much deeper way.

LAURA BERTONE has served in ministry for thirty years and is the "Bentorah" of Chaim Bentorah Ministries, having been Chaim's study partner for over a decade. She is currently going through the process of certification to become a foster parent, supervising the administrative work of Chaim Bentorah Ministries, and assisting Chaim in his word studies. Laura also copastors a cyber Messianic church through the subscription All Access online at HebrewWordStudy.com with Chaim Bentorah. Additionally, she is preparing podcasts and live classes on dream interpretation using the Bible and Hebrew as a basis for the interpretation. Laura has a passion for holistic living and nutrition and how it is reflected in the Hebrew language. She will be offering classes on the All Access website on dream interpretation, and the holistic nature, beauty, and design of Biblical Hebrew.

Chaim Bentorah Biblical Hebrew Studies

www.chaimbentorah.com

chaimbentorah@gmail.com